Work-Based Learning

The New Frontier of Management Development

Joseph A. Raelin
Professor of Management
Boston College

Prentice Hall, Upper Saddle, New Jersey 07458

Executive Editor: Michael Roche
Associate Editor: Ruth Berry
Editorial Assistant: Adam Hamel
Production Supervisor: Louis C. Bruno, Jr.
Senior Marketing Manager: Julia Downs
Senior Marketing Coordinator: Joyce Cosentino
Electronic Production Manager: Scott Silva
Print Buyer: Sheila Spinney
Printer and Binder: Banta Book Group
Cover Printer: Coral Graphics

This book is in the Addison-Wesley Series on Organization Development.
Consulting Editors: Edgar H. Schein and Richard Beckhard

Library of Congress Cataloging-in-Publication Data

Raelin, Joseph A., 1948–
    Work based learning : the new frontier of management development /
Joseph A. Raelin.
        p. cm.—(Addison-Wesley series on organization development)
    Includes bibliographical references and index.
    ISBN 0-201-43388-5
    1. Executives—Training of. 2. Employees—Training of.
3. Organizational learning. I. title. II. Series.
HD30.4.R33 1999   98-55917
658.4'07124—dc21   CIP

Prentice-Hall International (UK) Limited, London
Prentice-Hall of Australia Pty. Limited, Sydney
Prentice-Hall Canada, Inc., Toronto
Prentice-Hall Hispanoamericanan, S.A., Mexico
Prentice-Hall of India Private Limited, New Delhi
Prentice-Hall of Japan, Inc., Tokyo
Pearson Education Asia Pte. Ltd., Singapore
Editora Prentice-Hall do Brasil, Ltda., Rio de Janiero

Printed in the United States of America

10 9 8 7 6 5 4 3 2 1

Series Foreword

The Addison-Wesley Series on Organization Development originated in the late 1960s when a number of us recognized that the rapidly growing field of "OD" was not well understood or well defined. We also recognized that there was no one OD philosophy; hence, one could not at that time write a textbook on the theory and practice of OD, but one could make clear what various practitioners were doing under that label. So the original six books in the OD Series launched what became a continuing enterprise, the essence of which was to allow different authors to speak for themselves rather than to summarize under one umbrella what was obviously a rapidly growing and highly diverse field.

By the early 1980s, OD was growing by leaps and bounds and expanding into all kinds of organizational areas and technologies of intervention. By this time, many textbooks existed that tried to capture core concepts in the field, but we felt that diversity and innovation continued to be the more salient aspects of OD. Accordingly, our series had expanded to nineteen titles.

As we moved into the 1990s, we began to see some real convergence in the underlying assumptions of OD. As we observed how different professionals working in different kinds of organizations and occupational communities made their cases, we saw that we were still far from having a single "theory" of organizational development. Yet, some common premises were surfacing. We began to see patterns in what was working and what was not, and we were becoming more articulate about these patterns. We also started to view the field of OD as increasingly connected to other organizational sciences and disciplines, such as information technology, coordination theory, and organization theory.

In the early 90s, we added several new titles to the OD Series to describe important new themes: Ciampa's *Total Quality* illustrates the important link to employee involvement in continuous improvement; Johansen et al.'s *Leading Business Teams* explores the important arena of electronic information tools for teamwork; Tjosvold's *The Conflict-Positive Organization* shows how conflict management can turn conflict into constructive action; and Hirschhorn's *Managing in the New Team Environment* builds bridges to group psychodynamic theory.

In the mid-1990s, we continued to explore emerging themes with four revisions and three new books. Burke took his highly successful *Organization Development* into new realms with more current and expanded content; Galbraith updated and enlarged his classic theory of how information management lies at the heart of organization design with his new edition of *Competing with Flexible Lateral Organizations*; and Dyer wrote an important third edition of his classic book, *Team Building*. In addition, Rashford and Coghlan introduced the important concept of levels of organizational complexity as a basis for intervention theory in their book *The Dynamics of Organizational Levels*; in *Creating Labor-Management Partnerships*, Woodworth and Meek take us into the critical realm of how OD can help in labor relations—an area that has become increasingly important as productivity issues become critical for global competitiveness. In *Integrated Strategic Change*, authors Worley, Hitchin and Ross powerfully demonstrate how the field of OD must be linked to the field of strategy by reviewing the role of OD at each stage of the strategy planning and implementation process. Finally, authors Argyris and Schön provided an important link to organizational learning in a new version of their classic book entitled *Organizational Learning II: Theory, Method, and Practice*.

Now, as we continue to think about the field of OD and what it will mean in the 21st century, we have added several titles that reflect the growing connections between the original concepts of OD and the wider range of the applications of these concepts. Rupert Chisholm's *Developing Network Organizations: Learning from Practice and Theory* explores and illustrates the link between OD and building community networks. In their new book called *Diagnosing and Changing Organizational Culture*, Cameron and Quinn explore one model and technique of how to get at the crucial concept of culture and how to make this concept relevant for the practitioner. The theme of process consultation has remained central in OD, and we have found that it continues to be relevant in a variety of helping situations. In *Process Consultation Revisited: Building the Helping Relationship*, Schein has completely revised and updated this concept by focusing on process consultation as a general model of the helping process; his new volume pulls together material from previous work and adds new concepts and cases.

The newest member of the OD Series—and the first to bear a 2000 copyright—is *Work-Based Learning*, by Joe Raelin. This new book shows readers how to acquire learning in the midst of practice by exploring the intersection of knowledge and experience. Intended as a practical guide for a new generation of managers and executive educators, *Work-Based Learning* explores how to learn collectively with others who too wish to develop their own capability and how to engage one's reflective powers to challenge those taken-for-granted assumptions that unwittingly hold us back from questioning standard ways of operating.

Our series on Organization Development now includes over thirty titles. We will continue to welcome new titles and revisions as we explore the various frontiers of organization development and identify themes that are relevant to the ever more difficult problem of helping organizations remain effective in an increasingly turbulent environment.

New York, New York   Richard H. Beckhard
Cambridge, Massachusetts   Edgar H. Schein

Other Titles in the Addison-Wesley Series on Organization Development

Diagnosing and Changing Organizational Culture
Kim S. Cameron and Robert E. Quinn   1999 (0-201-33871-8)
This book helps managers, change agents, and scholars to understand, diagnose, and facilitate the change of an organization's culture in order to enhance its effectiveness. The authors present three forms of assistance for readers: (1) validated instruments for diagnosing organizational culture and management competency, (2) a theoretical framework for understanding organizational culture, and (3) a systematic strategy and methodology for changing organizational culture and personal behavior. This text is a workbook in that readers can complete the instruments and plot their own culture profile in the book itself. They can also use the text as a resource for understanding and leading a culture change process.

Process Consultation Revisited: Building the Helping Relationship
Edgar H. Schein   1999 (0-201-34596-X)
The latest addition to Ed Schein's well-loved set of process consultation books, this new volume builds on the content of the two that precede it while expanding to explore the critical area of the helping relationship. *Process Consultation Revisited* focuses on the interaction between consultant and client, explaining how to achieve the healthy helping relationship so essential to effective consultation. Whether the advisor is an OD consultant, therapist, social worker, manager, parent, or friend, the dynamics between advisor and advisee can be difficult to understand and manage. Drawing on over 40 years of experience as a consultant, Schein creates a general theory and methodology of helping that will enable a diverse group of readers to navigate the helping process successfully.

Developing Network Organizations: Learning from Theory and Practice
Rupert F. Chisholm   1998 (0-201-87444-X)
The inter-organizational network is rapidly emerging as a key type of organization, and the importance of the network is expected to increase throughout the 21st century. This text covers the process of developing these complex systems. The author uses in-depth description and analysis based on direct involvement with three diverse networks to identify critical aspects of the development process. He explains relevant concepts and appropriate methods and practices in the context of developing these three networks, and he also identifies ten key learnings derived from his direct involvement with the development process.

Organizational Learning II: Theory, Method, and Practice
Chris Argyris and Donald A. Schön   1996 (0-201-62983-6)
This text addresses how business firms, governments, non-governmental organizations, schools, health care systems, regions, and whole nations need to

adapt to changing environments, draw lessons from past successes and failures, detect and correct the errors of the past, anticipate and respond to impending threats, conduct experiments, engage in continuing innovation, and build and realize images of a desirable future. There is a virtual consensus that we are all subject to a "learning imperative," and in the academy no less than in the world of practice, organizational learning has become an idea in good currency.

Integrated Strategic Change: How OD Builds Competitive Advantage
Christopher G. Worley, David E. Hitchin,   1996 (0-201-85777-4)
and Walter L. Ross
This book is about strategic change and how firms can improve their perfor-mance and effectiveness. Its unique contribution is in describing how orga-nization development practitioners can assist in the effort. Strategic change is a type of organization change that realigns an organization's strategy, structure and process within a given competitive context. It is substantive and systemic and therefore differs from traditional organization development that produces incremental improvements, addresses only one system at a time, or does not intend to increase firm-level performance.

Team Building: Current Issues and New Alternatives, Third Edition
William G. Dyer   1995 (0-201-62882-1)
One of the major developments in the field of organization redesign has been the emergence of self-directed work teams. This book explains how teams are most successful when the team becomes part of the culture and structure or systems of the organization. It discusses the major new trends and em-phasizes the degree of commitment that managers and members must bring to the team-building process. It is written for managers and human resource professionals who want to develop a more systematic program of team build-ing in their organization or work unit.

Creating Labor-Management Partnerships
Warner P. Woodworth and Christopher B. Meek   1995 (0-201-58823-4)
This book begins with a call for changing the social and political barriers exist-ing in unionized work settings and emphasizes the critical need for union-man-agement cooperation in the present context of international competition. It demonstrates the shift from confrontational union-management relationships toward more effective and positive systems of collaboration. It is written for human resource management and industrial relations managers and staff, union officials, professional arbitrators and mediators, government officials, and pro-fessors and students involved in the study of organization development.

Organization Development: A Process of Learning and Changing, Second Edition
W. Warner Burke   1994 (0-201-50835-4)
This text provides a comprehensive overview of the field of organization development. Written for managers, executives, administrators, practition-

ers, and students, this book takes an in-depth look at organization development with particular emphasis on the importance of learning and change. The author not only describes the basic tenets of OD, but he also looks at OD as a change in an organization's culture. Frameworks and models like the Burke-Litwin model (Chapter 7), as well as numerous case examples, are used throughout the book to enhance the reader's understanding of the principles and practices involved in leading and managing organizational change.

Competing with Flexible Lateral Organizations, Second Edition
Jay R. Galbraith   1994 (0-201-50836-2)
This book focuses on creating competitive advantage by building a lateral capability, thereby enabling a firm to respond flexibly in an uncertain world. The book addresses international coordination and cross-business coordination as well as the usual cross- functional efforts. It is unique in covering both cross-functional (lateral or horizontal) coordination, as well as international and corporate issues.

The Dynamics of Organizational Levels: A Change Framework for Managers and Consultants
Nicholas S. Rashford and David Coghlan   1994 (0-201-54323-0)
This book introduces the idea that, for successful change to occur, organizational interventions have to be coordinated across the major levels of issues that all organizations face. Individual level, team level, inter-unit level, and organizational level issues are identified and analyzed, and the kinds of intervention appropriate to each level are spelled out.

Total Quality: A User's Guide for Implementation
Dan Ciampa   1992 (0-201-54992-1)
This is a book that directly addresses the challenge of how to make Total Quality work in a practical, no-nonsense way. The companies that will dominate markets in the future will be those that deliver high quality, competitively priced products and service just when the customer wants them and in a way that exceeds the customer's expectations. The vehicle by which these companies move to that stage is Total Quality.

Managing in the New Team Environment: Skills, Tools, and Methods
Larry Hirschhorn   1991 (0-201-52503-8)
This text is designed to help manage the tensions and complexities that arise for managers seeking to guide employees in a team environment. Based on an interactive video course developed at IBM, the text takes managers step by step through the process of building a team and authorizing it to act while they learn to step back and delegate. Specific issues addressed include how to give a team structure, how to facilitate its basic processes, and how to acknowledge differences in relationships among team members and between the manager and individual team members.

Leading Business Teams: How Teams Can Use Technology and Group Process Tools to Enhance Performance
Robert Johansen, David Sibbett, Suzyn Benson, Alexia Martin,
Robert Mittman, and Paul Saffo   1991 (0-201-52829-0)
What technology or tools should organization development people or team leaders have at their command, now and in the future? This text explores the intersection of technology and business teams, a new and largely uncharted area that goes by several labels, including "groupware"—term that encompasses both electronic and nonelectronic tools for teams. This is the first book of its kind from the field describing what works for business teams and what does not.

The Conflict-Positive Organization: Stimulate Diversity and Create Unity
Dean Tjosvold   1991 (0-201-51485-0)
This book describes how managers and employees can use conflict to find common ground, solve problems, and strengthen morale and relationships. By showing how well-managed conflict invigorates and empowers teams and organizations, the text demonstrates how conflict is vital for a company's continuous improvement and increased competitive advantage.

Change by Design
Robert R. Blake, Jane Srygley Mouton,   1989 (0-201-50748-X)
and Anne Adams McCanse
This book develops a systematic approach to organization development and provides readers with rich illustrations of coherent planned change. The book involves testing, examining, revising, and strengthening conceptual foundations in order to create sharper corporate focus and increased predictability of successful organization development.

Power and Organization Development: Mobilizing Power to Implement Change
Larry E. Greiner and Virginia E. Schein   1988 (0-201-12185-9)
This book forges an important collaborative approach between two opposing and often contradictory approaches to management: OD practitioners who espouse a "more humane" workplace without understanding the political realities of getting things done, and practicing managers who feel comfortable with power but overlook the role of human potential in contributing to positive results.

Designing Organizations for High Performance
David P. Hanna   1988 (0-201-12693-1)
This book is the first to give insight into the actual processes you can use to translate organizational concepts into bottom-line improvements. Hanna's "how-to" approach shows not only the successful methods of intervention, but also the plans behind them and the corresponding results.

Process Consultation, Volume 1: Its Role in Organization Development, Second Edition
Edgar H. Schein   1988 (0-201-06736-6)
How can a situation be influenced in the workplace without the direct use of power or formal authority? This book presents the core theoretical foundations and basic prescriptions for effective management.

Organizational Transitions: Managing Complex Change, Second Edition
Richard Beckhard and Reuben T. Harris   1987 (0-201-10887-9)
This book discusses the choices involved in developing a management system appropriate to the "transition state." It also discusses commitment to change, organizational culture, and increasing and maintaining productivity, creativity, and innovation.

Stream Analysis: A Powerful Way to Diagnose and Manage Organizational Change
Jerry I. Porras   1987 (0-201-05693-3)
Drawing on a conceptual framework that helps the reader to better understand organizations, this book shows how to diagnose failings in organizational functioning and how to plan a comprehensive set of actions needed to change the organization into a more effective system.

Process Consultation, Volume II: Lessons for Managers and Consultants
Edgar H. Schein   1987 (0-201-06744-7)
This book shows the viability of the process consultation model for working with human systems. Like Schein's first volume on process consultation, the second volume focuses on the moment-to-moment behavior of the manager or consultant rather than the design of the OD program.

Managing Conflict: Interpersonal Dialogue and Third-Party Roles, Second Edition
Richard E. Walton   1987 (0-201-08859-2)
This book shows how to implement a dialogue approach to conflict management. It presents a framework for diagnosing recurring conflicts and suggests several basic options for controlling or resolving them.

Pay and Organization Development
Edward E. Lawler   1981 (0-201-03990-7)
This book examines the important role that reward systems play in organization development efforts. By combining examples and specific recommendations with conceptual material, it organizes the various topics and puts them into a total systems perspective. Specific pay approaches such as gainsharing, skill-based pay, and flexible benefits are discussed, and their impact on productivity and the quality of work life is analyzed.

Work Redesign
J. Richard Hackman and Greg R. Oldham   1980 (0-201-02779-8)
This book is a comprehensive, clearly written study of work design as a strategy for personal and organizational change. Linking theory and practical technologies, it develops traditional and alternative approaches to work design that can benefit both individuals and organizations.

Organizational Dynamics: Diagnosis and Intervention
John P. Kotter   1978 (0-201-03890-0)
This book offers managers and OD specialists a powerful method of diagnosing organizational problems and of deciding when, where, and how to use (or not use) the diverse and growing number of organizational improvement tools that are available today. Comprehensive and fully integrated, the book includes many different concepts, research findings, and competing philosophies and provides specific examples of how to use the information to improve organizational functioning.

Career Dynamics: Matching Individual and Organizational Needs
Edgar H. Schein   1978 (0-201-06834-6)
This book studies the complexities of career development from both an individual and an organizational perspective. Changing needs throughout the adult life cycle, interaction of work and family, and integration of individual and organizational goals through human resource planning and development are all thoroughly explored.

Matrix
Stanley M. Davis and Paul Lawrence   1977 (0-201-01115-8)
This book defines and describes the matrix organization, a significant departure from the traditional "one man-one boss" management system. The authors note that the tension between the need for independence (fostering innovation) and order (fostering efficiency) drives organizations to consider a matrix system. Among the issues addressed are reasons for using a matrix, methods for establishing one, the impact of the system on individuals, its hazards, and what types of organizations can use a matrix system.

Feedback and Organization Development: Using Data-Based Methods
David A. Nadler   1977 (0-201-05006-4)
This book addresses the use of data as a tool for organizational change. It attempts to bring together some of what is known from experience and research and to translate that knowledge into useful insights for those who are thinking about using data-based methods in organizations. The broad approach of the text is to treat a whole range of questions and issues considering the various uses of data as an organizational change tool.

Preface

Isn't it high time that we return learning to a very natural location—to work itself? This book represents a modest attempt to start our new century with a fresh view about how to mobilize the management development process. It's time to get our managers, at least in part, out of the classroom and back into their work, not just to do their jobs but to reflect and learn continuously from their very practice.

Is this not a most natural, even an intuitive process? If so, why the need for a book on work-based learning? Unfortunately, we have forgotten how to learn in conjunction with experience. We have separated theory from practice, and we have prematurely decided that our tacit actions cannot be brought into consciousness to shape our knowledge. Hence, there is a need to catalog in one place the many thoughts and strategies available to us to demonstrate how we might recall that instinctive need to learn as we go. Yet, I am not prescribing a mere trial-and-error learning experience. Our work-based learning approaches, though elegantly simple and natural, have become sophisticated enough to accelerate our learning to learn. We now know how to learn collectively with others who also wish to develop their own capability. We now know how to engage our reflective powers to challenge those taken-for-granted assumptions that unwittingly hold us back from questioning standard ways of operating. We now know how to engage and then document the collective learning process to make it accessible to everyone and even contagious within the organizational environment.

The challenge of this book is to bring these ideas and strategies together to inspire a new generation of management and executive educators who will dare to experiment with this novel yet age-old, natural approach. The book might thus serve as both a practical guide and an inspiration to those ambitious enough to attempt work-based learning experiments in their own organization. In time, these experiments might turn into a continuous process of growth at the individual level, development at the team level, and renewal at the organizational level. Indeed, the promise of organizational development might be made a little more attainable through the accounts to be detailed in the pages that follow.

A project of this nature cannot be undertaken without a lot of support from many individuals and institutions. Two eminent publishing groups worked alongside me on this project. I am grateful to Mike Roche of Addison Wesley Longman for getting me started and to David Schafer of Prentice Hall for getting me to the finish. Lou Bruno placed his deft touch on production, and Michael Campbell has creatively coordinated marketing efforts. I would like to offer my appreciation to the OD Series editors, Ed Schein and Dick Beckhard, for including me in this historic set of volumes. I am also grateful to my own institution, Boston College's Wallace E. Carroll School of Management, for releasing me for a sabbatical in 1997 to work on this project. Helping me at the outset was my colleague Jim Gips, who funded an early initiative through our school's Andersen Consulting Fund. As I shall detail in the first chapter, I am also indebted to my own learning team—a core group of executive educators, called the Forum for Executive Learning, who worked with me throughout the project to help me refine my ideas and practices. I wish to acknowledge the reviewers of this manuscript, especially Chris Argyris and Warner Burke. Although this book represents an original contribution in almost its entirety, I have occasionally made use of some of my prior work that has appeared elsewhere. The sources are cited as appropriate, but I wish to thank the Institute for Operations Research and the Management Sciences (INFORMS) for allowing me to use a portion of my Vol. 8, No. 6 article from *Organization Science* in Chapter 4.

Finally, I am grateful to my students, clients, and colleagues who go unnamed here, but who have patiently allowed me to experiment with the ideas and practices in-the-making covered in this book. If the approaches now read as coherent and tested, it is only because of their good will and encouragement.

Boston, Massachusetts   J.A.R.

To my work-based learning tutors with gratitude

Chris Argyris—for your intellectual stimulation
Al Savitsky—for your friendship and sustenance
Abby Raelin—for your dedication and love

Contents

1

Introduction

*I took a great deal o' pains with his
education sir; I let him run the streets when he
was very young, shift for his-self. It's the only
way to make a boy sharp, sir.*

—Charles Dickens
The Pickwick Papers

What Is Work-Based Learning?

The sina qua non of organization development has become the need for continuous learning. Only learning can keep up with change; in fact, recalling a maxim of the inventor of action learning, Reg Revans, "the rate of learning must equal or exceed the rate of change." Learning is what creates, but also adapts, enlarges, and deepens knowledge. Without new or adapted knowledge, it is not possible to change either the meanings we attach to our actions or the actions themselves.

So, learning has to become a way of life in our organizational systems. As such, it has to be more than the sum of everyone's individual learning; it needs to become shared as part of an organizational ethic. That ethic requires the organization to deliberately unseat itself in order to cope with change, in order to "get smarter faster."

How can we introduce learning as an organizational property that extends to all managers? The answer lies in making learning arise from the work itself. Learning has to become natural, even fun. Unfortunately, we have become conditioned to a classroom model that separates theory from practice, making learning seem impractical, irrelevant, and boring. But what if we make our worksite a perfectly acceptable location for learning?

1

This is where work-based learning comes in. Work-based learning expressly merges theory with practice, knowledge with experience. It recognizes that the workplace offers as many opportunities for learning as the classroom. Such learning, however, needs to be centered around reflection on work practices. It needs to offer managers faced with the relentless pace of pervasive change an opportunity to overcome time pressures by reflecting upon and learning from the artistry of their action. It is no longer acceptable to offer the rationale, "We don't have a minute to think." Managers can no longer react to change; they must anticipate and work with it. Reflection with others offers the key to competing successfully in the twenty-first century marketplace.

Work-based learning uses many diverse technologies, but primary is the deployment of action projects, learning teams, and other interpersonal experiences, such as mentorships, that permit and encourage learning dialogues. Learning dialogues are concerned with the surfacing, in the safe presence of trusting peers, of those social, political, and even emotional reactions that might be blocking operating effectiveness.

There are three critical elements in the work-based learning process:

1. It views learning as acquired in the midst of action and dedicated to the task at hand.
2. It sees knowledge creation and utilization as collective activities wherein learning becomes everyone's job.
3. Its users demonstrate a learning-to-learn aptitude, which frees them to question underlying assumptions of practice.

Work-based learning, then, differs from conventional training in that it involves conscious reflection on actual experience. Fundamental to the process is the concept of metacognition (Meisel and Fearon 1996), which means that one constantly thinks about one's problem-solving processes. It is not enough just to ask, "what did we learn"; we must also ask, "what does it mean or how does it square with what we already know?" Hence, learning can be more than just the acquisition of technical skills. It also constitutes the reframing necessary to create new knowledge. Peters and Smith (1997) refer to programs of work-based learning as "throwing a net around slippery experience and capturing it as learning." Ohmae (1982) adds that learning of this type requires a combination of rational analysis with imagination and intuition. Using both hemispheres of the brain, one reintegrates information into new patterns.

Figure 1.1
Honey and Mumford's Learning Cycle and Learning Styles

Figure reprinted from *Capitalizing on Your Learning Style* © 1995 by Dr. Peter Honey and Dr. Alan Mumford. With permission of Organization Design and Development, Inc., King of Prussia, Pennsylvania.

Although I shall detail many examples of work-based learning experience in the chapters to follow, finishing with a prototype model in Chapter 11, it might be useful to get an early glimpse of what elements are normally incorporated into work-based learning programs. By adapting the prior work of Kolb (1984) on learning styles, Honey and Mumford (1992) provide us with such a glimpse of what a work-based learning experience might look like (see Figure 1.1). Within a work setting, the process might start by having a manager undertake an experience that is new or unique and attempt to learn what that experience meant to him or her and what it achieved for the organization. For example, a human resource (HR) manager might benchmark her hiring practices against a number of companies participating in a regional trade association. This is acting in what Honey and Mumford refer to as an "activist" role. However, they also recommend that the manager become a "reflector," which entails some deep reflection about the unique experience, brought about normally through public dialogue with some like-minded colleagues. Hence, the HR manager might assemble a small group of colleagues from the association to meet both in person and on-line to react to each others' practices, including their recruitment and selection procedures.

In the next role, the "theorist" role, the manager, continuing the public dialogue, interprets what the experience meant in context, perhaps by comparing it with other actions, comparing it with other theories, and so forth. Finally, in the last stage of the learning process, the manager in a "pragmatic" role plans what steps he or she might take next to extend the experience, keeping in mind how the learning already acquired might be applied. Completing our example, the HR manager would use the ongoing dialogue with her colleagues, in addition to other written sources, as a means of adding to her knowledge base. She would attempt to implement some of these new ideas into her work setting while continuing to reflect on these initiatives on her own as well as with her learning team and her worksite colleagues.

Work-based learning, then, is mindful and situated learning in the sense that it does not view preexisting knowledge as fixed but rather as provisional until tried out in a given context or in practice (Langer, 1997). Further, it recognizes that learning can occur spontaneously in a given situation. It is not akin to learning a set of facts to be stored and used later but rather to bringing new tools to bear in order to figure out how to cope with instant challenges arising from the practice field.

Derived from action itself, work-based learning may be thought of as a natural process tied to the human instinct to grow. In this sense, it is very much a part of our being. Accordingly, we might match it against seven unique criteria proposed by Peter Vaill (1997) for making learning a "way of being."

- *It is self-directed.* The learner has substantial control over the purpose, content, form, pace, and evaluation of the learning.
- *It is creative.* There is no preset goal, nor are there preset methods in work-based learning. The learner is asked to create on the spot to find and solve problems.
- *It is expressive.* Learning occurs in the process of doing it and expressing it. All nuances of the experience, especially tacit performance, are engaged. Unlike classroom learning and even in some experiential learning, we do not know

what will happen at the conclusion of our practice. Learning occurs in conjunction with experience, perhaps a little before, as long as we theorize about what we are about to do and compare our experience to it. Learning also occurs during and after the experience as we improve our often tacit behavior by reflecting on what we did, through peer advisement, or from instruction.

- *It involves feeling.* Work-based learning entails emotional involvement in the context itself. We care about what we do and what we have accomplished. We feel the learning as well as possess it intellectually.

- *It is on-line.* We do not learn in an artificial, sheltered environment; we learn within the fray of practice itself, within genuine operating environments.

- *It is continual.* Once work-based learning becomes natural to the learner, it becomes a never-ending process. We are always open to surprises, to new ways of doing things. Change is accepted as a given in life; hence, learning becomes part of our very being.

- *It is reflective.* We become not just more aware of our own learning processes, but also more aware of (and more interested in publicly commenting on) the processes of others.

The Uniqueness of This Book

Having read this far, you may begin to wonder what is unique about this book. How does it differ from the myriad of works out there on organization development? First, the field of work-based learning is new, although it has been recognized in the past through other labels, such as adult learning, vocational education, cooperative education, school-to-work, and so forth. Books in these fields typically come from the generic field of education and, thus, do not focus on management development.

Housed humbly within Addison Wesley Longman's distinguished OD Series, this book is about management and organizational development, but it approaches learning in a unique way. Although there are countless methods to help managers develop their organization to be more effective and more humane, or to help managers develop themselves or their associates, most of these methods come in the form of a recipe. The recipe is like a tool that has been devised by someone else but that can be successfully applied within the user's organizational or team culture. For example, we have reengineering and quality tools, we have access to socio-technical systems, and the like. This book presents very few such tools. Why? It is because the philosophy of work-based learning does not specify the methods of practice *in advance*. Rather, the methods of work-based learning are developed concurrently with work practices themselves. If there is a recipe to be afforded here, it is one that merely prescribes how to set up various experiences that make use of the organic and reflective processes embedded in work-based learning.

In this way, this book parallels some of the recent work in organizational learning; yet here too there is an important difference. Organizational learning characterizes a set of activities that allow organizations to grow and learn in order to sustain themselves and improve. The learning organization characterizes the type of organization whose internal structure and process allow organizational learning, which, in other words, allow it to grow and learn. Work-based learning characterizes those developmental activities and educational efforts within the organization to help it establish a culture of organizational learning.

The closest parallel to work-based learning is, of course, action learning, and a close second would be action science. However, these so-called "action strategies" have developed along distinct epistemological traditions, as have such interrelated methods as mentorship, journalizing, or the emerging field of community of practice. As yet, there has not been any attempt to distinguish the commonalties across these approaches and to bring them together as part of a new yet comprehensive tradition, which we can now refer to as work-based learning.

A Special Source: FEL

Throughout 1997, I was granted a one-year sabbatical from my academic duties at the Wallace E. Carroll School of Management at Boston College. During this time period, I organized a virtual learning community of corporate educators interested in sharing their best practices in work-based learning. This virtual network was called the Forum for Executive Learning (FEL). The dialogue exchanged in the FEL network produced many insights, some of which readers will soon notice have made their way into this book. There was no set agenda for discourse among FEL members, but as members exchanged information, they would post their comments according to evolving topics. Many of these topics became quite relevant for the development of the emerging field of work-based learning. Hence,

FEL has served as a sounding board for the field's evolving theory and practice. FEL also constitutes one of the data sources for the book. Readers will note from time to time that particular citations will be attributed to FEL members. Each time you see such a citation, you can be assured that the comments were made by an on-line exchange through the Forum for Executive Learning at Boston College.

The Plan for the Book

Before we plunge immediately into the applied world, it is important that we first consider the theoretical and practical context of work-based learning in order to understand its rationale. We shall start, then, in Chapter 2 by considering what I am calling the "new" learning, a work-based process that, based on reflective principles, may be the one way to successfully overcome the frenetic pace of our corporate world. In Chapter 3 the emerging tradition of work-based learning will be compared to other familiar and closely allied management and organization development approaches—in particular, the movement of organizational learning. Chapter 4 is my theory chapter and hence may be one that some of my less sympathetic readers may choose to skip. It develops a comprehensive conceptual model that integrates the learning styles embedded in work-based learning.

Three of the most popular learning styles or strategies of work-based learning that evolve out of my conceptual model will be detailed in Chapter 5: action learning, community of practice, and action science. In Chapter 6, I pay special attention to the fundamental basis for work-based learning—public reflection. It is only through public reflection that we can create a collective identity as a community of inquiry. From there, we embark in Chapter 7 on a discovery of four specific reflective practices known to be quite representative of work-based learning experience: learning teams, journals, developmental planning, and developmental relationships. A separate chapter is subsequently devoted to the art of facilitation in work-based learning, especially as applied to learning teams. In Chapter 9, the most popular of all work-based learning techniques, the action project, is discussed at length. Chapter 10 is devoted to those organizational officials who, having sold the concept of work-based learning in their organization, now have to prove it by sound management practices and reliable measurement techniques. Finally, the last chapter, Chapter 11, displays a prototype work-based learning program and incorporates many examples of such programs in current use today here and abroad.

2

The Grounds for Work-Based Learning

What one knows is, in youth, of little moment;
they know enough who know how to learn.

—Henry Adams

The World of the Busy Executive

Executives live in a world of frenetic activity. They tend to see the world around them as hostile and dependent but for their intervention. Action is required. Delaying decisions is seen as a sign of weakness, even if the delay may subsequently produce a better decision. Yet, is it possible that the frenetic activity of the executive is a drug against the emptiness of our organizational souls? Constant action serves as a substitute for thought.

Meanwhile, reflection and its counterpart, listening, receive short shrift in society. We don't seem to be interested in the whole story, in the data. We even perfect the art of interruption so that we can show our "pro-activity," and to gain the boss's attention. There was a time before instant replay when humans had to get the whole message or it would be lost forever. We seem to have lost the art of listening, and we seem to be unwilling to perfect the art of public reflection, in which we show a willingness to inquire about our own and our friends' assumptions and meanings.

One rationale for this action obsession is that in our current global economic system, we face the imperative of "grow or die." According to John Adams (1993), who is a member of our FEL network, the growth mantra has become an addiction, along with deadlines. It produces a mass denial that we can continue on as we are, with no ill effects. Its essence is an inner need to prevent awareness of the connection between our behavior and its consequences. As with all addictions, recovery requires a willingness to confront the pain that's being avoided. However, as long as we continue to operate on narrow, short-term growth cycles, we will continue to think about life as "having," not as "being." We will continue to go for what is tried-and-true, not what is unknown or risky. We will continue to live in a myth of "positive thinking," which externalizes, which sees the good life as a matter of outer arrangements, not as a balance of both success and inner well-being. Caught in our own insecurity, we will feel that we have to be the hero, to create rather than co-create with others.

Under the constant stress of the office, few permit themselves the time for introspection or self-assessment, let alone public reflection. But if we are to make learning a response to the pace of our world and yet a natural extension of ourselves, we will need to slow down. We might recall the remake of the film *Sabrina*, which starred Harrison Ford as a high-speed CEO named Linus, and Julia Ormond as the maid's daughter, Sabrina, who upon maturing finally obtains the notice of the executive. As they develop their relationship, at one point Sabrina completely stymies Linus with one simple question, "Linus, where do you live?"

In an emotionally charged exercise that my colleague Robert Leaver and I orchestrate, called "Actors and Reflectors," corporate participants demonstrate to themselves the contradictions of a pure action orientation (at all costs) at work. People are asked to volunteer to sit in either a chair marked "action" or one marked "reflection." Sitting opposite each other, taking opposite positions, they debate from their respective frames. The actors demonstrate how the workplace is going at warp speed. The reflectors demonstrate what can be done to slow down the pace of the workplace. At the conclusion of the exercise, participants reflect upon the factors in our life that compel us to reflect about

- the quality of our work and personal experience;
- what others at work are saying about the intense pace of the workplace;
- our desire for personal reflection time;
- our desire for more genuine conversation in a group or with a colleague;
- what the community is saying it needs from business;
- what the Earth is saying in her painful cry.

The New Learning

Who among the readers of this book have not experienced at least one of the following changes in their organization: top management change, restructuring, sudden competitive threat, technological transformation, downsizing, merger, spin-off, divestiture? The list could go on and on, but the pace of change will not let up. Twenty-first century organizations need to be highly nimble, able to deploy new teams of employees in ever-changing organizational configurations to respond to ever-changing market conditions. What can managers do about these changes? Survival itself will consist of absorbing the forces of change and responding with the correctly forecast organizational response. In other words, it requires learning, for only learning can keep up with change; in fact, recalling again the maxim of Reg Revans: the rate of learning must equal or exceed the rate of change.

The learning we are talking about will need to differ markedly from our age-old conceptions. The skills we "learned" in school become typically obsolete by the time we find a job or develop a career. It is thought that most young people now preparing themselves for the job market will experience some six or seven different careers in their lifetime, each requiring new skills. In fact, the whole notion of skills as a set of technical abilities to perform a job has itself become obsolete. Replacing skills is the new idea of learning, which will be commingled with the notion of work itself. The most valuable employee will be the updated one who can shift with the organizational environment.

In a similar vein, the notion of apprenticeship, though fundamental to learning, needs a reinterpretation to be viable for twenty-first century careers. A workplace learning process that dates as far back as the history of work itself, apprenticeship inducts trainees into a community of practice. What makes it distinctive from classroom education is that the master's or teacher's practices constitute the standards of performance for the apprentice (Berryman, 1992). In addition, apprenticeship offers a number of advantages over classroom learning (Jordan, 1987):

- The activities to which the apprentice is a witness are organized around work to be done; hence the mastering of tasks is appreciated for its immediate use value.
- There is a temporal ordering of skill acquisition from the easy to the more complex.

- Skill acquisition derives from the ability to do rather than the ability to talk about what to do.
- Standards of performance are built right into the work environment in which the novice participates.
- Teachers and teaching are largely invisible; to a large extent, the person who judges the apprentice's performance is the apprentice.

Yet apprenticeship cannot be a proper metaphor for the new learning in modern society unless it is modified in two critical ways: First, work in the twenty-first century, be it management, machine repair, systems engineering, or law, entails more cognitive or implicit knowledge than physical or observable knowledge. Therefore, apprenticeship requires the talent of "externalizing" processes symbolically. For example, fixing machines equipped with microprocessors requires technicians to represent structures and processes. Second, traditional apprenticeship presumed relative constancy in the activities being learned. However, modern work activities often hold few constants or routines. We need learning processes that can entertain volatility in the work environment.

Consequently, to be vocationally successful, people will need to replace the idea of skill or competence with the "meta-competence" of learning. By "meta-competence," I am referring to competence that transcends itself. It is not any particular skill that is critical but the change of that skill to adapt to the environment. Another way of putting this is to say that the most important skill or meta-competence is that of "learning-to-learn." Rather than learning job-specific skills, workers will be asked more and more to learn situation-specific principles attending to a given work domain. By mastering these principles, workers can be expected to handle ongoing variability in work demands.

The learning I am addressing here, the "new" learning, will also have a personal, even spiritual, side, as it will be based on the self-reflexive principle of becoming. Personal learning of this character (which I will continually refer to in this book as the practice of reflection) allows us to investigate our precarious nature. It also invites others to review our nature under the assumption that exposure is oftentimes preferable to concealment. None of us wish to make our lives an open book. The T-group movement of the 1960s proved that total disclosure doesn't really free us any more than utter stoicism. Yet we need to err on the side of more disclosure as we attempt to develop ourselves and try out new roles. Our growth is measured not just in quantitative but also in qualitative terms. We are as concerned about the human qualities of dignity and integrity as with our competitor's market share. In this sense, our obligation is that we do the only thing that we ultimately can contribute of ourselves, that we grow and become who we want to be.

The Basis for the New Learning

Let's consider how the new learning widens and thus changes our entire conception of the learning process. Keep in mind that work-based learning, compared to conventional learning modalities, such as training, is designed to be consistent with the new approach. First of all, let's recall that *learning* is a verb—an action verb that is concerned with a phenomenon in motion. Hence learning is continuous; like fish, if it stops it dies. I am always puzzled by corporate educators who depict knowledge as a competitive advantage. Learning is what creates and also adapts, deepens, and transfers knowledge. Since learning is ongoing, knowledge by itself cannot constitute a competitive advantage. Once it is acquired, it will become stale if not continually renewed. It is learning, then, in its active sense, that constitutes the competitive advantage.

Learning is both a cognitive and a behavioral process, although it is cognition that is both the sufficient and necessary condition for learning to occur. On the other hand, a behavioral manifestation may be necessary to distinguish learning from knowing. Consider, as an example, that most of us know that our bodies need exercise. We also know what foods make for a healthy diet. Learning may not become apparent, although it may have occurred, until we process that knowledge in a way that leads us to exercise regularly and eat healthy foods consistently.

How does learning evolve? Learning begins when we attend to information. At that instant, information from the environment or from within the self is compared to cognitive frames that we already hold. For example, we may come in contact with data that challenge existing patterns or meanings. As this process of comparing meanings unfolds, we may or may not change our behavior. This is why behavioral change is elective insofar as learning is concerned. We may choose not to change after having experienced a cognitive reinforcement of what we already know. We may also use the new information to change our frames or patterns of relationships, but we may not change behavior or even need to change behavior at that moment. However, the new meanings now stored in memory could eventually produce new behavior.

Learning can take place at three levels, though we tend to associate it most with the first. In first-order, or single-loop, learning, new data produce a direct challenge to current actions. As we question our prior actions produced from reliable frames, we may choose to try new actions. In this way, first-order learning resembles what we commonly think of as "trial-and-error." We are essentially moving from using preexisting habitual responses (zero-order learning) to learning about such responses.

In second-order, or double-loop, learning, we learn about contexts sufficiently to challenge the standard meanings underlying our habitual responses. Thus, using second-order learning, we find ourselves capable of transferring our learning from one context to the other. By third-order learning, we become aware that our whole way of perceiving the world has been based on questionable premises. We learn about the "context of contexts" such that our entire assumptive frame of reference can be challenged. Indeed, it is conceivable that without third-order learning, the potential for transfer of learning characterized by second-order learning may be limited as practitioner actions and even adjustments become habitual and unwittingly inflexible (Freire, 1970; Burgoyne and Hodgson, 1983). For example, in the midst of action, we may begin to rely on preconceived criteria for appropriate action. Unfortunately, this tendency limits our innovation in working through irregularities in certain contexts. Using third-order learning, one holds a virtual reflective conversation with one's situation. In this way, we attempt to uncover the underlying assumptions guiding our work and readjust our practice.

Consider an example: The executive staff of a large company determines that in order to stay lean, the company will need to reduce head-count. They appoint a task force to "learn" how to proceed with a rational restructuring of the company: Should they lay off workers across-the-board; should they concentrate on weak operating units; should they rely on natural attrition; or should they make specific cuts? Working thus far at the first order of learning, perhaps someone on the task force might pose a second-order thought or question: "I'm wondering whether we have a real productivity problem." "On what basis has the decision been made to make us more lean?" "What evidence is there that restructuring through layoffs is the correct solution to begin with?" "Maybe there's another way to attack the problem." "Maybe we don't even have a problem to begin with but we are on the verge of creating one."

In third-order, or triple-loop, learning, or what Ackoff (1994) has termed "dissolution," basic premises are questioned. In this case, someone might ask why it is that reductions-in-force or restructuring constitutes the set of usual alternatives proposed whenever there's a concern about productivity. Someone might also ask why the organization permits disquiet at the top of the company to lead to knee-jerk implementation efforts or what prevents individuals from raising these types of questions to the executive staff to begin with.

Just-in-Time Learning

Work-based learning, then, is concerned with learning at each of these three levels, but it is particularly interested in providing a setting for third-order, or triple-loop, learning to emerge. As such, learning-to-learn will become more critical than learning specific topics. Second, as we acknowledge that individuals learn in different ways, we will need to accommodate diverse learning styles and contexts in introducing new ideas. Third, and perhaps most important, learning will gradually become disentangled from the idea of the classroom.

The classroom will no longer need to be the sanctuary for learning. Indeed, consistent with the orientation of this book, the workplace can be viewed as a prime location for learning. In fact, we are even moving away from an old presumption that one has to travel to a place in order to obtain one's learning. Learning can occur in the very work that we do in our own organization. Peter Francis, president and chief executive of J.M. Huber, a $1.4 billion industrial and natural resource products company based in Edison, New Jersey, offered the following perspective at a roundtable sponsored by *Chief Executive* magazine (1995) and Arthur D. Little Company:

> Many people equate organizational learning with school, and they respond, "Yuck!" Yet everybody I know has something they love to do, whether it's crocheting, playing the banjo, reading, or traveling. They must feel the joy of learning when they're doing it. The challenge is creating—and perpetuating—that love of learning in your organization.

In this way, learning can be viewed as responding to the individual's needs and preferences and being delivered just-in-time to be of use to one's work, to one's thinking, and to one's feelings. Note that the role of teacher must also be reconceptualized. Teachers are not necessarily instructors who provide information to captive audiences. In the new learning described here, teachers are just as likely to be mentors, group project leaders, learning team facilitators, and designers of learning experiences (Twigg, 1994).

With the new learning comes the realization that learning involves active engagement in the action at hand. One doesn't become "learned" by simply spouting formulas or proofs. Citing prepared answers to standard questions will do little to establish one's expertise. Learning occurs not so much within the classroom as within a community of scholars or practitioners in which one becomes familiar with the real questions of practice. In fact, knowing only the explicit formulas is what gives the outsider away. Those on the inside know more. Brown and Duguid (1996) characterize this action form of learning in this way:

> People don't become physicists by learning formulas any more than they become football players by learning plays. In learning how to be a physicist or a football player—how to act as one, talk as one, be recognized as one—it's not the explicit statements, but the implicit practices that count.

In the domain of executive education, companies are gradually turning toward pedagogical approaches that address immediate corporate issues rather than those that subject their executives to lengthy and lofty theoretical lectures or even worn-out case studies (Wines, 1996). Such companies believe that general business principles are best illustrated by weaving real-life corporate strategies and problems into the curriculum. The thinking behind this approach is in fact the classic business formulation of ROI, return on investment. Participants in programs derive personal learning while simultaneously working out creative solutions to current corporate dilemmas.

In a study involving interviews with 74 executives from 65 corporations, 48 consultants, and 52 university leaders, Fulmer and Vicere (1995) found that the majority of new corporate educational initiatives were relying less on classroom time and more on facilitated, small-group, action learning applications. The classroom is increasingly being seen as just a temporary station for illustrating a concept or tool that must then be applied to a current challenge or issue on a real-time basis to complete the developmental experience.

Consider how Symmetrix, the management consulting firm, approaches learning during its heralded "Friday meetings" (Driscoll, 1995). Every Friday, a three-hour forum is held not just for company employees but for clients, prospects, and job candidates. The meeting that ensues is not your typical corporate meeting; in fact, people attend under one condition. They must participate in vigorous discussion. An associate might offer a brief presentation on a new technology, a partner might lay out a vexing problem confronting a new client, but whatever the topic, people come to realize that it is all right to challenge their colleagues' assumptions and reasoning. At one Friday forum, the chief executive officer, inspired by an associate's dilemma, jumped up to argue against his own conclusions on an earlier case. The president of Symmetrix says of the Friday meetings, "They allow us to see reality through multiple eyes. This helps us generate collective knowledge; it assures that as a firm we keep on learning."

How Managers Traditionally Have Learned

Up to now, I have made reference to the conventional management development approach, but let's give it a closer look. First, I'd like to consider training. We spend literally billions of dollars on management training throughout the world. One study placed the tab for U.S. executive education at about $12 billion (Fulmer and Vicere, 1996). At the same time, there is growing concern that we are not netting a sufficient return from this considerable investment. Tannenbaum and Yukl (1992) found that while most trainees enjoyed their training classes, any performance effects were at best short-lived. Transfer of learning to the job was quite low; in fact, in some cases, less than 5 percent of trainees claimed to have used their training on the job. According to Sveiby (1997), after five days, most people remember less than 10 percent of what they heard during a lecture. When activities are used involving seeing and hearing, the retention climbs to about 20 percent; however, when trainees learn from doing, people remember 60 to 70 percent of what they practice. It is no wonder that, according to a *Human Resource Planning* benchmarking survey of best-in-class companies (Olian et al., 1998), there has been a noticeable trend toward incorporating learning into the job itself. General Mills, one of the best-practice corporate respondents, indicated that only about 10 percent of its training now occurs away from the job.

The problem with classroom training is that it tries to make neat an activity that is normally messy—be it technical work that is found in the trenches or the very practice of management itself. Neatness and order derive, in turn, from control, so it is no surprise that most training activities are under the fairly precise control and pacing of the trainer, not the trainee. Management, furthermore, is a complex practice since problems change from one setting to the next. It is no wonder that executives who travel off to residential training experiences, though personally transformed by the training, find it almost impossible to influence their organizations in the "transformed" way when they get back. The problem is that the transformation is individual in scope. The executive may have been transformed, but the organization and its departments and divisions have remained in their familiar patterns while the executive was away. Clearly we need a management education approach that appreciates the contextual variety in management practice.

The way Werner Ketelhorn (1996), professor of strategy at the International Institute for Management Development (IMD) in Lausanne, puts it, training equips trainees with toolkits. He goes on, "But a manager who plays a memorized tape each time he or she encounters a problem is not going to solve that problem. A tool cannot replace thinking. And training to use tools cannot replace education."

According to Brinkerhoff and Gill (1994), there are five scenarios out of six that could make the typical training program not only ineffective but highly inefficient. The sixth successful scenario centers on employees receiving the right training when they need it. The other less propitious scenarios, which the authors feel are unfortunately common, are

1. Employees receive the right training, but it is too late to use.
2. Employees receive training that is irrelevant to their work environment.
3. Employees are forced to wait for training that they need.
4. Employees wait for training that they do not need.
5. Employees attend training to escape a punishing work environment.

Items 1, 3, and 4 address the issue of learning being just-in-time, as noted earlier; in other words, learning must occur as one encounters a problem. Knowledge or skills provided after they are needed may be wasted, forgotten, or, worse, poorly transferred if they are no longer relevant (Brinkerhoff and Gill, 1994). While the fifth item needs no explanation, the second item suggests that training resources may be wasted if they are not tailored to the situation confronting the employee. When courses are provided off-site by trainers not familiar with the organizational environment, further waste may occur if the training content is delivered without knowledge of the firm's or unit's cultural and political idiosyncrasies.

A fairly typical account of a training department's response to a managerial need was reported by Stamps (1997) as he described how Xerox initially attempted to integrate three of its separate customer service departments at its Texas customer service center. The consolidation was expected to take two years because the corporate training department, which is in Leesburg,

Virginia, would have to craft separate curricula—each involving weeks or months of design—for each aspect of the various customer service jobs. The reason for requiring this much time at the outset was due to the need to place training department officials on-site to determine training requirements, which would then, in turn, be handed off to the curriculum designers back in Leesburg. Once the curriculum was written, there would be the training itself, which was expected to take 52 weeks.

Unfortunately, once the training was delivered, the trainees reported that they spent too much time on tasks that they never or seldom performed and far too little time on some of the most crucial aspects of the job. Their trainers, although good platform presenters, were not themselves customer service reps, so they trained on the basis of a carefully crafted curriculum, not on the basis of actual experience. There was also no time for trainees to practice what they were taught during the three to four weeks of training. As a result, when they finally got back to their job, they had forgotten most of what they had been taught. For example, trainees were put through 11 weeks of lectures on credit procedures before they were allowed to take their first call.

Having considered the pitfalls of training, let's look at the other principal method of developing managers and executives—through experience per se, that is, by rotating them through a wide range of experiences so they can learn the broad task of managing the whole organization (Vicere, Taylor, and Freeman, 1994). In practice, managers are often given a variety of so-called "stretch" assignments to season them and to expose them to various operating areas to help them learn "general management" skills. Unfortunately, these assignments, though often challenging, do not necessarily come with any consistent form of mentorship; nor is the assignee given much chance to reflect with others on the skills presumably being learned. Experience, in other words, tends to teach in private, reinforcing the notion that learning is done individually, not collectively, in organizations.

Nevertheless, experience can be a very effective learning vehicle and has some clear advantages over formal courses. In particular, as Bunning (1992) points out

- Experience is not a scare commodity. It occurs naturally on an everyday basis for all managers involved.
- It is not artificial or isolated from the actual work itself. It occurs simultaneously with the actions of managers as they carry out their regular work roles.

- It is unquestionably relevant. Any learning that results from the experience is highly likely to be applicable to the work situation from which it arose.

There are ample lessons available to managers in their everyday experience; all they have to do is take advantage of them. Gerber (1998) points out, for example, that workers can learn from such practices as making mistakes and learning not to repeat them, solving problems, interacting with others, being an advocate for one's colleagues, offering leadership to others, or practicing quality assurance. Unfortunately, unless these practices are brought out into collective consciousness, much of what is learned may not be generalizable or transferable. From cognitive research, moreover, we know that experience, though producing formal and informal knowledge of one's organization, may not necessarily help executives learn from the tacit skills that they will actually be using in accomplishing their tasks effectively.

Consider the common use of job rotation, which is thought by many human resource managers to be the most effective route into general management. Job rotation assignments expose so-called "high-potential" managers to a cross-section of operating departments in both line and staff roles. After completing the assignments, the cream supposedly rises to the top. Yet why is it that many of these aspiring managers fail in their first general management assignment? Unfortunately, though they may have exhibited effective skills in their job rotation experiences, there is typically little opportunity for them to reflect on and process these skills and competencies, *even when they were performed effectively*. When confronted with new situations calling for the use of these same skills, therefore, they haven't learned sufficiently to know that these implicit skills can be applied (or not applied, as the case may be) in the new context.

As an example, perhaps one of the assignments given to a trainee is to work with a management negotiating team to hammer out a labor agreement with one of the company's powerful unions. During the course of the negotiations, the trainee may have picked up some valuable bargaining skills. When placed in his first general management job, the former trainee faces the challenge of staffing a new project group within a matrix structure. Unaware that he is in a negotiating environment, he selects people from the various functional organizations—accounting and control, operations, market research, quality—to staff the new project team, only to find resistance from each appointee and often from the appointee's boss. He attempts to circumvent the resistance by asking his boss to intervene on his behalf, only to find his boss astonished that he hadn't solved the problem already.

What happened here is that our trainee hadn't learned sufficiently about contexts to apply techniques that he had, in fact, learned. His learning, however, was at a technical first-order level, which did not translate into the new environment. Was our trainee learning disabled? I would contend that it was not necessarily an intellectual gap that caused this trainee's downfall. Rather, the organization itself may have set him up for failure by disregarding the need for ongoing reflective practices throughout his training, which was based only on experience.

In addition to experience per se, some training departments like to use so-called "experiential" activities to attempt to simulate real-life experience. As I shall point out in Chapter 4, these simulated endeavors, often referred to as experiential learning, can be quite effective in giving trainees a taste for the use of concepts in action. However, simulated experience is just that—simulated, not real. Simulation is not designed to be real, but in fact to simulate reality as a way to give trainees a taste of what might ensue in real experience. Experiential learning thus has a valid role to play as a precursor to real work-based experience; however, it cannot be a substitute. Ultimately, we need to move from having learners think about how others would act in certain situations, to having them think about how they themselves would act, to having them act.

Simulated experience often makes reality appear to be tidy or logical. Trainee actions seem to generate their desired effect. Yet trainees do not obtain necessary reflection in how their plans and actions get misinterpreted once placed in the woolly world of action. Likewise, human contacts often seem to lead to agreements in simulations, even in those that involve tough negotiations. Real experiences seem to lead to a higher degree of disagreements and failures and require reflective practices to help practitioners overcome these unplanned disturbances.

A More Radical View

There is another set of reasons why formal training may not be working as well as we might like in our management development programs, but they have more to do with psychology and politics than with pedagogy. Let's start with the proposition that although educators, whether in formal university classrooms or in corporate training facilities, have every good intention of teaching about management, quite often their students—practicing managers—go to great lengths not to learn what is taught. This contradiction by no means suggests incompetence on the part of university or corporate instructors; in fact, both make every effort to make their sessions active and practical. For example, classes tend to be packed with a variety of hands-on activities, cases, and exercises. There is maximal emphasis on practical techniques and normally minimal coverage of theoretical concepts.

Unfortunately, an implicit theory guides the foregoing pedagogical approach. It is that managers themselves are actually passive learners under the assumption that they cannot take charge of their own learning and cannot use conceptual knowledge unless it is reinterpreted for them and delivered using carefully reconstructed methods (Salaman and Butler, 1990).

The passivity of learners is reinforced by the long-standing assumption that the role of the teacher is to rescue learners from their state of "not knowing." Teachers collude in allaying learner anxiety by structuring the curriculum to minimize unexpected or anxiety-provoking occurrences and by controlling the class to prevent destabilizing dynamics, be they irrelevant discourses from students, emotional outbursts, or even silences. The last thing expected from teachers is to confront students with their own state of not knowing and to help them face the fears that such not knowing can produce. Otherwise, such a practice would be akin to abdication of one's responsibility as a teacher to meet students' dependency needs (Raab, 1997).

Beyond preconceptions about practitioners' learning needs, further disjunction between the theory of teaching and its actual practice evolves when the knowledge in management education does not jibe with organizational realities. Although the delivery of courses may cover leading-edge content, it often presents perspectives that might not yet be embraced by the organizational hierarchy. Hence, although well-presented by instructors and consequently well-understood by students, the new knowledge may be strategically tucked away by these students for fear that its use would be punished if practiced in that same hierarchy. This very condition was acknowledged by Chief Learning Officer Steve Kerr as the basis for changing GE's Leadership Development program when he quipped that "It's Organization Development 101. You never send a changed person back to an unchanged environment" (Rifkin, 1996).

We might also propose a more sinister view regarding why students may purposely not learn from their courses. The adoption of management education programs is normally planned by the top of our knowledge dissemination industry. Top managers discuss with trainers in advance the apparent content to be covered in training sessions. Department chairs and their faculty review the course curriculum to decide what should be included; but, the knowledge that gets disseminated and even produced conforms to a worldview that is often disparate from the locus of its implementation—operating management. Meanwhile, there is a well-known tendency on the part of operating managers, at various levels within the hierarchy and representing different sub-units that compete for resources, to intentionally distort information passed down from the top (Lawler et al., 1980; Argyris and Kaplan, 1994). Coming back from courses, they know too well which knowledge they can put into effect and which is better left aside or even intelligently rejected.

An Integrative View

The previous, radical view notwithstanding, there are many effective management development programs that are legitimately and democratically offered to very eager consumers of the knowledge and skills provided. In such programs, managers may be given ample opportunity both to try out and to implement any new methods directly into their workplace. In such instances, work-based learning can and should be allied with traditional methods of management development. At the same time, work-based learning can correct some of the limitations of classical training methods. In closing this chapter, I will depict nine flaws that I believe to be associated with conventional management development and show how work-based learning addresses each of these weaknesses (Raelin and Lebien, 1993; Raelin, 1997a). To bolster some of my arguments, I will refer to a study I conducted at Lancaster University in the United Kingdom of three graduate-level programs, each of which used the form of work-based learning known as action learning.

1. *Lack of opportunity to practice and transfer training experiences.* As I have depicted, in conventional training trainees attend a course or workshop and then are expected to practice or put into effect the training principles or skills as soon as they return to their job. In distributed training models, sessions are spaced apart; hence, time is occasionally allotted in subsequent classes to discuss the impact of any personal or managerial changes. Although the latter approach addresses the issue of transference, it is normally not a key component of the training

experience, as most courses require students to move on in order to cover new content. In work-based learning, however, the application of course principles and skills is fundamental to the experience since students are expected to use them in their project work. The issue of transference is directly tackled in learning teams as participants debate their successes and disappointments in implementing course-based ideas. Furthermore, as they encounter resistance to their plans and actions, compared to general training programs, they now have the opportunity to bring back their experiences to their colleagues for further reflection. After completing a program, students have thus not only studied managerial theory but have tried it out in practice and have reflected on its utility as well. The workplace is the classroom. In the research study of the work-based learning programs referred to previously, fully 78 percent of the program participants and 66 percent of their on-the-job colleagues reported that the theory and practice components of their respective programs blended. Among the most critical benefits reported by the respondents were the subject matter and the intellectual stimulation. Participants truly found the material to be both interesting and yet relevant to their work.

2. *Paucity of leadership and other competencies.* The evolving global marketplace has increased competition and subsequently increased the demand for flexible and experienced managers. Consequently, in-house training is shifting its focus to competencies such as leadership, strategic thinking, visioning, ethical judgment, and versatility. Unlike traditional development programs, work-based learning can have a positive and noticeable impact on a manager's development in such areas. In project work, for example, participants could be required to employ resources throughout the company, using all the people skills and political acuity they can muster; take the risk of making a major decision; and then present and defend that decision in a professional, yet convincing, manner to upper management. The leadership and behavioral strengths and weaknesses of each manager soon become apparent, providing participants with the opportunity to learn from their experience. Among the research findings, colleagues of the participants mentioned that

they had noted some significant behavioral changes. In particular, participants were noted to have markedly changed in the area of questioning behavior, especially at the strategic organizational level, although within the work unit as well. Participants were also reported to have developed a renewed openness to new experiences and greater sensitivity to others. These behaviors would appear to signify leadership competencies that are unlikely to be learned from passive educational experiences. Indeed, being able to question and learn from new experiences and from other people represent hallmarks in the search for quality management.

3. *Lack of business and organizational relevance.* Management development departments frequently attempt to make coursework relevant to their business and to their organizational culture by tailoring their offerings. Nevertheless, at times it is more economical to use "off-the-shelf" programs. A familiar criticism of such offerings is that though well-presented, they may not relate well to one's own culture. When work-based learning programs deploy projects in the participants' own organizations, it is unlikely that business or organizational relevance would even crop up as an issue since the focus is on real problems.

4. *Absence of learning-to-learn.* Many managers attend courses in management education and development out of necessity or obligation. They obtain their credits or certificates and then move on to do their job perhaps slightly better prepared than they were prior to the training. More often than not, they are not inspired to continue learning on their own; if a deficiency arises, there's always another course. Since work-based learning only whets the participants' appetite in relevant theory, they almost automatically seek more information as they embark on their projects. The search process becomes fundamental to learning since past experience may not suffice as a guide. It teaches a fundamental proclivity of learning-to-learn that tends not to be disregarded once the training is over. Indeed, in the research study, 87 percent of the participants committed themselves to continue the learning process after completing the program.

The experience seemed to have stimulated some genuine intellectual curiosity such that business books would now compete with trashy novels for reading "at those holidays in Spain" (as one respondent wryly commented).

5. *Insufficient time for interaction.* We know that one of the most favorable side-benefits from training is the opportunity that executives get to share experiences, trade tips, and build their networks. Yet this is normally considered a secondary objective, not a primary goal of the experience. Work-based learning makes collegial interaction and conversation a fundamental component of the program. Participants are not only encouraged but obliged to discuss their project experiences with one another. Naturally, during this time they also engage in informal networking and sharing. Oftentimes, their exchanges entail a fair amount of self-examination and candid feedback, which tend to lead to more realistic self-perceptions. When asked what they liked the most about their action learning experience, the most popular response among the participants in the research study was the opportunity to network with like-minded colleagues. This was the case regardless of whether the program was consortial, expressly assembling participants from different settings, or company-based. In the latter instance, participants reported using their contacts from the program to help them get things done in their own company.

6. *Meager executive-level training.* One of the common perceptions about management training is that executives sponsor it for all levels in their organizations except for their own. Among the reasons offered for their modest appetite for training is the time commitment, especially for classroom-type experiences. Two of the three programs chosen for the research study were executive development programs, although they could be also characterized as "high-potential" programs for junior executives rather than for CEOs. Nevertheless, the results seem to support a genuine commitment to the experience among the participants and their executive sponsors.

7. *Cynicism.* As I pointed out previously, if training outcomes are not considered a normal part of operating behavior, participants may sense a disjunction between

course content and everyday organizational life and become cynical about course attendance (Salaman and Butler, 1990). Although this kind of thinking can never be eradicated totally, it is less likely to arise in work-based learning settings since managerial legwork is required to launch the program in the first place. If executive sponsors do not want certain practices performed in their organization, then they won't sanction the respective projects. However, once they endorse a work-based learning effort, they tend to be prepared for double- and triple-loop learning challenges. Hence program participants are likely to know early on whether their learning will be considered valuable and legitimate and appropriately rewarded.

8. *Avoidance of diversity issues.* We have heard so much about the changing demographics of the workforce. Because their opportunities to acquire sophisticated skills are sometimes limited by circumstance, language, or even bias, nonmajority workers present a special training dimension. Work-based learning promotes adaptive behavior as well as the more traditional technical skills, encouraging employees to face the challenge of working within a diverse workgroup head-on. For example, learning teams expect members to engage in free and open exchanges, leading in many instances to disclosure about feelings toward one another. It is natural in this setting to inquire about diversity in cultural viewpoints.

9. *Excessive costs.* Often traditional programs are held off-site and require enormous outlays to pay for high-overhead vendors. While the instructional component of work-based learning may be held off-site, projects and learning teams are often assembled on-site. Facilitators and mentors can be recruited from within the company. Material costs such as books and videos tend to be modest. Although participants may spend time away from their regular jobs, as in traditional courses, they typically work on significant projects that could reap substantial benefits for the organization. In Chapter 10, I will devote an entire section to how the returns of work-based learning compare to its costs.

3

The Distinctiveness of
Work-Based Learning

*It is what we think we know already that
often prevents us from learning.*

—Claude Bernard

Having established the grounds for work-based learning, we now need to examine its distinctiveness compared to other familiar and closely allied management and organization development approaches. Most affiliated with work-based learning is the organizational development movement known as organizational learning. I have already suggested in the Introduction that work-based learning might be considered the engine of organizational learning in that it furnishes the developmental activities and educational efforts to help an organization establish a culture of organizational learning. In this chapter I will provide an overview of organizational learning and then demonstrate its connection to work-based learning. In a similar way, though less extensively, I hope to demonstrate how work-based learning relates to the competencies movement and how it might alter educational policy. I also consider in this chapter the characteristics of individuals and organizations that might predispose them to work-based learning. I conclude with a special section on the relationship between work-based learning and leadership.

Work-Based Learning and Organizational Learning

Just as individuals need to learn in order to actualize their being, to engage with their environment, to grow and become, organizations need to learn to maintain themselves and, of course, to improve. Any organization that has survived within our current turbulent global environment is already a learning organization in one form or another. Some pundits sell "organizational learning" as another recipe for competitive advantage, but in fact it is more than that. It is a way of organizational life that will keep the organization intact, that will allow it to be ever adaptable to its surrounding environment. Redding and Catalanello (1994) consider it to be a survival ethos: Those organizations that will survive are those that can absorb what is going on in their environment and act on that information appropriately. Essentially, such organizations "learn their way out" of environmental challenges.

So, organizational learning can characterize a set of activities that go on in a learning organization. And what is a learning organization? According to Vaill (1997), it is a type of organization whose internal structure and process is marked by imaginative flexibility of style in its leadership and by empowered contributions from its membership. It is constituted to learn and grow and change. Its members engage in a continuous process of discovery and experimentation. In such organizations, learning becomes a way of life. Members feel free to challenge the governing values of their practice. Structures and standards can change to accommodate new information. These organizations tend to be involved in a continuous process of discovery and experimentation. Perhaps Al Flood (1993), Chairman of the Canadian Imperial Bank of Commerce, said it best when he noted that in a learning organization, the company doesn't "force employees to learn, but creates a context in which they will want to learn."

Learning organizations also work to maintain a fit within their environment. The way Hayes and Allinson (1998) put it is that members of learning organizations diagnose their organization's predicament, integrate this information into a shared mental model, and then use that mental model to modify, as required, the rules that guide decision making and action.

Learning is thus the critical link between plans and operations, between our thinking and our doing. We learn what worked and what didn't work. Further, if the process is continuous, if we can challenge the organization to deliberately engage in a steady diet of reflection, we can learn constantly. Trial-and-error learning occurs only after failures; true organizational learning should just as likely occur after breakthroughs or after successes. We shouldn't need a crisis to point out the gap between our plans and our execution. We are just as interested in learning what went right as what went wrong.

There is a natural tie between organizational learning and the emerging practice of knowledge management that encompasses generating, disseminating, and assimilating the intellectual assets within the organization. As I noted, the learning organization with its emphasis on organizational learning engages in activities that stress the generation of new knowledge through free exchange of information, experimentation, and the sharing of existing knowledge. The main difference between organizational learning and knowledge management seems to reside in the relative emphasis on technical versus behavioral explanations. Some knowledge management practitioners tend to focus on improving accessibility to information through such technical means as networking technology. Others, more aligned with the organizational learning school, are concerned with cultural and behavioral processes inside the organization that can induce or impede creativity and learning.

In this chapter I am not as much concerned with differentiating these approaches as with showing how work-based learning can serve as an engine for transforming an organization to be receptive to learning. First, we need to understand the process of organizational learning, for which some familiar knowledge management concepts can be instructive. Consider the three-step approach proposed by DiBella, Nevis, and Gould (1996):

1. *Knowledge acquisition.* This is the development or creation of skills, insights, and relationships.
2. *Knowledge sharing.* This involves the dissemination to others of what has been acquired.
3. *Knowledge utilization.* This entails the integration of knowledge so that it can be assimilated, made broadly available, and generalized to new situations.

Let me describe these three steps in a little more depth. In knowledge acquisition, new knowledge is created through the development of new ideas, made available through internal or external sources. If the knowledge in question is formal, then acquisition entails the provision of documents, reports, or on-line information from personal or institutional repositories either inside or outside the organization. If the knowledge is tacit, then the creation of new knowledge requires a formal elicitation of this less structured information into a usable format.

Choo (1998) believes that "sense making" is the key driver of knowledge acquisition. Changes in the environment of an organization create internal discontinuities (Weick, 1979). People begin to challenge their usual interpretations of phenomena. They may find that "doing things the way we always have" may no longer work, causing a rethinking of how to manage new contingencies. A case of effective sense making was reported by Meyer (1982) at a San Francisco community hospital that in 1975 suffered a major physician strike due to an abrupt cancellation of the group's malpractice insurance. The administration of the hospital anticipated the strike two months before it happened. They collectively developed a scenario that projected the consequences of the strike, distributed it to all department heads, and then asked each to develop new knowledge to cope with the contingency of a major work stoppage. When the strike hit and occupancy sank to 40 percent, the hospital was ready. In fact, cost cutting was so effective that the hospital actually made money during the strike!

Knowledge sharing means getting the information into the hands of people who might need it, though they may not even realize the need. Hence, the knowledge carrier has to be aware of and learn how to work through a good deal of organizational interference, such as local language idiosyncrasies or inattentiveness. In fact, Dixon (1995) recommends that carriers may need to spend some time in another person's space before there is a willingness to accept the new knowledge. The organizational culture itself may also present a barrier to knowledge dissemination since it often exerts conformity, exercises control, and otherwise deters learning except for what is delivered according to accepted norms (Hendry, 1996). Since new knowledge may be disruptive, users have to be prepared to reframe their problems or to confront dilemmas between their espoused beliefs and actual practices. Further, the organizational culture needs to be shaped to encourage everyone to share their knowledge. For example, compensation and performance evaluation can be linked for purposes of sharing knowledge.

The knowledge infrastructure within the firm should thus be user-friendly; in other words, employees should find it easy to connect with one another, be it through internal e-mail or intranet platforms, so that they can swap information with one another. Francis O'Brien, Senior Manager at Ernst and Young's Knowledge Management Solution Team, also advises appointing a knowledge team that includes a chief knowledge officer, whose role it is to set knowledge policies and procedures and to champion and shepherd them through the organization. In addition, people need to be appointed at the department level to ensure that everyone knows how to contribute to the knowledge database.

Knowledge utilization continues the dissemination process to another level, for this is where knowledge can be widely integrated throughout the organization. Grant (1996) refers to this process as "knowledge capability." It is one thing to have new knowledge lodged within the specialties that directly use it; it is another to integrate this knowledge throughout the organization. Perhaps Chris Argyris (1982) has been most instrumental in providing organizations with methods to circumvent the barriers to knowledge utilization in his advocacy for so-called Model II behavior. In a Model II world, organizational members make free and informed choices about change based upon valid information, and they maintain, as a consequence, a high internal commitment to any new behavior that they adopt. Therefore they feel free to make their reasoning explicit and to reveal their inferences, because they know that their colleagues and peers will do the same. They regard assertions as hypotheses to be tested, challenge errors in others' reasoning, and openly explore differences with others even to the point of bringing up the "undiscussables."

A good example of knowledge utilization comes from the United States Army at its Center for Army Lessons Learned (CALL) at Fort Leavenworth. CALL sends teams of experts into the field to observe missions firsthand—collecting, analyzing, and integrating insights from dispersed sources—and then works with both line and staff organizations to disseminate the knowledge in various forms (Baird, Henderson, and Watts, 1997). CALL's knowledge management system was put to the test in 1994 when it was called upon to prepare troops for both combat and peacekeeping operations in Haiti. Using observation and analysis of prior engagements as well as actual deployments of troops in Haiti, CALL developed 26 scenarios likely to be faced by the troops, complete with video footage, virtual simulations, and scripted responses. In actuality, the troops in Haiti ultimately faced 23 of the 26 scenarios developed.

Knowledge Transfer

Integral to the organizational learning processes described in the previous section is the notion of knowledge transfer. Learning organizations make it their business to see that knowledge is freely transferred throughout their organization from department to department. Lex Service in England, for example, has created a "virtual university," where managers from different lines of business and in different areas of the country can communicate with each other about diverse operating problems (Arkin, 1996). This has to be done in such a way, however, that one unit can make sense of the data received from another. In many instances, more than a database is needed. A representative from a unit, say manufacturing, might be made available to a design unit to help interpret a particular transferable process. Sharing resources in this way might even be required across similar functions that are located in different regions of the country or the world. Daniel Tobin (1998) reports about an unusual but highly successful knowledge-sharing practice used at Buckman Laboratories, a Memphis-based specialty chemicals company with business in 80 countries. The company asks its salespersons to write up one unique case history of how one of its customers developed a unique application of a Buckman product, most likely one that had not been suggested in the product manuals or training programs. As these case histories make their way around the company, salespeople in different regions begin adding these applications to their sales calls. Access to the cases is as simple as logging on to the company's knowledge network. Besides maintaining a library of case studies, Buckman's network also provides employees with a set of interactive forums through which employees can dialogue with others, no matter where they might be in the company, to get answers to their operating questions.

Learning-oriented companies are beginning to deploy knowledge "shepherds," whose job it is to collect and diffuse learning throughout the organization. These shepherds are not industry experts per se; rather, their job is to make sure that queries from interested parties get answered. For example, Columbia/HCA maintains electronic repositories of documents detailing their most successful business processes. Users at Columbia's 340 hospitals nationwide can search and retrieve information through the company's intranet. But how is the information acquired? In the case of ambulatory care, an internal team of shepherds regularly visits each of the company's 147 ambulatory surgery centers, identifies best practices, and describes them in pages posted on the intranet. Shell's Learning Center employs 10 subject matter specialists who comb both internal and external sources for leading-edge practices, which are then contributed to the company's Knowledge Management System (KMS) repository. Similarly, at Monsanto, topic experts are appointed to sift through and contribute material on particular topics. Shepherds are also assigned to ensure that dialogues are carried out among different departments (Hibbard, 1997). At PricewaterhouseCooper, so-called knowledge "concierges" maintain some 25 internal databases. They regularly purge, add, and reorder information such that any consultant in the firm can tap another's knowledge by accessing the relevant database (Halper, 1997).

Knowledge shepherds often operate in conjunction with internal benchmarking or best practice teams. Benchmarking teams are typically formed to export and adapt outside practices for the organization. Best practice teams tend to be part of the ongoing networking structure of the organization charged with identifying and transferring existing internal practices. At Chevron, the best practice teams are coordinated by functional experts called "process masters," who act as internal consultants assisting with the transfer (O'Dell and Grayson, 1998).

The Use of Experts

The most basic form of knowledge transfer is the familiar master-apprentice relationship (Polanyi, 1966). The master shows how things are done, the apprentice imitates the process, and the master evaluates the effort. As apprentices begin to apply the rules inherent in the work process, they begin to look elsewhere for inspiration, perhaps from explicit sources or from other experts. Once they become very skillful, they might become experts themselves. What is it that characterizes expertise?

We know that experts are able to revise their cognitive patterns or frames quite flexibly in response to changes in environmental cues (Schön, 1983; Dreyfus and Dreyfus, 1986). Indeed, they do not as much stop and think (of which theory and procedure should be used next) as keep alive, in the midst of action, a multiplicity of views of the situation (Hoshmand and Polkinghorne, 1992).

Expert practitioners are thus able to enrich their inquiry by examining competing frames of reference of particular situations in order not to reduce their perception to a single, all-inclusive perspective (Morgan and Ramirez, 1983). Experts possess wisdom that is far more than knowledge, for it characterizes what you are rather than what you have. Wise people consider what *needs* to be explained.

The novice and even the learned craftsperson typically know in advance the job that needs to be done. Their task is akin to a jigsaw puzzle: They must merely put the pieces together in an organized manner. The master, or what in Anglo-American societies is often referred to as the wise "professional," does not view the task as a jigsaw puzzle, for he or she recognizes that the task is not set in advance. The master, therefore, develops new "tools" or new ways of thinking about the job before being able to complete it satisfactorily. Invented on the spot, these new tools are designed to fit the requirements of the job at hand. Using wisdom, the master is thus able from time to time to make something that was never dreamed of before rather than solving something that was already there.

Although we treasure our masters as a basis of knowledge transfer, at the same time we also need to reduce our dependency on experts. All experts are not necessarily competent in or even interested in teaching; many prefer, in fact, to work on their own except for occasional professional exchanges with peers outside the organization (Raelin, 1991). So, it becomes critical to spread expertise around the unit or organization as much as possible. This can be accomplished by allowing cross-functional deployment of staff, which allows workers to do more than one job. Piggybacking can also be used. According to Sveiby (1997), piggybacking is a structure in which senior professionals may display their skills for juniors to imitate. At *Affärsvärlden*, a Swedish magazine, for example, junior writers accompany senior journalists to interviews and press conferences in order to learn some of the tricks of the trade. Sveiby also recommends making more use of open-space offices to promote more face-to-face open communication of tacit knowledge. Professionals and individual contributors who do wish to share their expertise can participate in work-based learning experiences through mentorships.

Expertise may be available from sources not only inside but also outside one's organization. Novices can learn a great deal from merely observing interactions between experts. Once they get their feet wet, they might be able to draw lessons from stories or anecdotes shared between other workers in their presence. In time, they might also be able to learn tricks of the trade from members of the community outside their particular specialty. Gherardi, Nicolini, and Odella (1998) report in their study of the construction industry that novice site managers learn much from both observing and talking with bricklayers, architects, machine operators, technicians, dealers, and commercial representatives and officials.

The Engine of Change

Work-based learning can be the format of preference to establish a culture of organizational learning. First, work-based learning arms the organization with the proper skills to establish a community characterized by inquiry. In particular, participants in work-based learning programs, by being asked to reflect regularly on their practice experience, develop the confidence to challenge fundamental assumptions about their actions and those of others. Work-based learning also breeds teamwork characterized not just by mutual task work but by consideration of others. The reflective orientation of work-based learning supports the simple yet overlooked practice of giving time to one's work colleagues (Newton and Wilkinson, 1995). As members of a learning team prosper from the support of their colleagues, they become inclined to extend the culture of learning to others. Once a critical mass of people have experienced work-based learning, the organization as a whole may develop the necessary will to embark on a mission of learning. Finally, work-based learning provides the necessary structure or platform for organizational learning to occur. For example, executives will begin to notice the impact of action learning project teams, the emergence of communities of practice, the development of informal mentoring relationships, and other manifestations that enable the process of organizational learning.

Susan Wyatt (1997) uses very similar logic in discussing how individual learning can be transferred to team learning and then to organizational learning. The process begins with public reflection, which she describes as occurring when members of a team suspend judgment and begin to observe and reflect on their common experience. Public reflection then leads to shared meaning, which involves reaching mutual understanding by refining shared vision and values and updating members' mental models. Once shared meaning is acquired, members of a team can begin to work on a transition plan to transfer their learning processes into the workplace. This can be accomplished by using the very work-based learning techniques discussed in this book—that is, by reflective practices that attempt to introduce "sustained, collective inquiry into everyday experience."

Work-based learning can also be a complement to or even a substitute for expertise in a work unit or in the organization as a whole. It can create a shift in the organizational culture from dependence on expertise to learning with and from fellow learners. The knowledge made available arises not from a fount of available expertise but naturally from the collaborative inquiry of fellow learners deciding through experience what to do next. Work-based learning, then, calls for a partnership in learning (Botham, 1997) wherein different people with different ideas engage whole-heartedly with each other in order to resolve each others' problems as partners-in-adversity. To be effective, the partnership needs to be both supportive and, at the same time, challenging, deeply caring, yet questioning. Those participating find that they have not only addressed a pressing problem but have engaged in a continuing process of professional and personal development.

Hence, consistent with our view in the last chapter regarding the need to update the concept of apprenticeship, the expertise of the master in work-based learning is not so much an instruction as a tacit guidance (Rogoff, 1990). In fact, the responsibility for structuring the learning process is shared between master and apprentice. The dialogue between the two helps both to interpret and to articulate experience. Without the inquiry of the apprentice, the craft knowledge of the master—largely a knowing-in-action—remains for the most part unarticulated.

Knowledge transfer does not occur naturally in management development. Unless the instructor makes provisions for trainees to share with one another, the learning that takes place tends to be passive and individual. Any knowledge transfer that does occur goes on in the interstices of the training experience. In lauding the knowledge transfer properties of management development at Shell, for example, Arie de Geus (1997) admitted that course attendees evaluating their experience gave explanations such as this: "It was not so much what I learned in the official sessions but what I picked up from my colleagues during the breaks that was important."

Work-based learning attempts to bring these "off-line" conversations, often considered by trainees to be the most useful segment of their training, into the learning experience itself. Conventional classroom training tends to segment the formal learning from the informal, and in many cases, doesn't even acknowledge the value of the latter. In work-based learning, the informal learning that transpires in learning teams, in significant developmental relationships, in unplanned crises that erupt in project experiences, and so on is made a centerpiece of the experience. Formal learning is as much developed to support the inquiry process in behalf of problem solving as it is for its own sake.

The initiation of work-based learning processes can begin quite modestly, perhaps with some experiments in remote parts of the organization, to build credibility for the idea that learning and work can be synonymous. In organizations already attuned to a climate of risk, work-based learning projects can take place at the highest strategic levels of the organization. At KPMG Netherlands, Ruud Koedijk, the firm's chairman, facing a shrinking market in the auditing business, made a bold move in 1994 of establishing a "strategic integration team" of 12 senior partners and 100 professionals from different levels and disciplines (Heifetz and Laurie, 1997). Divided into 14 task forces, the team developed learning projects in three areas: gauging future trends and discontinuities, defining core competencies, and articulating the learning challenges facing the entire firm. Each task force was housed on a separate floor with its own support staff. As the experiment took hold, work-based learning, taken as a whole, led to changed attitudes and behaviors at KPMG. Curiosity became more valued than obedience to rules. People no longer deferred to the senior authority figure in the room. Genuine dialogue replaced deference to authority. In all, the task forces identified more than $50 million of new business opportunities and primed the firm to be a more nimble player in its professional service markets.

In a similar vein, MCB University Press, thought to be the world's largest management journal publishing house, chose to use a work-based learning approach in transforming its very structure from an academic ownership model to one involving more professional management. Accordingly, six- to nine-month action projects were chosen from across the company to enable managerial growth and ownership succession. These projects transformed the company's strategic vision and produced many valuable functional changes, such as the development of a computer-based integrated customer environment, initiation of a new electronic production system, the restructuring of the acquisitions and new launches units into a business development center, development of an electronic publishing initiative, and the endorsement of a multifunctional team dialogue process (Gore, Toledano, and Wills, 1995).

Work-Based Learning and Competencies

Another tradition in organizational learning—the competency movement—has a number of parallels to work-based learning. In brief, the intent of the competency movement is to identify and develop competencies or behavioral characteristics of managers that are specific, observable, and verifiable (Jacobs, 1989; Schroder, 1989). Once in practice, competencies are thought to lead to superior managerial performance if performed well (Albanese, 1989). Although some competency apologists, such as Boyatzis (1982), understand that these competencies need to be adjusted for contextual factors, such as environmental and internal organizational conditions, most competency writers believe that there are certain tasks required of all managers in any organization. Competencies labeled "generic" are thought to be applicable to an entire class of managers across organizations and positions (Powers, 1983). On the other hand, "organic" competencies (Raelin and Cooledge, 1995) constitute those that apply to particular managerial jobs and are specific to the context and language of the organization. It is my view that only organic competencies can have the specificity and fluidity to represent meaningful categories of managerial work.

The generic competency movement seems to be operating, unfortunately, under the methodological flaw known as "multiple causality." As has already been purported, managers need to respond to an unpredictable environment through an unabiding commitment to learn. Rather than emphasize predictability, they need to look for patterns that lurk beneath seemingly random behavior. Hence, causal links, such as the one proposed between competencies and performance, are unlikely to be tenable. Although some competencies might contribute to effective managerial performance, surely there are other attributes, tangible and intangible, controllable and uncontrollable, that also cause effectiveness.

The real issue at the heart of the generic competencies debate is whether competency attainment is necessary to be a good manager. Competencies that might lead to effective behavior for one job in one company may not translate into effectiveness for that job in a different organization or even for a similar job in the same organization.

Assuming one could identify relevant competencies for a given managerial job, the applications within management development are legion. Competency models have been used in all phases of human resource strategy, including recruitment, selection, performance management, team development, process improvement, and compensation, as well as development and training. Indeed, competencies are thought by some managers to represent the language of their strategic human resource policy, allowing the organization to match its available human resources against its strategic needs (Woodruffe, 1991). In particular, the development function benefits from tailoring competencies to one's own environment. Development here does not refer merely to positioning oneself for a rapid ascent up the managerial hierarchy. It refers to learning those skills that will inspire both individual and team performance. Competencies used for development, however, need to take context into consideration. They should be "organic," arising from the specific context of the individual, job, and organization rather than from an artificial list. Organic competencies offer a language for purposes of feedback discussions. By preserving the local idiom, managers can recognize identifiable categories of performance.

Pedler, Burgoyne, and Boydell (1978) identified three overarching categories of competencies, each of which incorporated generic as well as situational components. The first category represents basic knowledge used in managerial decision making and action. Besides mastery of managerial techniques and functional competence, basic knowledge also requires working knowledge of the organization and its policies. The second category constitutes specific skills and attributes that directly affect behavior. Here again, generic competencies— be they interpersonal sensitivity, leadership, team development, or initiative—are combined with contextual attributes, such as organizational and political awareness. The third category constitutes "meta-qualities," such as ingenuity, open-mindedness, and self-awareness, which allow managers to develop the situation-specific skills that they may need.

Work-based learning operates at all three levels identified by this seminal work. In their project work, participants are challenged to work within and then stretch the boundaries of their local operating context. They are virtually prevented from being effective if they plunge ahead unaware of their surrounding organizational culture. To the extent the program also furnishes conceptual foundations in functional management domains, these ideas or theories can find immediate application in the everyday working environment. The utility of these theories, however, is tested against their actionable relevance. How do participants recognize the effectiveness of their knowledge and competencies? They not only obtain feedback from milestones in their project work, but their workplace peers and their learning team peers are always present to offer a reading of their ongoing performance.

Meanwhile, the skills and attributes brought out in the workplace, whether in their project work or in their regular operating responsibilities, are also placed under constant scrutiny. Participants in the safe environment of the learning team actually look forward to bringing out examples of their managerial practices for examination within the group. Where the program also institutes self-assessment vehicles, participants match their performances both in the job and within the group against assessed strengths and weaknesses.

Finally, the meta-competencies receive special consideration in work-based learning. This is no more apparent than in the public reflection called for in learning teams and in other development relationships built into the program. Participants are asked to challenge their fundamental assumptions about their practices, even when such challenge can precipitate some uncomfortable behavioral change and soul-searching. In order to proceed in this kind of learning environment, the development of such meta-qualities as open-mindedness, ingenuity, and interest in self-development is encouraged.

Work-Based Learning and Educational Policy

It is interesting to note that the words "work-based learning" are expressly used in U.S. legislation called "The 1994 School-to-Work Opportunities Act." The act provides funds for activities that are classified as work-based learning as well as those that are termed school-based learning. Although there are separate goals for each component and separate listings of activities (e.g., work-based learning has a pedagogical goal of presenting students with "real world" application of concepts), school-to-work proponents acknowledge that pedagogical benefit occurs only if work-based learning activities are well-coordinated with the classroom. Early assessments of the program recommend that work-based learning activities be carefully planned and dovetailed with the classroom components. It has been my contention in this book that work-based and school-based learning should *not* be segmented. Work-based activities are not meant to be accomplished once students have learned their lessons. Rather, they offer an opportunity for students to apply their classroom principles immediately into work as well as to reflect on their work practices.

At the level of higher education, there is a fundamental lack of understanding of how to surface the learning in work-based learning. A report by State Higher Education Executive Officers (Van Horn 1995) found overwhelming support for the use of "experience-based learning" as the best way to help graduates make the transition from college to work. Yet the only method cited as an example of experience-based learning was the use of internships and cooperative education. Hamilton and Hamilton (1997, p. 682) warn that "simply placing young people in workplaces does not guarantee that they will learn," and Gordon (1997) points out that there is little evidence that practices of this kind can lead to a specific career path. Further, Kevin Hollenbeck (1997) suggests that if one of the intents of the school-to-work legislation—that of restructuring education to consider the value of contextualized learning—is to be achieved, there is a need to offer professional development to teachers and counselors to help them effectively operationalize this new form of learning.

Perhaps of most concern to the readers of this book is the relevance of work-based learning to educational policy as it relates to management development and management education. Oddly enough, there once was a time, in fact up until the 1960s in the United States, when managers prepared for their craft by first becoming intimately connected with their industry and organization. Some would obtain a grounding in liberal arts education but most would learn the tools of the trade on the job. Unfortunately, there was little opportunity for public let alone private reflection on their work practices save for occasional function-specific training experiences. Moving into management entailed a commitment to work with and through others to accomplish the organization's or organizational unit's goals. As new challenges presented themselves—new products or processes, technological advances, international trade, or competitive pressures—novice managers would learn to cope by plunging into the problem and getting their feet wet as well as by committing themselves to a lifelong learning experience in the problems of management in their industry. Lifelong learning was implicitly endorsed by the corporate community (Raelin, 1990).

Many cultures around the world still prepare their managers in this way. In the Anglo-American countries, however, in societies that are "profession-conscious," academics and educational leaders associated with management education have sought to advance the professionalism of management. Professionalism does not necessarily mean increasing the service ethic of the field or expanding the commitment to one's client. It means gaining respectability, especially in academic circles. In fact, four pivotal studies, two in the United States (Gordon and Howell, 1959; Pierson, 1959) and two in the United Kingdom (Constable and McCormick, 1987; Handy et al., 1988), called for a process of professional and academic qualification through the acquisition of standardized managerial knowledge and skills. In order to upgrade management education, the American studies essentially advised mimicking the academic process prevalent in the esteemed graduate programs of the social sciences. The reports reasoned that increased managerial professionalism could be obtained by extending the coursework required of students and by more careful screening of their instructors, whose credentials would now require a full-scale research program—one that would hold up under scrutiny by most any accredited, liberal arts academic department.

If a graduate program is designed to professionalize its education, then it should endeavor to enroll students as early as possible into the program. There should be no floor establishing a minimum age or experience. It needs to initiate students in the knowledge, skills, and values attending to the profession before they can practice it. According to this model, professional students, in order to experience total immersion in their field, should be segregated from those studying other disciplines (Raelin, 1991). They should be bound by the unique concepts and language of their discipline as well as by sheer propinquity. As they face their rites of passage, marked by milestones of examinations, boards, and clinical trials, they will naturally band together. As an intact group, they will be exposed, through a protracted period of study prior to entering their chosen profession, to the discipline known as management.

As is self-evident, this professional education model was based on the notion that knowledge in a field can be substantially learned prior to entering one's profession. One would not practice the profession first and then return to school to learn what he or she did right. The need to have education precede practice in the professions, however, does not have to be replicated in an experientially based, messy, interdependent occupation such as management. Education, especially lifelong learning, may be required, but it need not be provided as an intensive first experience. There may even be a floor establishing the amount of experience required before any intensive education would be worthwhile. Managers cannot be effective by learning a set of systematic "professional skills"—skills to be applied once the learning is over. In fact, the learning needs to be constant, interactive, and quite often nonsystematic. It needs to be organization- and industry-specific, and as much behavioral as technical. It requires, in sum, the contribution of a work-based learning modality.

Predisposition Toward Work-Based Learning

Are there certain types of individuals and organizations that are predisposed to work-based learning? I have found that in terms of individuals, those likely to derive useful benefits from these programs tend to be looking for a challenge, to be committed to their organization, to be consistent in their beliefs and actions, and to be risk-oriented (Raelin, 1997a). Bunning (1992) adds that such individuals need to be curious in their outlook, creative and innovative, and collaborative. They are also likely to be opportunistic (in their learning) and collectivist. An opportunistic learner is someone who is committed to learning in life from whatever source is available—reading a novel, being engaged in conversation, observing an interesting display. Such a learner doesn't need proof that learning can occur as much from experience itself as from the formal discipline of teaching. Opportunistic learners also are curious about which circumstances seem to produce the most efficient and effective learning for themselves (Honey and Mumford, 1992).

Individuals with a collectivist orientation are people who have a general propensity to cooperate with others in group endeavors (Eby and Dobbins, 1997). Whether it be in project work involving others or in learning teams, work-based learning tends to require a commitment to work and learn in the company of compatriots. Those with individualistic orientations, who prefer to work on their own and also to learn on their own, tend to object to the groupwork contingent in successful work-based learning programs.

FEL member David Ashton asserts that a simple diagnostic question, merely asking people to describe their work, can be quite revealing in diagnosing predispositions among potential learners. Managers who describe their job by merely listing the duties or responsibilities attending to their job description tend not to be interested, at least in their current setting, in their own personal and professional development. On the other hand, managers who like to describe the broader context of their work as it affects other functions in the organization tend to be committed to contextual learning.

Elena Antonacopoulou's work (1995), though not concerned specifically with work-based learning, can be quite instructive regarding the predispositions of individuals toward company-based educational efforts. She distinguishes between philomathic and mathophobic learners. Philomathia describes individuals who maintain positive attitudes toward learning and a readiness to explore and improve through learning. Mathophobia describes individuals who are reluctant to or lack confidence in their ability to learn. Moreover, mathophobics often refuse to take personal responsibility to develop themselves, have little sense of direction, and are typically unwilling to explore different learning avenues. What makes someone mathophobic? In her study of a major bank in the United Kingdom, Antonacopoulou found that these anti-learning managers were not just passive in the face of learning opportunities but in some cases were actually fearful of admitting their ignorance because it might be disclosed in a public setting. They also felt that they were unable to influence the learning environment in the organization.

Besides these internal factors, Antonacopoulou also found that organizational norms and policies could affect individuals' predispositions to learn. Most dampening to personal learning habits was the company's inconsistency between its espoused support of development activities and its actual implementation of this policy. A female manager in personnel noted, "When people at the top pay lip service to aspects they breach, they do not give the example for others to follow." Other organizational factors revealed in the research were incompatibility of learning style between company and individual, lack of support from one's boss and from one's other colleagues, and discontinuity and lack of clarity concerning the organization's expectations.

Weinstein (1995) suggests that work-based learning seems to be most effective with individuals who can release a so-called "inner learning cycle." These people do more than merely recall experience; through internal processes, they make themselves open to personal transformation. The processes she describes incorporate an awareness of, a desire to, and the personal courage to change on the basis of personal insight.

In terms of the organizational qualities that facilitate work-based learning, I found that cultures that value collaboration over individualism and organizations that are clear on their mission and goals seem to produce better work-based learners. Bunning (1992) also contributes some additional qualities in the organizational domain; in particular, work-based learning outcomes are enhanced in organizational cultures that value

- organizational nondefensiveness
- learning as a basic norm
- process-oriented leadership in addition to a focus on content
- reflective self-examination by individuals and teams
- commitment to change

Honey (1994) as well defines a series of behaviors on the part of managers and staff that he feels need to be present if the culture is to support the approach that I have referred to as work-based learning. Among these behaviors, three stand out expanding on those already mentioned. In particular, in learning-oriented cultures, people tend to (1) ask a lot of questions, (2) explicitly talk about learning, and (3) freely admit their inadequacies and mistakes.

Work-Based Learning and Leadership

This chapter, which has attempted to show how the tradition of work-based learning connects to other management and organizational development approaches, would not be complete without reference to the critical topic of leadership. Work-based learning, as I have established, supports a different form of organization than the classic bureaucracy. Bureaucracy, by definition, is concerned with rules and regulations that are devised to impose order on an organization. The learning organization, on the other hand, though recognizing the value of some order, at the same time reassesses it by challenging closely held assumptions and structures. It upends standard ways of doing things by encouraging independent thinking from the factory floor to the executive suite. It recognizes that knowledge becomes stale as soon as it is used and requires learning, as I have pointed out, to adapt, deepen, and transfer it.

If work-based learning contributes to turning the structure of bureaucracy upside down, then it should come as no surprise that it also tends to disrupt the classic definition of the leader as the one "who stands out in front." We must not take everything away from the classic definition, since it can be agreed that leaders do mobilize others. However, in the learning environment, rather than providing answers, leaders reinforce and join others in the search for questions. French statesman Alexandre Ledru-Rollin once said, "There go my people. I must find out where they are going so I can lead them." Leaders in the current era similarly must be designers of the future. They question old patterns and act with courage when faced with conditions of ambiguity, complexity, and stress. The leader of the future is thus cast as someone who has direct working experience with so many people in the organization that he or she knows their abilities and thus can use this knowledge to direct resources where they are needed (Hesselbein et al., 1996).

Hence, leaders are just as likely to create meaning as to provide solutions (Drath and Palus, 1994). Meaning is not the same concept as divine vision, which is possessed only by the leader. Rather, meaning refers to an expression of common interests and commitments that resonate throughout the entire community. In searching for meaning, leaders engage everyone in actions that enhance learning. Oftentimes, their job is to balance action with reflection. More specifically, they engage in explicit acts of learning creation. Meisel and Fearon (1996) offer four components:

1. *Finding a gap in the information needed by the organization.* Leaders amplify the "hearing" of coworkers. They appreciate that doubt or uncertainty can be seen as an opportunity for learning, not just a state of anxiety to be remedied.

2. *Accepting the risk to experiment on various new courses of action.* This means that they are willing to stop action at times in order to ask or accept uncomfortable questions that may lead to the exploration of very new ideas. They are also willing to face conditions that have been suppressing learning, even if these conditions have been known in the past to be successful.

3. *Organizing a search for the acquisition or creation of new information.* In this search, they release everyone for a while from work per se to engage in the learning work of the organization. Learning leaders recognize that we are all knowledge workers; we are all co-learners. In a concept known as "open-book management," employees are asked to view themselves as partners in business. At

Springfield ReManufacturing, CEO Jack Stack, co-author of the *Great Game of Business* (1994), believed in this concept so deeply that he gave every employee access to the company's financial information system so that they could understand their role in the overall performance of the company. Similarly, Republic Engineered Steel's CEO, Russell W. Meier, regularly shares economic data with employees. Meier believes this gives his workers "a better understanding of the economics of the company and the pressure we face every day in the marketplace" (Robertson, 1995).

4. *Converting new information into workable knowledge.* Leaders don't relax when solutions are found. Instead, they recognize and are willing to explore the discontinuities between solutions and implementation. They are supportive of those willing to experiment with new ways of doing things, even when such newer methods challenge the status quo.

The learning orientation of leaders is also context-dependent. Although the competency of meaning creation is generic, it takes on a different form depending upon the culture one is in. Corporate leaders are not interchangeable parts and cannot be transported willy-nilly from one company to another. They need to be bred into their own culture, understanding its subtleties and dynamics. Work-based learning contributes to the home-grown orientation of learning leaders by exposing them to company-specific problems. They undertake projects in their own environment and they deal with corporate-specific business issues, not those from other companies found in case studies.

Dotlich and Noel (1998) make note of some additional leadership competencies that tend to be acquired through work-based learning:

- *Working flexibly.* Being comfortable working with all types of people in all types of teams, including virtual teams that cut across geography, time, and function.
- *Using a breakthrough mentality.* In addition to making incremental improvements, having the courage to ignite breakthrough ideas in product development, applications, systems, and people.
- *Increasing learn/stretch capacity.* Displaying the ability to reach for high goals even while lacking plentiful resources to achieve them.

- *Knowing oneself.* Possessing insight about one's strengths and weaknesses so as to self-manage stress and recharge oneself when running low on energy.

In characterizing the learning leader, Chris Boylan, of Beth Israel–Deaconess Medical Center and a member of FEL, notes that work-based learning tends to produce perhaps the most important competency of reflective practice.

> . . . those who do not just jump to provide the answer to the problem all the time. The usual mode of providing an answer to a staff problem is much quicker, especially compared to developing staff to reflect and come up with the answer themselves, which they usually have anyway. It takes much more time to do this, but in the end is more effective and satisfying.

In a similar vein, Lex Dilworth (1996, p. 52) reports on the group processes of action learning teams organized to support the project component of the Adult Education and Human Resource Development program at Virginia Commonwealth University (VCU). Learning teams are designed to help learners reflect together on the plans and actions they undertake in their project work. VCU's staff deliberately do not assign formal leaders to the learning teams; rather, they let the teams work out the issue of leadership on their own. Supporting the notion of leadership as a shared phenomenon, one of the team members noted the following in her final report:

> The one role that seems to have been of most concern to the greatest number of non-group members was that of our set's leader. Everyone wants to know who it was. So here is the answer to the big mystery— we were all leaders and we were all followers as the group needs dictated. We were, and are, the only ones not concerned about it because we had faith that someone would step up to fill the role. And someone always did; it wasn't always the same person.

Hence work-based learning, with its focus on subjecting one's assumptions to public scrutiny, supports the creation of a new paradigm of leadership consistent with the co-creation theme presented here. Heifetz (1994) expresses it as the person who can orchestrate the conflicts among stakeholders to reach a community of interest, who works with people to face their own tough realities. Perhaps the best personification of this ideal is Jan Carlzon, the legendary CEO of Scandinavian Airlines Systems (SAS). He expresses the mission of leadership as getting people on the executive team to listen to and learn from one another. . . . People can learn their way to collective solutions when they understand one another's assumptions. The work of the leader is to get conflict out into the open and use it as a source of creativity (Heifetz and Laurie, 1997).

Block (1993) refers to this ethic as "stewardship" or "servant leadership." Consistent with Gandhi's trusteeship concept, stewardship means that we have no automatic right to power, that power is merely granted from those below, that we embark on our task of management in trust to those to whom we are ultimately accountable. In work-based learning, leadership builds capacity in organizations by releasing people to develop themselves to their fullest capabilities.

4

Theory of Work-Based Learning

The only person who behaves sensibly is my tailor. He takes new measurements every time he sees me. All the rest go on with their old measurements.

—George Bernard Shaw

It may well be that some readers, as I suggested at the outset, will choose to skip this chapter, which will focus on the theory of work-based learning. However, if as a reader you are willing to entertain some academic thought, you might find that, as Lewin once alluded, the theory [of work-based learning] is actually quite practical! One problem with omitting reference to theory is to leave an impression that work-based learning is "vocational," which unfortunately has come to mean suitable for those who don't like to learn in the classroom. Work-based learning, as I shall repeat often, is not antagonistic to theory; it respects and uses theory. Therefore, it should make sense that it has its own theoretical tradition. This chapter is an attempt to portray this significant tradition in epistemology.

Theory vs. Practice Modes of Learning

Those of us concerned with management development live in two worlds. We speak two different languages. We occasionally come together and exchange views. Although we talk to one another, we are hardly aware that we are not sharing our conceptions of reality. We tend to part company thinking that we had a mutual exchange, but we then go back to our respective worlds for the most part unaffected by the so-called exchange.

We come from the two worlds of theory and practice, and with but few exceptions we have not figured out how to merge them, how to speak in a language that not only informs each other but also advances our mutual preferences. Theory is depicted as the world of thought, and practice refers to the world of action. Other depictions are less dispassionate. Theory is often construed by practitioners as impractical or as "academic" or "ivory-towerish." Meanwhile, practice is viewed by academics as banal and atheoretical. In normal science, the dominant approach to inquiry is represented by a strategic separation of theory and practice. Theoreticians develop hypotheses, empiricists do theory testing, and practitioners apply the results. In the Academy of Management, the major professional association of management professors, three separate journals are published: the *Academy of Management Review* for theory-building, the *Academy of Management Journal* for empirical testing, and the *Executive* for executive practice.

We are only now beginning to understand the epistemological tradition of work-based learning. By "epistemology," I refer to the very foundation of what makes up knowledge itself. For years, educators were imbued with a tradition that split knowledge from activities in the world. We now are more accepting of the view that knowledge (and especially its more dynamic agent, learning) is always occurring. It is part of our everyday life. As Wenger (1998) suggests, if we believe that knowledge is something that is stored, be it in a library or in a brain, then it makes sense to package it and present it without distraction in a succinct and articulate way to receptive students. However, if knowledge is viewed as arising as much from active participation in the very apparatus of our everyday life and work, then we have to expand our conventional format of the classroom and, indeed, interpret the home and the workplace as suitable loci of learning.

Work-based learning is much more than the familiar "experiential" learning that consists of adding a layer of simulated experience onto conceptual knowledge. In work-based learning, theory may be acquired in concert with practice. Theory building, for instance, may be viewed as a practice since those in practice are fully capable of producing theory. The informal activities and patterns of practice can themselves be formalized and disseminated to others in the field (Mott, 1996). The theory produced by the practitioner may be more a practical, commonsense theory, but a theory nonetheless. According to Schön (1988), practitioners build theory as they consciously reflect on challenges of their practice; reiteratively engage in problem posing, data gathering, action, evaluation, and reflection; and then share the knowledge produced with others in practice.

Consider, in my own field of higher education, how a department chairperson performs his or her job. Except for academics coming out of schools of education, there is a dearth of formal preparation in learning how to manage academic professionals and departments. Yet managing in a professional bureaucracy is an enormous challenge since faculty members often behave as individual entrepreneurs rather than as members of a team. In spite of the lack of academic training, some professors nevertheless become very effective chairpersons. Others often make very good mentors to junior faculty or even to incoming chairs. How do they develop their expertise? How do they know how to work through sticky problems?

Oftentimes, they can be found improvising new theories on the spot, theories without the backing of a sustained literature, but theories nonetheless. If an incoming chair were to face resistance to a department initiative from a senior faculty member, for example, she might be advised by a mentor to recruit support from another senior professor first who could, in turn, persuade the recalcitrant. What would be the rationale for this approach? The mentor might be using an implicit theory that suggests that peer encouragement based on a professional relationship works better than administrative exhortation. Although such a theory might find support in the literature, in this instance, it most likely was formulated through years of practice and reflection as part of an actionable knowledge base to be shared with others.

Although there is now a rich source of knowledge to help us understand how work-based learning occurs and may be facilitated, we need a model that might integrate the many traditions underlying its construction. In developing such a model, we need to incorporate two dimensions fundamental to the process of work-based learning: theory and practice modes of learning, and explicit and tacit forms of knowledge. Since theory can be viewed as a frame in which to challenge the assumptions of practice, it makes most sense as a mode of learning when combined with action. Indeed, the connection between the teacher's intentions and the students' understanding is best achieved through action. Practice, meanwhile, is the process by which individuals acquire and practice artistry (Schön, 1983).

Unfortunately, as noted earlier, a disjunction occurred between theory and practice. Its derivation has very much to do with a view of knowledge espoused by the modernist tradition in epistemology (Bernstein, 1976; Hanfling, 1981; Rosenau, 1992). Although modernism has itself branched into multiple forms, its essence is that through the use of reason, the course of civilization can be tamed, and progress through the regulation of innovation and change controlled (Bell, 1974). It also holds that human beings, through the commonsense of ordinary discourse, can reach consensus on a reality that exists outside of human thought (Cooper and Burrell, 1988). In probing reality, modernists need to separate themselves from their viewpoints so that they can "know" an objective world.

Among the many branches of modernism, positivism (or logical empiricism, as it is commonly known), is the one most associated with the view that facts or reality are based on the "positive" data of experience. Moreover, reality can be described and explained through the manipulation of theoretical propositions using the rules of formal logic (Lee, 1991). As new theories are introduced and current ones are subjected to greater scrutiny and revision, scientists are able to map and predict reality more accurately and thus sustain progress in human endeavors (Popper, 1959).

Positivists were generally of the view that knowledge revealed through science was superior to that produced from values, feelings, or untested experience because of its adherence to scrupulously objective and unbiased methods. Consequently, theory, which afforded testable propositions, was deemed best separated from practice. Teaching was also separated from learning as it became seen as the process of transferring information from teacher to student. Learning would occur when that information was successfully received, stored, and recapitulated. The teacher's role was to focus on theory without taking into consideration the context. It was the students who, once in practice, would have to make the link between the previously learned theory and their current workplace problems. On their own, they might also discover the reasoning behind their practice. Through all this, knowledge assumed a connotation of abstraction and permanence.

But we now know that knowledge undergoes construction and transformation, that it is as much a dynamic as a static concept, as much a collective activity as individual thought (Lave, 1993). Abstract knowledge cannot help but be affected by circumstances, and frames of situations are at best inconclusive until verified by their effectiveness in action. Work-based learning, then, must blend theory and action. Theory makes sense only through practice, but practice makes sense only through reflection as enhanced by theory.

Explicit vs. Tacit Forms of Knowledge

So far, I have contended that work-based learning requires a new epistemology of practice that seeks to explore not just the explicit instructions and guidelines available in the workplace but also the tacit processes invoked personally by practitioners as they work through the problems of daily management. Let's explore in more depth what I mean by the terms "explicit" and "tacit" knowledge. Explicit knowledge is the familiar codified form that is transmittable in formal, systematic language. Tacit knowledge is the component of knowledge that is not typically reportable since it is deeply rooted in action and involvement in a specific context (Polanyi, 1966). In other words, although individuals may be knowledgeable in what they do, they may not have the facility to say what it is they know (Pleasants, 1996). Ryle (1945) made the distinction between "knowing how" and "knowing that." "Knowing how" represents the tacit dimension that often eludes our capacity to abstractly frame our action.

Another useful distinction proposed by Anderson (1983) is between declarative knowledge and procedural knowledge. Declarative (explicit) knowledge represents our conceptual understanding of phenomena, whereas procedural (tacit) knowledge represents our skill in doing something, be it mentally or physically.

Even though tacit knowledge may not be expressed or codified, it may be teachable. For example, a competent trainer might provide an observable model of tacit skill for the trainee to follow and imitate. The tacit skill would thus be apprehensible and observable in use, even though not articulated or put into words (Wright, 1994).

Conventional learning methodologies tend to be theory-based classroom experiences relying on explicit knowledge. Unfortunately, they suffer the risk of leaving inexperienced students with the impression that eventual field problems can be nestled into neat technical packages. But, as Robert Reilly (1982) asks, can these students once in practice think independently, function without sufficient data or extrapolate beyond given data, change their approach in mid-stream, negotiate, and continually reflect and inquire? In a compelling example, he depicts the shock of a fresh MBA-trained manager who finds out that a product line divestment decision has less to do with marginal cost analysis than with personal affinity to the line on the part of the CEO who began his career with the brand.

Work-based learning is interested in both explicit knowledge and tacit knowledge. Heretofore it was thought, especially by classroom epistemologists, that tacit knowledge couldn't be taught; it had to be "picked up" by trial and error at work. However, knowledge creation has been depicted by Nonaka (1991) as transforming what is implicit into something that is explicit, especially through spirals of ongoing interaction between individuals, work teams, and organizations.

The neglect of tacit knowledge arose because it is not necessarily mediated by declarative knowledge; however, it serves as the base for many of our conscious operations. It is perhaps at its most accessible point when we think of our actions as intuitive. This is when we have a sense of the correct action or response but are incapable of explaining why we behaved the way we did.

In using tacit knowledge, it is often preferable to leave one's performance unanalyzed. We wouldn't expect musicians in a concert, for example, to concentrate attention on their fingers since it might disrupt their playing. It is after the experience that one might attempt to bring the inherent tacit knowledge to the surface. In so doing, we might not only improve but even permanently alter our understanding of the situation and, as a result, our actual performance (Polanyi, 1966; Reber, 1976). The critical issue for an epistemology of practice seems to be not whether but *when* to introduce explicit instructions and reflection into the field to yield optimal performance (Howard and Ballas, 1980; Lewicki, 1986).

The Conceptual Model

Using these two dimensions of modes of learning and forms of knowledge, we can construct a conceptual model of work-based learning provided we also consider a third dimension: level of activity. One learns through work at an individual level, since the intersection between the learning modes and knowledge forms challenges personal frames of action. However, learning in the workplace requires an extension of learning out to the collective level defined as one's coworkers—be they within or even outside the present work unit. My emphasis in this book is clearly on the collective level of activity, but I will digress here briefly to describe the learning styles afforded by the model at the individual level.

Table 4.1
A Model of Work-Based Learning (Individual Level)

Modes of Learning	Forms of Knowledge	
	Explicit	**Tacit**
Theory	Conceptualization	Experimentation
Practice	Reflection	Experience

Work-Based Learning as an Individual Property

In Table 4.1, the four individual learning types, resulting from a matrix of the two learning modes and two knowledge forms, are depicted. Astute readers will immediately see a similarity between the labels used here and those depicted in David Kolb's well-known learning style inventory (Kolb et al., 1995). In fact, the processes operating in the work-based learning model and Kolb's learning from experience are compatible. However, since Kolb first produced his inventory, much more research has been done on tacit knowledge, especially by the discipline of cognitive psychology, leading to a deeper understanding of learning processes while working. Furthermore, Kolb's framework was also designed as a way of gaining insight into one's style of learning, which in turn could provide an indication of career interest (Kolb and Plovnick, 1977). The learning types produced in the first matrix of the model of work-based learning do not so much characterize styles as processes that individuals may deploy to learn effectively, efficiently, and critically within work. Although like Kolb I contend that individuals are predisposed to a learning type, all four should be used to engender the most learning in the shortest amount of time. Effectiveness of work-based learning results from the comprehensiveness of facets to which the learner is exposed. It is not sufficient to learn only through theoretical exposition, nor is it sufficient to engage in tacit practices without making one's mental models accessible. Meanwhile, efficiency of work-based learning results from selective attention to each of the four learning types. For example, as we shall see, experience solidifies the learning made tacit in experimentation but may lead to mastery more quickly when subjected to reflection. As we move from reflection back into conceptualization, we hope to achieve criticalness, defined as the ability and dedication to question our underlying assumptions within the learning process. The four sections that follow demonstrate how each of the four learning types contributes to a solid foundation for work-based learning on the part of individuals.

Conceptualization. Basic theory has contributed a great deal to management practice. Not only does theory challenge the assumptions underlying practice but, according to Thorpe (1988), as a way of illuminating and describing action it provides practitioners with a common language and wide powers of analysis. They learn to perceive even standard problems in a new light. Furthermore, by introducing practitioners to new principles, conceptualization gives them a means to tackle new and different problems in different contexts. A consultant who has successfully used the theory of the experience curve in one setting might find it to be equally applicable in a second.

Theory might also reveal problems heretofore undiscovered or left fallow for lack of recognizable solutions. It allows practitioners to explicitly reflect upon and actively experiment with their practice interventions. Consequently, it is virtually necessary in work-based learning if learners are to adopt the capacity to deal with change and with the future—indeed, if they are to imagine.

Conceptualization is often criticized as not being sufficiently real-world, meaning not capable of being translated into practice. As Maclagan (1995) has shown; however, it is possible that individuals use theories to help them with their reasoning but purposely keep them implicit in communicating with others. In fact, since theoretical language may not be accepted in some cultural settings (consider the tolerance toward using ethical jargon), individuals may choose to translate otherwise obscure concepts into everyday language. It is also possible that theorizing is used by practitioners to help them with their decision making but is kept hidden from consciousness. As noted, conceptualization can also provide a basis for subsequent reflection on and reappraisal of actions.

Experimentation. In his day, Dewey (1916) warned educators that mere "doing" or activity was not enough to produce learning; rather, doing should become a trying, an experiment with the world to find out what it is like. At the same time, students need the opportunity to try out their conceptual knowledge so that it becomes contextual or grounded—in a word, that it becomes "do-able." Reliance on conceptualization alone may limit our problem solving since most new or real problems are not yet sufficiently coherent to be organized into theory (Polanyi 1966).

Once they enter the field, students normally encounter a dissonance between their theory and practice. Argyris and Schön (1974) refer to this inconsistency as a difference between one's "espoused theory" and one's "theory-in-use." The espoused theory is the theory with which one enters a situation; therefore, it might well be the conceptual knowledge that a student brings to bear on the situation. Once in action, however, we tend to modify or vary our espoused theories even unconsciously as we employ our theories-in-use. It is important that students have the opportunity to engage in experiments to bring these two theories into alignment. This would be the purpose of experimentation, which often takes the form of case studies, role-plays, in-basket exercises, simulations, and the like.

Consider the plight of a nursing student who enters her clinical experience with visions of attending to the needs of the whole person only to find that the pressing demands of the unit combined with her sheer exhaustion allow her to attend merely to the urgent, physical needs of her patients. A case study or simulation revealing the demands on an emergency ward nurse might help ground the student's conceptual foundations. Experiments such as these serve to make our espoused theories tacit, applicable to the situation at hand, and more understandable to ourselves.

Experience. Learning often occurs through experience. Learners first need to undergo a particular experience and then, as they reflect upon that experience, learn from it (Long, 1990). Learning by experience is important to new practitioners because once they enter the world of practice, no matter how hard they try to apply theoretical criteria, use advanced analytic techniques, or recall a case study, they confront a host of unexpected contingencies associated with organizational life.

Experience reinforces the tacit knowledge acquired in experimentation. It can also be thought of as nonconscious intellectual activity. Practitioners who rely on nonconscious acquisition of information can often not only process more quickly than their more "thoughtful" counterparts but can handle more sophisticated data, such as multidimensional and interactive relations between variables (Lewicki et al., 1992). We all know of athletes who always seem to be at the right place on the field, rink, or court, who are amazingly intelligent in practice but almost totally hamstrung when it comes to articulating their performance. This kind of knowledge, as I pointed out earlier, is not necessarily mediated by conscious knowledge. There is no abstract theory guiding performance in these cases. We act because we are familiar. Subsequently, we can form an impression, a theory perhaps, of our expert activity.

Learning acquired through experience is often referred to by cognitive psychologists as implicit learning, meaning the acquisition of complex knowledge that takes place without the learner's awareness that he or she is learning (Hayes and Broadbent, 1988; Green and Shanks, 1993). Implicit learning is thought to be the foundation for tacit knowledge and can be used to solve problems as well as make reasonable decisions about novel stimulus circumstances (Reber, 1989). Knowledge acquired during implicit learning is often not amenable to verbal report, whereas explicit learning, which proceeds with the subject's awareness of what is being learned, is verbally reportable. It is conceivable that implicit learning serves as the base for conscious operations. It is perhaps at its most accessible point when we think of our actions as intuitive (Reber, 1989). This is when we have a sense of the correct action or response but are incapable of explaining why we behaved the way we did. The subsequent step of reflection allows us to bring our intuitive actions to the surface.

Reflection. Reflection constitutes the ability to uncover and make explicit to oneself what one has planned, observed, or achieved in practice; therefore, it is concerned with the reconstruction of meaning. In particular, it privileges the process of inquiry, leading to an understanding of experiences that may have been overlooked in practice. Thus reflection, as pointed out earlier, especially public reflection, is fundamental to all work-based learning practices. Introduced here as a discrete individual learning type, it becomes all the more critical at the collective level.

Unfortunately, most practitioners are unable to develop a cohesive theory and explanation of their work, though they may be very skilled (Viljoen et al., 1990). As a result, as noted earlier, they have difficulty explaining their interventions to themselves or to others. Reflective practitioners, on the other hand, become sensitive to why they performed in a certain way, the values that were being manifested, the discrepancies that existed between what was said and what was done, and the way in which forces below the surface may have shaped actions and outcomes. Rather than follow prescribed methods, they question whether new approaches could have led to better solutions. Reflective practitioners are thus critical thinkers who have the intellectual discipline to avoid confusing viewpoint and reality. They probe whether a socially approved decision is ethically justified and whether a suggested action is ultimately consistent with the very values that they espouse (Argyris and Schön, 1978; Marsick, 1988; Paul, 1992; Raelin, 1993a).

Reflection is thought by cognitive psychologists to contribute as much to learning as experience itself to the extent learners are active observers. In fact, people often learn behavior from observing others before performing the behavior themselves (Bandura, 1986). According to social learning theory (SLT), individuals tend to anticipate actions and their associated consequences. Hence, before trying out new or altered behaviors, they first pay attention to others and develop mental models or cognitive maps to guide their trials (Bandura, 1977). Perhaps you may have noticed, that when you are introduced to a new skill involving some dexterity, such as making a wrist shot in hockey, you prefer seeing someone else demonstrate the activity first. That way you can develop a mental picture of what the skill entails before trying it yourself.

Patricia King and Karen Kitchener (1994) have developed a reflective judgment model that is developmentally sequenced based upon increasingly complex ways of understanding and resolving ill-structured problems. Individuals progress through the stages of the model on the basis of a number of epistemic assumptions: the extent to which they investigate the facts of a situation; the strategies they use to obtain information; their degree of acceptance of divergent interpretations; and the degree of uncertainty they feel about whether a problem has been solved. By the last stage, reflective judgment entails acknowledging that one's understanding of the world is not a given but must be actively constructed and interpreted. Knowledge is understood in relationship to the context in which it was generated.

Mezirow (1991) distinguishes three forms of reflection. Content reflection is based upon what we perceive, think, feel, or act upon. Initially grounded in Dewey's notion of "critical inquiry" (1933), reflection on content involves a review of the way we have consciously applied ideas in strategizing and implementing each phase of solving a problem. Process reflection, on the other hand, is an examination of how we go about problem solving with a view toward the procedures and assumptions in use. Premise reflection goes to a final step of questioning the very presuppositions attending to the problem to begin with. In premise reflection, we question the very questions we have been asking in order to challenge our fundamental beliefs.

Consider an example of these three reflection forms. Let's say I wish to consider Jim for a job, but I am concerned about his age. I can't ask him directly how old he is because of fair hiring policies, so I need to invoke my content reflection—how can I get a handle on his age? I might ask him when he graduated from college or I might take a closer look at the lines in his face. Yet these data can be deceptive. My process reflection, considering the assumptions in use, might lead me to posit that Jim may have gone to school later in life or that he might look older than he is. Finally, my premise reflection may be invoked when I consider the more provocative question challenging the presuppositions of my query: What if age doesn't matter in the first place regarding Jim's qualifications for the job?

According to developmental psychologists, such as Broughton (1977), premise reflection or "theoretical self-consciousness" is only available to adults. It is only in adulthood that one becomes capable of recognizing paradigmatic assumptions in our thinking. However, adults need to engage and to evoke their reflective consciousness, to learn at this level. Mezirow (1981) calls this learning "transformative" —that is, learning that takes us into new meanings. Transformative learning can help us review and alter any misconstrued meanings arising out of uncritical half-truths found in conventional wisdom or in power relationships. Since higher-level reflection may not occur naturally, educational opportunities need to be provided within the workplace to provoke critical reflection on current meaning perspectives. As Kegan (1982) has noted, however, such a practice can be threatening unless accompanied by an environment that intellectually and emotionally supports individuals in their learning and development.

Work-Based Learning as a Collective Property

Having explored work-based learning at the individual level, we can now turn to the processes of learning within work in the company of others. In Table 4.2, four different learning types are displayed at the collective level, resulting from a matrix of the now familiar dimensions of learning modes and knowledge forms. As we shall see, each type tends to be derived from a distinct epistemological tradition. Yet these four types should also be integrated, as in the case of the individual level of activity, in order to produce effective, efficient, and critical learning. In the next section of this chapter, I review the contribution of the first collective type, applied science, to the model. Because the remaining three types—action learning, community of practice, and action science—offer robust practical implications for developing actual programs in work-based learning, they will be

Table 4.2
A Model of Work-Based Learning (Collective Level)

Modes of Learning	Forms of Knowledge	
	Explicit	**Tacit**
Theory	Applied science	Action learning
Practice	Action science	Community of practice

expanded upon in the subsequent chapter. Although an essential building block, applied science does not receive much attention here only because it constitutes the classic and familiar approach to learning used in most of the world. For purposes of this book, we are most concerned with its contribution to the emerging tradition of work-based learning.

Applied Science

Although experiments under the carefully controlled conditions of the scientific method can proceed in the domain of learning and work, most academics in the management field tend to dedicate their science to instrumental or applied problems. However, as good scientists, they tend not to waver in their commitment to sound empirical methods. Using the guidelines proffered by logical positivism, as introduced earlier in the chapter, they contend that they can gain insight into an objective knowledge or reality that exists outside of human thought (Bernstein, 1976; Hanfling, 1981; Rosenau, 1992).

In an attempt to find areas of objective knowledge still left undiscovered, scientists further explicitly detach themselves from the situations that might reveal elements of this knowledge, they selectively test out preordained patterns of conceptual relationships, and then they draw conclusions that might generalize to other similar situations. The knowledge subject to this intensity of inquiry has these features: (1) it becomes truer or more valid as it undergoes the rigorous methods of theory testing; (2) it becomes expressed as a series of logical relationships often defined using mathematical language; and (3) it invites reformulation as its precepts and procedures are subjected to further scrutiny (Hoshmand and Polkinghorne, 1992). By explaining their methods and elaborating on their data in detail, scientists are willing to have other investigators assess the results of their experiments for themselves. Others may also offer alternative explanations and propose tests of competing theories. Through this empirical debate, a form of detached community of inquiry is formed that seeks to distinguish valid from invalid claims on our knowledge base (Putnam, forthcoming).

Although scientific knowledge has led to a bifurcation between theory and practice and has resulted in disciplinary isolation, applied science—in particular, applied social science—can contribute a great deal to collective knowing (Sutton, 1989). Active theory can inform spontaneous inquiry. What can be most helpful to practitioners is not a pure scientific method that attempts to objectify all organizational phenomena but an applied science that takes into consideration the cultural, political, and moral dilemmas within our social systems (Toulmin, 1990; Wilmott, 1993). We need to correct and qualify what we learn in one discipline by what we learn not only in other disciplines but from everyday life as well (Paul, 1992).

Applied science can make an important contribution to practice by offering theories of action that are systematically tested using the rigorous conditions of hypothetico-deductive logic. At the same time, practitioners have to be allowed to contribute to theory and comment on gaps between formal research and processes in the field. In this way theory can be united with the practice world consistent with the philosophy of praxis (Vazquez, 1977). The history of science and human thought clearly makes room for the contribution of human activity. Conversely, praxis benefits from theory construction and verification (Hoshmand and Polkinghorne, 1992). Our work-based learning methods, for example, as I shall detail especially in Chapter 10, require measurement and evaluation to ensure they are delivering minimally the service they attest to deliver. Work-based learning, then, would benefit most from an applied science that deliberately introduces its methods into the practice field and that solicits the contributions of practitioners.

A Comprehensive Model

Although I have yet to detail three of the collective learning types— action learning, community of practice, and action science—I would like to sketch what the conceptual model of work-based learning might look like as a whole, incorporating both the individual and collective levels of activity, but depicted more dynamically than in a 2 x 4 matrix

(Raelin, 1997b). The now comprehensive model of work-based learning (Figure 4.1) illustrates the interplay between the types of knowledge and the modes of learning at both levels. But, as learners in practice do not step into a discrete space to perform experience or reflection, the model cannot rigidly classify these behaviors. Rather, the model of work-based learning must represent the integration of these styles. For example, conceptualized knowledge ultimately requires the test of tacit experimentation. Pure tacit experience, representing beliefs-in-action, requires the test of reflection.

This approach recognizes that practitioners, in order to be proficient, need to bridge the gap between explicit and tacit knowledge and between theory and practice. Work-based learning subscribes to a form of knowing that is context-dependent. Practitioners use theories to frame their understanding of the context and simultaneously incorporate an awareness of the social processes in which organizational activity is embedded.

Each of the eight types of learning needs to be brought into consideration if learners are to achieve proficiency and criticalness of their learning. Although there is a logic to the choice of neighbors among the types, there is no precise rotation that is recommended. For example, experiments of theory are often tentative or successive, requiring frequent reversion to theory, especially during early stages of development. There are also links represented between the levels. For example, reflections lead to theory testing, which can contribute to science. Furthermore, isolated reflection tends ultimately to incorporate the surrounding social context. Individual learning can proceed independently for a while but it may be illusory to think of oneself as autonomous (Brookfield, 1993). Most of us work with others, and so we need to inquire as to how they see us in action and how they interpret workplace phenomena.

Readers should be able to envision the workings of the model at the collective level even though elaboration of the principal collective learning types awaits coverage in the next chapter. In brief, action learning, one of the most popular of work-based learning methods, places theory into tacit use by having managers learn from their peers while they are all engaged in the solution of real-time problems. Community of practice, an emerging domain of work-based learning, recognizes and encourages the development of tacit collective practices of individuals as they develop a common enterprise and shared ways of doing things. Action science seeks ways to illuminate our practices, especially our untested thoughts and assumptions, so that we can make better choices and enhance our capabilities for effective action.

The collective level is not meant to describe merely group-level phenomena. Although reflections from practice may be shared with an intimate community, the very process of sharing may ultimately spiral out to other communities. Communities of practice, for example, often need to consult with customers and suppliers to expand their understanding of tacit behaviors. Hence, although the model has a modest focus on learning through work, it can contribute to the more encompassing domain of organizational learning.

Each of the work-based styles of Figure 4.1 performs an important function, but various intersections are required to achieve comprehensive learning. A perfectly tacit community of practice may exist in a given work setting seemingly requiring minimal intervention. In fact, efforts to intervene may not only be rejected but may actually interrupt the work flow. However, communities of this nature cannot function as closed systems. In the next chapter, we will examine how new processes, some of which are adopted from action science, and technology might accelerate their learning and performance.

Figure 4.1
A Comprehensive Model of Work-Based Learning

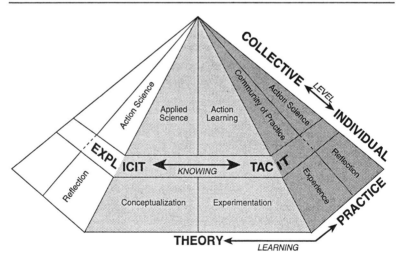

Reprinted by permission, Raelin, J., A model of work-based learning, *Organization Science*, Volume 8, Number 6, Nov.–Dec., 1997. Copyright 1997, The Institute for Operations Research and the Management Sciences (INFORMS), 901 Elkridge Landing Road, Suite 400, Linthicum, MD 21090.

Work-based learning as a framework serves to bring together a number of otherwise disparate learning processes, each of which has its own justification as a basis for learning within work. By integrating these processes, we gather insight into the dynamic interplay of forces that can impede or facilitate learning in the workplace.

5

Three Collective Work-Based Learning Types

A problem is an opportunity in work clothes.

—Henry J. Kaiser

For those readers who braved the conceptual account of work-based learning in the last chapter, we are now ready to examine the three principal collective learning types: action learning, community of practice, and action science. It you're just joining us now in midstream, this chapter will detail some of the action strategies that integrate the learning processes inherent in work-based learning.

Action Learning

Action learning describes an educational strategy, used in a group setting, that seeks to generate learning from human interaction arising from engagement in the solution of real-time (not simulated) work problems. It can take place either in a formal program offered through a university or as part of a corporate management development effort. It emphasizes learning by doing. The application of real experience cannot be overstated in action learning; its exponents sincerely believe that the real world needs to be considered the most auspicious location for learning. Since practitioners are stakeholders in the problems that they attempt to solve, real problems should become the focus of study (Korey and Bogorya, 1985; Raelin, 1997a).

Active or experiential learning devices, which attempt to introduce a spirit of procedural knowledge into traditional lectures—whether through case analyses, action research using consultancy, field research and observation, or multimedia methods—are useful, but they are not sufficient to help students convert theory into tacit knowledge or to learn how to challenge and reflect on their own theoretical assumptions. Students need to take real positions, make moral judgments, and defend them under pressure. Dealing exclusively with simulated events risks defusing or abstracting live conflicts. Cooperation typically is obtained where it otherwise may be impossible, and emotionally laden, complex problems get neatly analyzed into solutions. As Brown and Duguid (1991) have aptly put it, a critical issue in action learning is becoming a practitioner, not learning about practice.

It is not unusual to find that practitioners confuse action learning with experiential learning, because the word *action* might point to any curricular adaptation that allows trainees to become active rather than passive consumers of dispensed information. However, *action* learning differs from *active* learning. In *active* learning, trainees "actively" try applying course ideas or theories—typically by engaging in experiential or simulated exercises. In *action* learning, learners learn with others by working on and then reflecting on actual "actions" occurring in their real work setting.

Practitioners thus need the opportunity to merge theoretical principles with an understanding of the social construction of the organizations in which they work. Most principles about organizations, for example, cannot anticipate the particular circumstances unique to each organization. In action learning, principles become most useful when they help learners become more effective in action. Further, practitioners often learn best by sharing their theories and experiences with each other. Another way to put this is that organizational members need to enter each others' area of operation in order to provide new perspectives and stimulate inquiry regarding practice experiences (Nonaka, 1994).

In action learning, real-time experience, especially problems occurring within one's own work setting, constitutes a good part of the subject matter of the lesson. Opportunities are also provided for substantial debriefing of the real-time experience so that the participant may inquire how others reacted to his or her handling of the situation. Any actions taken are also subject to inquiry about the effectiveness of these actions, including a review of how one's theories were applied into practice. Action learning, therefore, relies on feedback, which by focusing on the participant's values and behavior ensures that any actions are seen not as neutral stances but as positions with points of view and anticipated consequences. Most action learning apologists believe, however, that the "action" in action learning is there as the pathway to *learning*. Solving the problem is fine, but it isn't as critical that there be problem resolution as much as that there be learning from the experience. It is preferable to fail at finding a solution to a problem yet obtain learning than to fail to learn while obtaining a solution to the problem.

Bob Garratt (1991) expresses the epistemology of action learning in this way.

> Adults learn best from live projects; from the support and construc-
> tive criticism of colleagues; from rigourous self-reflection leading to
> serious reinterpretation of their previous experiences; and from a
> willingness to test their hypotheses in action.

In Revans's original conceptualization (1982), learning results from the independent contributions of programmed instruction (designated *P*) and spontaneous questioning (designated *Q*). *P* constitutes information and skill derived from material already formulated and is presented typically through coursework. *Q* is knowledge and skill gained by apposite questioning, investigation, and experimentation. For Revans, *Q* was the component that produced most behavioral change and learning since it results from interpretations of experience and knowledge immediately accessible to the learner. These interpretations are bolstered by feedback from mutual learners who participate in a debriefing of the learner's workplace experiences. Hence, actions taken are subject to inquiry, as stated earlier, about their effectiveness.

In a typical action learning program, a module or series of modules constituting programmed instruction might be presented on a designated theory or on several theoretical topics. Concurrent or subsequent to these presentations, participants might be asked to apply the theories to a real-live project that is sanctioned by organizational sponsors and that has potential value not only to the participant but to the organizational unit to which the project is attached. Participants might work on projects individually or in groups. Either way, other organizational members and stakeholders not directly affiliated with the action learning program may be drawn into the project. Projects span any number of critical problems arising in the organization, such as a strategic decision to enter a new market or a new application connected to one of the company's functional areas. Projects have recognized clients—the departments and respective executive managers from which they originate. Clients take a genuine interest in the assignments and are expected to apply normal business pressures to ensure a high-quality outcome within a particular period of time.

As might be expected, not all organizational problems are solved or are even meant to be solved in action learning. Moreover, proposed solutions may be deemed by management to be too costly in time or money. It is even possible that participants may realize that no quick solution is available. Thus, the experience tends to confront participants with the constraints of organizational realities, leading oftentimes to their discovery of alternative and creative means to accomplish their objectives (Pedler, 1991; Weinstein, 1995). Projects almost always require some kind of output that can be evaluated. Often, a lengthy written statement detailing project aims, performance, and recommendations is prepared. This report, however, is not merely meant to describe the "results" but to detail the learnings and competencies addressed in the experience as well as the real constraints that may have blocked proposed interventions.

The advantages of working on such "real" problems, therefore, become obvious. Participants are forced to find real, workable answers, not easy, hypothetical ones; leadership and teamwork skills are developed along with the more technical skills; the company benefits immediately from the participants' contribution to the project; and the lessons learned from the experience tend to stay with the participants longer than if they had learned them from a book or lecture. Moreover, solving problems per se is not necessarily as much the focus in action learning as "dissolving" them. Consistent with Ackoff's notion of "messes" (1981), organizational problems are rarely stand-alone events but rather messy, dynamic, interdependent entanglements. Action learning participants might just as readily change the nature of the system or the environment in which the problem resides as directly "solve" the problem.

In this way the impact of the action learning project as well as the infusion of organizational members "trained" under this approach can be pervasive. In the PHARE program, a middle-management action learning program funded by the European Union and run by the International Management Center (IMC), the action learning process models reflection for the managers involved, especially in that the whole process, such as the presentations at the end of the program, entails reflective behavior. According to some of their consultants, whom I have met with, the program tends to produce managers who question everything. Some projects have also led to changes in the entire philosophy of the respective organizational unit.

The Leadership for Change program at Boston College's Carroll Graduate School of Management features six-month projects that procedurally observe action learning principles and that substantively invoke leadership efforts attempting to achieve social as well as economic corporate goals. Participants develop their own projects in conjunction with in-company sponsors. As in the PHARE program, Leadership for Change catalyzes change at many levels of performance; the managers emerge as leaders of change efforts and the organization obtains a project that tends to produce residual humanizing effects on its culture. To give readers a sense of some of these projects, three of them are described here in the participants' own words (though the names of the sponsoring companies are disguised).

Project A: "Maximizing Flexibility: Easing the Work/Life Conflict at 'Big Bank'"

Project Description: The project was developed to help address the issue of balancing work and life at a corporate level as part of a comprehensive benefits package. The study started by citing several reasons for the pressures in today's economy on both the individual and on the corporation. These pressures included the globalization of the economy, technological change, customer expectations, downsizing, and family values. These issues were used as a backdrop for an internal survey that identified why the work/life crisis exists, what its dynamics are, and why, in the case of "Big Bank," the benefit structure needed to be changed to bring about a holistic approach to work. Several proposals for work/family balance were introduced as part of the benefit package; some of which were later adopted as part of the bank's human resource policy.

Project B: "The Search for a Simpler Way: Cultural Emergence"

Project Description: This project intervention addressed the issue of how to engage employees in the development of a communications plan for disseminating the results of the Job Review process, a critical part of the reorganization that took place after the merger of "Beta" and "Delphi" Companies. The long-term goal of the intervention was to create a culture that supports open communication by sharing information, building relationships, developing a mutual identity, and nurturing the creation of a culture that values employee empowerment. The most immediate purpose was to improve communication within the division by communicating the Job Review process at both the group and individual levels such that employees would have a sense of ownership of the instrument as well as the process of job review.

Project C: "Creating a Balanced Scorecard for 'Well-Being Hospital'"

Project Description: The project created a simple set of financial and nonfinancial performance measures and developed a process to share the information on a regular basis, called the Period Performance Report. Through surveys and in conjunction with a team of staff, the project identified seven factors to be measured and developed measures for five of them. It also drafted an employee survey to aid in the measurement process.

In terms of our comprehensive model of work-based learning, detailed in the last chapter, action learning occupies that cell where conscious theory is placed into tacit practice. So in action learning, theory becomes contextualized. Context becomes important, however, not only as a basis to evaluate theory but also to evaluate plans and actions. An activity that might be seen as harmless in one context can be viewed as antagonistic in another. For instance, it might be acceptable to confront an action learning team member about her overuse of questioning behavior, but that same confronting style might be viewed itself as hostile in one's work team. Hall (1977) suggests that in analyzing contexts, we not only consider the subject of an event but the situation in which it is occurring. Further, he suggests that we come to understand the roles of those involved, our past experiences in the situation, and, finally, the way the situation is defined by the broader culture within which it is occurring.

Thus, if we're interested in attempting to export a technology used in our unit into another corporate unit, we need to know how that technology might be deployed in the new situation, who might help us champion its conversion and what their role might be, how well our units have cooperated in the past, and what this transference means in terms of the larger culture of our organization. Hall's guidelines can be useful as action learning participants think through the implications of project interventions.

The primary vehicle for providing collective reflection in action learning is the learning team or set, a group of five to seven participants who support each other in their workplace project activity. I will devote an entire section in Chapter 7 to discuss the reflective modality of learning teams, but an introduction is in order here. Learning teams are constituted of participants who, along with a facilitator or coach, help each other make sense of their action learning project experiences in light of relevant theory. Set members become skilled in the art of questioning in order to challenge the assumptions underlying planned interventions in members' projects. Subsequent actions taken tend to be clearer, better informed, and more defensible as a result of the set dialogue (McGill and Beaty, 1992). Johnson (1997), reporting a conversation in a set in which he participated, recalled a quip from one participant: "Your advice at the beginning was useless, your anecdotes were boring, but your questions really helped me."

Participants in action learning, then, learn as they work by taking time to reflect with peers who offer insights into each other's workplace problems. In recent years, there seems to also be a revival in interest in the overlooked P in Revans's formulation. Programmed instruction and theory can inform spontaneous inquiry and offer alternative frames of problems (Smith, 1988; Sutton, 1989). Conceptual frameworks, for example, can help set members work through problems in their project work. Moreover, creative devices, such as synectics and counterinduction, can be introduced to stimulate group and individual problem exploration. Many standard group process techniques are also available to advance the development of learning teams, resulting in improved functional efficiency and effectiveness (Raelin, 1993b).

An example of a conceptual process that learning teams can deploy is Smith's "Performance System Model" (1997). Three elements are introduced: focus, will, and capability. When congruent with one another, they form a self-reinforcing system. Focus calls for a clear definition and understanding of the task in question. Will, associated with attitudes, emotions, and mindsets, represents the strength of intent to action, so it may represent a participant's commitment to a project initiative. Capability refers to the skills, infrastructure, budgets, tools, and physical assets to carry out the project—that is, the necessary interpersonal skills to deal with a reluctant sponsor.

There are many examples of the use of action learning teams in executive education (Houlder 1997). Ashridge Management College has a program called The Action Learning for Chief Executives. It is described as a "supportive and confidential forum in which to review current practices and formulate new ideas. It provides an opportunity to discuss issues with colleagues who understand your problems but are not part of your company." The program organizes participants into groups. Each group then sets its own timetable and subject matter, although everyone brings specific issues to the sessions.

Another organization that uses learning teams is The Executive Committee (TEC), which has three thousand members worldwide. TEC coordinates regional groups of 12 to 15 chief executives who meet one day a month for sessions with a speaker, followed by a discussion of individual business issues. According to TEC, the aim is to provide "a supportive peer group in which chief executives meet for education and counsel."

The Academy for Chief Executives is a similar organization recently founded by a former facilitator from The Executive Committee. It runs groups with a maximum of 14 members. The aim is to provide updates on business developments and help executives continuously improve their personal skills.

Finally, a Global Institute for Leadership Development has been founded by famed educator and lecturer Warren Bennis and the CEO of Linkage, Inc., Phil Harkins. The institute features a week-long intensive experience with related pre- and post-workshop activities. Most interesting in terms of action learning is the use of learning teams, which meet throughout the institute both before, during, and after the program.

Before the program, participants are grouped into teams of 15 to 20 members on the basis of seniority and responsibility. Participants also choose whether to be on a cross-functional or function-specific learning team. Using an exclusive Internet Learning Team Forum, members decide on the common leadership and functional challenges or issues they would like to address during the week of the program.

During the program, the teams meet continuously and are facilitated by a learning team leader. Suggested topics beyond the pre-selected agenda include: process-oriented dialogues concerning that day's main competency, knowledge, and perspective presentations; customized simulations, case studies, and team-building exercises also keyed off the presentations; and problem-solving sessions devoted to actual leadership and functional problems that individual team members are confronting.

After the program the participants remain in contact with team members via the Internet Learning Team Forum. They can turn to fellow team members for reactions to current leadership issues and business problems. In addition, the learning team leader contacts each member within six months to ensure that the development process begun at program registration continues.

One of the members of our FEL community, Robert Kittrell, describes how he manages his learning teams at Leadership Solutions, using a slightly different mode than those above.

> 1) We limit our groups to seven participants (compared to TEC's 12 to 15); I have learned that if I do an effective job of pre-interviewing and bringing together the right mix of CEOs, they will have among their collective number ample expertise, experience, and wisdom

with which to deal with any problem or case presented by any of the members. For my own custom-made groups, I feel strongly that a dozen participants would clutter the lines of communications, as in too many people and too little air time.

2) Each participant in one of our groups, in turn, takes a three-hour session in which s/he presents either a work-related problem for which s/he wants to get new ideas and options, or s/he presents some item related to executive development that s/he wants to examine or improve. After the formal presentation to the group, I meet one-on-one with the presenter to go over the ideas and responses offered by the group. Out of these I work with clients to develop one or two strategy statements, along with a timeline, to which they will commit to accomplishing. Then, at the next meeting of the group they go over their written strategy statement(s), also committing themselves to informing the group of their progress.

It is the step of writing out the strategy statement, and committing one's self to be accountable to the group for future progress and results that mobilizes action learning. Our method provides our clients with constancy, support, and positive reinforcement. It asks them to choose what they want to work on, and then it asks them to be responsible, with help from friends, for the learning process. My work, and the group's, is to hold up a mirror to each participant, challenging him/her to think critically about what is working well and what needs additional work.

Community of Practice

Through action learning we know that learning teams can become a principal vehicle to introduce work-based learning into the work environment. However, we need to consider whether learning teams can also become work teams, or vice versa. Among the most referenced of authorities on work teams are Katzenbach and Smith (1993), who in their *The Wisdom of Teams* define a team as "a small number of people with complementary skills who are committed to a common purpose, a set of performance goals, and an approach for which they hold themselves mutually accountable." In short, when it comes to work teams, such as task forces, there is a focus on the achievement of performance goals. Learning is equivalent to deriving better methods so as to become more efficient and more effective in working together and in producing useful outcomes.

There is, however, another type of team that, though potentially interested in workplace problems, at least initially is even more interested in learning; we've called this team a learning team. Not only are learning teams used in action learning, but as we shall see, they are also relied upon in action science interventions. While individual members may be working on problems in their own work settings, the reason for their coming together is not only to work on these problems but to use the learning team itself to help them examine and possibly revise their reasoning and behavior in their back-home groups. Thus the focus is more on the development of individual capability than on explicit problem solving.

Now, what gets interesting is the question of what happens when one merges these two types of teams. A work team may come together to perform a discrete assignment and eventually disband after completion; however, during the entire process of completing the task, the group may never have congealed as a community of practice. They may never have created meaning together; they may never have focused their attention on their mutual learning or *collective* capability. It could be that only after the task was completed did some of the original members of the task group decide to stay together in a form of learning community that we call a community of practice.

Communities of practice evolve as people united in a common enterprise develop a shared history as well as particular values, beliefs, ways of talking, and ways of doing things (Drath and Palus, 1994). They come together not so much on the basis of formal memberships or job descriptions as by being involved with one another in the process of doing a job. Hence they don't have an agenda as much as an enterprise. Although their reasoning and behavior become shared, there is considerable variation from standard practices. In time, their efforts as a community become natural. Problem solving becomes more of a social activity than an analytically detached process. Although the knowledge produced is often tacit, community members are capable of surfacing it when needed through dialogue (Nelson and Winter, 1982; Bohm, 1985; Scribner, 1986). In other words, their practices become interpersonally instinctive and natural. Meanings are negotiated and the result of such negotiations typically is learning itself. Practices in communities of practice may take such forms as subtle cues, recognized hunches, intense verbal and physical give-and-take, rules of thumb, stories, or shared worldviews.

Wenger (1998) cites three dimensions that together create the conditions for the emergence of communities of practice. First, there must be *mutual engagement*. Membership is not just a matter of social category, role, or title. A community comes into existence because people are engaged in actions whose meanings they negotiate with one another. Members are included in what matters. Beyond engagement, they also consider themselves to be part of a *joint enterprise.* They find a way to work together, to be accountable to one another, to live with their differences, and they coordinate their individual aspirations to become part of a community. Finally, they develop a *shared repertoire,* including routines, words, tools, ways of doing things, stories, gestures, concepts, and the like that symbolize their shared practice.

One of the members of our FEL community reported on his work on a special operations project team that was charged with building new factories for his company. Initially, team members just saw themselves as performing a job, but over the course of time, the unit jelled in a special way. They took on a unique identity or a "face" to the outside world of the rest of the company. They became enmeshed with each other in practice. Over the course of time, they developed particular ways of doing things, and continually added to their knowledge base. Members of the team also created a database of problem resolutions so that newcomers would not have to reinvent the wheel every time they came up against a new problem. Newcomers were not automatically accepted as part of the team, but gradually learned, and even added to, the symbolic routines that defined how the team operated. The team was self-replicating in that before members would leave the team, they would bring in newcomers who could replicate their work performance. The team would also meet off-site once a month to debrief and discover how they could improve their processes. They would also conduct a two-week debriefing after they completed a project.

There is some dispute in the literature about whether communities of practice can be created or designed or whether they are "emergent" (Galagan, 1993). Emergent groups evolve informally and are often on the periphery, where innovation often lies. For example, groups sometimes form around an interest in technology. "Members" may see themselves as current experts who choose to communicate with one another and who may make it their business to become unofficial gatekeepers of the new technology. It is important to note that these emergent groups may cross organizational boundaries if not formal divisions within the same organization. Linn and Snyder (1997) reported on the successful use of groupware and informal communication in a very large international chemical company by a group merely interested in leveraging their expertise to solve customer problems occurring in their worldwide operations.

Andersen Consulting Education, the four-hundred person educational organization of Andersen Consulting, comparing its community of practice approach to the development of professional associations, uses a formal structure to facilitate the formation of so-called community of practice "interest groups" (Graham, Osgood, and Karren, 1998). In particular, the Andersen program features:

- an advisory committee that sets policy for the program;
- a management champion who provides leadership and support;
- an administrative team that handles communication and organizes activities;
- a written charter that stipulates a basic set of rules and guidelines for participation;
- a team of interest group leaders who develop their leadership skills and discuss ways to continually energize the interest groups.

Communities of practice may also arise out of necessity among formally constituted groups. What makes them a community of practice is both their function and their absolute need to commit to one another in order to "perform" their function. Such teams truly represent a collective mind to the extent that it is virtually impossible to detect individual virtuosity. On the other hand, each member of the team possesses partial knowledge of the job to be done. What is critical is how they contribute their partial knowledge to the team so that the collective entity has the full body of knowledge. Moreover, the members of a community of practice have learned how to work with each other as part of their mutual tacit understanding of what needs to be done (Badaracco, 1991; Choo, 1998).

Consider three examples supplied by Kenneth Labich (1996). The first example is the team represented by the U.S. Navy SEALS (Sea Air Land). Even though SEAL recruits arrive for training as tough physical specimens to begin with, only about three of every ten recruits make it. The one surefire way to wash out is to try to get by without the help of your fellow recruits. SEALs never operate on their own; their commitment to each other is and has to be total. Indeed, no dead SEAL has ever been left behind on a battlefield. This same dedication to one another can be found among members of the world renowned Tokyo String Quartet. No member ever even thinks about showing off his individual talent or technique, even though each is skilled enough to be a virtuoso soloist. They realize that they must project as one and maintain the quartet's personality. As a team, they blend their skill by instinctively knowing each other's moods, talents, and preferences.

A third example of a formally constituted community of practice is the pit crew at the Winston Cup races, where, given that races are often settled by fractions of a second, the facility of the crew can determine the outcome. A top crew made up of between 15 to 17 people—7 over the wall working on the car itself, the others on the other side handing them things—can change all four tires, power-pump 21 gallons of fuel, clean the windshield, and give the driver a drink all in less than 21 seconds.

Reaching the state of a community of practice can be achieved without a pronounced leader or a facilitator, but facilitation might potentially accelerate the process. Using some of the techniques described in action learning or action science (as will be disclosed in the next section), the facilitator might assist members of the team to reveal more of their hidden assumptions about themselves and about others. Members might learn more about how the group as a whole is functioning and how to improve its process. Facilitation might also reveal that the leadership role can be shared and that every member has the opportunity at various times and under certain conditions to perform a leadership function.

Consequently, although there is seemingly little agreement about when and whether the facilitator of a learning team ought to make explicit interventions, clearly for a learning team to function well the task of managing the learning has to permeate the entire team. Hence, in a community of practice, which operates in part as a learning team, anyone assuming a facilitator role may reach that proverbial point of "working oneself out of a job." Getting to this point, admittedly, may take far longer than the straightforward accomplishment of a task by a work team. Although a work team may share a common goal, typically the accomplishment of an assignment or project, it may not require its members to probe to the depth of their underlying assumptions about their values or about their feelings for each other. They may also require a pronounced leader who distributes the tasks without argument.

Team members who have never experienced a community of practice may question why one has to reveal assumptions and even inferences if the job is to accomplish a task. Indeed, for mere task accomplishment, such "deeper" processes may not be required. If learning and creating become as important as doing, however, then group members will realize the value of exploring the deeper dimensions of their behavior. As Janov (1995) puts it, it is not enough just to understand oneself; to make meaning together in a community of practice, one needs to understand oneself in relationship to the team.

In fact, meaning making becomes the primary basis for holding a community together. Members of such a community realize that it is not as critical that they report on what happened but rather that they commit themselves to interpret what an event that occurred *means*. They realize that each one of them may interpret events differently and that learning in their community can only occur once they share how they see things in a joint manner. Discovering what happened is less important than constructing their own reality together as a community. Further, it is not so much a question of their arriving at the right answer as much as their arriving at a mutual understanding (Berger and Luckmann, 1967; Bolman and Deal, 1997). Once a team reaches this level of mutuality, not only does the role of facilitator fade away, but so does the role of explicit leader. In fact, leadership becomes everyone's responsibility in the sense of reminding group members of their meaning together, be it in accomplishing traditional responsibilities or in facing new work.

Boody et al. (1998) provide an apt example of the process of building a community of practice in their account of a group of teachers who became interested in reflecting together and improving their teaching practice. They each took turns describing their actions and mutually drawing each other out to explain the assumptions behind their choices of teaching strategies. Despite a conscious effort to maintain the focus on the presenter, at times the questions posed by the other group members would trigger reflective statements about their own practices. At some point in the process of the group, it appears that with the permission of the presenter, the presumed digression was allowed as an episode in what they referred to as the "group thinking together." The thinking in this case was not something that resided in each member's head but represented an open space in the middle of the group. In time, the dialogue took the form of a shared cognitive space. In the course of posing a critical question to the presenter, it became permissible to turn the question on oneself. This process allowed the members to focus both on themselves and on their practices as a collaborative venture for change.

Are there mechanisms for executives and managers involved in potential communities of practice to facilitate their formation and development? The emerging literature on the subject is mixed on this account, with some writers believing that external intervention can actually risk destroying what might evolve naturally. Clearly, minimal intervention is called for, but there are ways to "fertilize the soil" (Stewart, 1996). The Institute for Research on Learning (IRL) makes available such tools as video analysis, simulation, and observation to help community members see themselves in action, helping them learn even more quickly than if their development were to occur naturally. National Semiconductor, which has probably gone the farthest among U.S. companies in promoting communities of practice, has advanced a number of methods, such as distributing a toolkit to help rank-and-file technologists build their own communities of practice and, once formed, encouraging them to build their own home pages on the Web (Brown and Gray, 1995). It has also created a Communities of Practice Council to provide advice, offer technology support, and lobby for funding for projects.

So, whether through deliberate human or computer programming, collective learning can be accelerated. Compared to nonconscious performance, programmed collective learning can expand the consideration of new conditions and perspectives. It introduces practitioners to a language that is capable of uncovering personal conventions of practice that without programming would not otherwise add to collective memory.

Programmed learning in a community of practice bridges to the next learning type—action science—when implicit behavior is made explicit using cognitive and artificial intelligence technologies. Strategies for mobilizing collective learning of this nature can be both formal and informal. A method known as "cognitive task analysis" has begun to analyze the knowledge and performance requirements for jobs that involve complex cognitive skills (Ryder and Redding, 1993). It can help novices accelerate the acquisition of automatic job skills that tend to be associated with the unconscious actions of experts (Fisk and Gallini, 1989).

Much less formal is the ethnographic approach used by the aforementioned Institute for Research on Learning (IRL). In Chapter 2, I reported on the case of Xerox's attempt to create an integrated customer service center at its Louisville, Texas facility. A two-year training program was not getting the job done for many reasons, among which was the proverbial complaint that the training content did not match the requirements of the job. Using a community of practice approach, researchers from the IRL were able to shorten the training time dramatically with superior results (Stamps, 1997). What was their secret? It was merely collocating service reps in groups of six or seven so that they would be in constant contact with one another. Workers began to teach each other how to do their respective jobs; sales reps shared what they knew about selling; account administrators explained how to maintain a customer database. Their learning was constant and exciting. One of the reps described her experience in this way.

> We shared information with each other all the time. Even when we weren't asking for help, we were leaning because we could hear other people in our work group on the phone with customers, and we'd pick up tips about how they handled certain kinds of calls. (Stamps, 1997)

Another well-known case in informal collective learning was depicted by Orr (1990) in his account of photocopier technicians who, as most of us working around offices have seen, need to skirt around training manuals as they confront idiosyncratic workplace problems. Designers obviously cannot predict the social context in which the machines are used, so they must rely upon the technicians to understand the user environment. In many instances, problems arise because of operator use or misuse not predicted by the designers. So the knowledge that is acquired here is social, as if the technicians are participants in a group mind. Nelson and Winter (1982) point out that operator communities build up "routines" that transcend the sum of individual actions and capabilities. Problem solving becomes more of a social activity than an analytically detached process. It also becomes a natural exercise. Scribner (1986) described workers in a commercial dairy, showing how the packers, for example, were able to configure mixed orders using calculations based upon changing base numbers depending on the item and its pack size. Their calculations, which were error-free, seemed effortless.

The social and tacit infrastructure of workers is not always productive or even collective. Hence, remedying ineffective team behavior where differences become polarized, for example, requires team members to learn to observe and experiment with their own collective tacit processes in action. Bohm (1985) suggests that breakdowns in team effectiveness be handled through a dialogic process in which participants learn or relearn to reason and act together. In dialogue, members of a team begin to act in an aligned way, rather than segmenting thought into categories with each member presenting a particular position. The dialogue process initially calls for a suspension of judgment of extreme points of view followed by a gradual commitment to inquire together as new insights and meanings unfold.

In the Tokyo String Quartet, mentioned earlier, the members reported that they were rescued from a sense of complacency, which can arise among community members all too familiar with one another, when in 1981 Canadian Peter Oundjian joined the group. Bringing an outsider's perspective, he questioned everything the group did, from musical selections to tour dates. Had the group not been functioning as a community, such a challenge from an outsider might have brought it down. However, the other three found Peter's suggestions to be enriching and chose to learn with him, leading them to even greater heights of performance (Labich, 1996).

The expertness of the community of practice as a learning community should not be overlooked. As an element of work-based learning, it often supersedes the formal scientific documentation that can be found in training manuals or designs that are "downskilled" to operating levels. Learning becomes "enacted," that is, constructed on the spot as new information comes on-line (Daft and Weick, 1984). Documenters often assume that the problems their manuals are designed to debug are relatively predictable. Unfortunately, tools such as manuals are mere abstractions, which often fall short in comprehending the complexity of actual field practices (Brown and Duguid, 1991). Typically, it is necessary for field workers, through their informal interactions or war stories that represent repositories of accumulated wisdom, to bring coherence to an otherwise random set of conditions.

So the notion of community of practice places knowledge into its context. As a model of work-based learning, it suggests that learning is built out of the materials of the local situation and that it is often collective. Hence students cannot be segregated from the communities in which they are to work. Apprenticeships, for example, cannot be complete if training is conducted in merely simulated work conditions. Apprentices must have the opportunity to observe and even participate in collective practices. Their job is to learn when, how, and what is to be done according to particular intrinsic practices. They also need to be able to give a reasonable account of why it is done and what kind of person one must become in order to be accepted as a competent member of the community (Wertsch, 1985; Blackler, 1993; Gherardi, Nicolini, and Odella, 1998). The knowledge used in a context is often practical as opposed to theoretical, and it is often elegant in its simplicity. In her study of the dairy, Scribner (1986) reported that drivers maintained a nearly perfect on-the-job accuracy rate on pricing problems, but when given standard arithmetic tests, they made many errors on decimal multiplication problems nearly identical in format to their pricing problems.

Meanwhile, journeymen or regular members of a community of practice need to literally practice together in order to develop their mutual expertise. We would not expect an orchestra to perform without rehearsal, so why should a work team be expected to perform without practice? In communities of practice, time needs to be taken to experiment and reflect on the team's practice in a safe environment.

Communities of Practice as Organizations

A new variant of communities of practice is the controversial notion of producing a community of practice in an entire organization. Many observers might suggest that this is at best an idyllic, illusive vision that can only be strived for, never to be achieved. There are too many barriers in human systems, especially considerations of power when mass collections of people assemble, to create a community where everyone constructs meaning together. Nevertheless, there have been successful experiments in creating at least temporary communities by placing the "whole system in the room." Such experiments represent processes that bring up to three hundred organizational members and their stakeholders together for several days to work through critical organizational issues.

There are a few tenets that these large-group interventions have in common. Most critical is that all stakeholders concerned about the problem be present and actively participate in their remediation. Second, it is important that the meeting be structured in advance so that both productive conversation and reflection can ensue in order to generate new ideas and perspectives and to allow people to dream and feel purposeful (Bunker and Alban, 1997). Consistent with work-based learning approaches, these approaches recognize the value of private and public reflection to absorb the enormous amount of information exchanged during the meetings. Marvin Weisbord, co-originator of the *Future Search* technology (Weisbord and Janoff, 1992), talks about the need for "soak time" to give participants a chance to process the network activities both privately and publicly. It is also important that the experience be structured to see how all the parts of a community interact to produce what happened, to help people recognize multiple perspectives, and to give them an opportunity to work together to manage a better future. What large-group interventions attempt to do is to allow multiple voices to engage in dialogue and thus to learn to create meaning together.

Nancy Dixon (1997) gives an account of a future search conference held for a group of 70 people from a grocery chain, including store managers, employees, customers, and suppliers. The chain had been struggling with the question of whether to continue its expansion strategy. The store managers voiced their concern that such a strategy would adversely affect quality and other issues. However, through organized discussions held throughout the three days of the conference, they realized that the long-term viability of the chain required continued growth. This realization occurred to them collectively as all conference members expressed their expectations for the future viability of the business. Other outcomes were likewise produced, such as the need to hire a national purchasing director to centralize buying, all from having everyone in the room learning how to reason together, not necessarily to find a right answer.

There has been a burst of innovation in creating designs for large-system interventions (see Bunker and Alban, 1997), such as the Conference Model (Axelrod, 1992), Participative Design (Emery, 1995), The Search Conference (Emery and Purser, 1996), and Open Space Technology (Owen, 1993). As FEL member David Hardy describes it, in Open Space Technology, people in large-group settings are given the opportunity to champion a discourse around an area of concern of their choosing. As long as at least two people are interested, they can continue to meet. Reports to the large community are built into the process.

Open Space Technology has also been shown to be very efficient, most likely because it engages the passion of participants in a way that can produce practical results. A 23-person team was given the charge prior to the 1996 Summer Olympics in Atlanta to redesign a pavilion that could accommodate seventy-five thousand visitors. The team had already used Open Space Technology to design the original pavilion that had a capacity for only five thousand visitors. It was so impressive that the Olympic Committee had asked the team to move it to the center of the Olympic Village. Again relying on Open Space Technology, within 45 minutes the group developed a completely new concept, started the necessary architectural drawings, and made phone calls to have supplies shipped to Atlanta. The design team did in 2 days what had previously taken them 10 months (Ventetuolo, 1998).

Art Kleiner and George Roth (1997) invented the "learning history" to operationalize the collective memory of an organization. In their terms, "a learning history is a written narrative of a company's recent set of critical episodes: a corporate change event, a new initiative, a widespread innovation, a successful product launch, or even a traumatic event such as a major reduction in the workforce." Through interviews, a consultant team prepares up to a one-hundred-page document detailing the episode through direct quotes placed on the right-hand side of the document. On the left-hand side, the consultant team and some knowledgeable insiders, as "learning historians," draw out the recurrent themes, assumptions, implications, and even "undiscussables" from the narrative. The learning history is then used as a basis for group discussions. Kleiner and Roth's technique draws on the ancient practice of community storytelling, wherein individuals would offer their recollections of events and a shaman might comment on the narrative to draw out its significance. Reexperiencing the event together, the group learns collectively. In today's corporate world, the learning history can spark conversations and knowledge-sharing across divisions. It can also generate trust and permit more open discussions about difficult issues. Most critically, it represents a unique way to have organizational members make meaning together.

By studying these large-system technologies, we might learn what the ingredients need to be to experiment with communities of practice for whole organizations. Dixon (1997) has already identified six elements: (1) reliance on discussion, not speeches; (2) egalitarian participation; (3) encouragement of multiple perspectives; (4) nonexpert-based dialogue; (5) use of a participant-generated database (primary data that are shared by all members present, not as reports from others); and (6) creation of a shared experience.

Virtual Team Learning

A critical question in the domain of work-based learning is whether distance learning methods, especially those using electronic communication, can be successfully applied to create collaboration and reflection. There may be occasions when teams might need to coordinate tasks or reflect on past or current practices but are too geographically distant to hold meetings. In particular, communities of practice, evolving as they often do around function, may by design be constituted of members who cross organizational boundaries. What keeps them together might initially be their substantive interest or expertise, not their proximity. They may also wish to discuss real-time work issues in an effort to learn from one another.

Accordingly, communities of practice may find it convenient to make use of electronic means of communication. Using e-mail or more sophisticated technologies, such as web conferencing or desktop videoconferencing systems, members can keep up-to-date with one another regardless of space or time. On the other hand, without some initial and then quite frequent face-to-face meetings, members may not be able to sufficiently warm up to each other. Peter Hillen, a partner with Congruity Corp., a consulting firm in Los Altos, California, puts it this way: "No one yet has invented a technology that replaces a pitcher of beer" (Stamps, 1997).

Although virtual communities allow plenty of opportunity for private reflection, there is a concern that they may not represent a conducive environment for public reflection on members' practices and assumptions. In particular, dialogue is often impeded by a lack of nonverbal cues and by a reduction in the exchange of social-emotional information. As a result, although virtual teams may handle task-oriented exchanges well, they tend to be slow in developing relational links among members (Chidambaram, 1996; Warkentin, Sayeed, and Hightower, 1997). Finally, although they may help work teams as they address their functional or operational concerns, can they be useful for managers to help them work through fundamental questions of culture and change?

Perhaps, as Coutu (1998) reports, it comes down to a need to build trust, especially when people cannot interact directly with one another. Hence, substituting for the luxury of face-to-face encounters, virtual teams might need to begin their interactions with a series of social messages, such as introductions, before focusing on the task at hand. Virtual team members might also need to assume designated roles, helping them to establish their identity and commitment, and to make explicit some of their norms and expectations especially in regard to goals, tasks, and results.

When it comes to preparing members to participate effectively in virtual endeavors, the very competencies addressed in work-based learning are the ones that need development. It is often not very difficult to instruct people in the use of computer-based technologies, but it is challenging to develop skills in interpersonal relations, team contribution, and intercultural communication. For example, team members need to be, at least initially, more sensitive to how their messages might be received because they do not have the benefit of nonverbal expression. Because team membership also tends to be fluid, effective teams require members who can quickly assimilate into a virtual social structure. Teams also need members who can comfortably communicate with people of diverse cultures (Townsend, DeMarie, and Hendrickson, 1998). Having experience in project and learning teams that systematically deploy skills to accelerate learning can be critical when it comes to participating in virtual communities.

Experiments are underway to consider the extent to which work-based learning can be delivered on-line as a virtual community experience. At Xerox, a Management Institute sponsors two learning programs for senior and mid-level managers worldwide based upon virtual learning principles (Henderson and Casey-Higgins, 1997). The programs address such fundamental challenges as broad industry knowledge, knowledge of finance, strategic thinking skills, teamwork, employee empowerment, and use of an outside perspective. But what is most interesting is that the managers, especially those in the senior-level program, meet their peers— who happen to be in different business units from all over the world—on-line and work in teams on business problems that have a corporate-wide strategic thrust. The program takes between 10 and 12 months to complete. Participants spend between six and eight hours a week on assignments.

Gwen Casey-Higgins, one of the Institute's program managers, believes that the program works because managers address real business challenges. They need to find the right stakeholders, market their ideas, and push forward with implementation plans. Second, because the participants meet on-line, they can address issues within their own sphere of business activity without having to leave their work space. Using virtual learning, participants are paired with managers who are at different levels and seniority in the company, who have different strengths, and who reside in a different part of the business. This allows for cross-fertilization of ideas and for new synergies in business strategy to emerge. Further, the projects, as in most work-based learning programs, can produce significant economic consequences for the company either in savings or revenue growth.

It appears that cross-organizational communities of practice need to take advantage of electronic technology by necessity; otherwise, there would be excessive gaps in their contact. The key strategic issue seems to be how and when to structure some face-to-face time. The Xerox project teams come together when they need to visit a business client or when they need to present their business plan. An Ann Arbor consulting firm, Dannemiller Tyson Associates (DTA), though a virtual company with its partners working out of locations scattered across the United States, designs face-to-face joint learning opportunities. Each quarter, for example, the partners take turns running in-house programs so they can continually learn from one other. They also use these and other occasions to work on mutual projects and to collaborate on writing books, articles, and other firm publications (Rose 1998).

Electronic technologies can be used in a variety of ways to support communities both in their processes and in their task endeavors. For example, the computer-based application known as group support systems (GSS) can be used to facilitate group development. Mennecke, Hoffer, and Wynne (1992) propose that because of GSS's use of collective procedures, tools, and heuristics, team building can be accelerated. For example, GSS can be used for electronic brainstorming or for idea organization. In the latter, group members may work in parallel to converge on key issues raised during a brainstorming session. GSS also features electronic voting, group outlining, group writing, shared drawing and diagramming, and structured alternative evaluation. One of the advantages offered by GSS in building a community of practice is that it allows everyone to "talk at once," overcoming the natural effect of losing the train of thought, be it of one's own ideas or those of others. Strong or loud personalities don't have an opportunity to dominate as they would in a totally open forum. All participants have an equal opportunity to contribute, and ideas are considered on their own merits rather than on their sources (Briggs, Ramesh, Romano, and Latimer, 1994-1995).

There are many applications of electronic communication as a knowledge management resource. In particular, communities of practice can find the data storage and retrieval facets of technology to be critical to their work. Consider how collective experience is captured for on-line examination using the computer-aided maintenance system (CAMS) at General Motors. Given the complexity of repair due to the increasing diversity and customization characterizing the automobile industry, it has almost become impossible to rely upon written repair manuals to assist mechanics in performing their job. What CAMS does is reproduce the collective memory of mechanics who have derived useful routines or heuristics in solving planned but also unforeseen breakdowns in vehicle performance. The mechanics, whether novice or expert, can use each other's experiences when trying to fix new problems associated with new components on new vehicles.

Another car maker, DaimlerChyrsler Corp., has developed a collaborative electronic system for its engineers across the globe. Called the Engineering Book of Knowledge (EBOK), the system provides best practice information on car design and building processes, ranging from door panels to tail lamps to engine parts (Halper, 1997). In a similar vein, GE has established an Answer Center, which has programmed 1.5 million potential questions and complaints into a computerized database system (Nonaka and Takeuchi, 1995). Xerox's Palo Alto Research Center has developed an electronic "knowledge refinery" called Eureka (Brown and Gray, 1995). Eureka, a relational database of hypertext documents, essentially organizes and categorizes tips generated from the field by its tech reps. Andersen Consulting also maintains a large database of practices to ensure consistent service provided by its consultants. Called ANet, Andersen's electronic network links 82,000 employees in 360 offices in 76 countries (Quinn, Anderson, and Finkelstein, 1996). Finally, Hewlett-Packard's corporate education division supports a Lotus Notes database, which is thought to be particularly effective in transferring tacit knowledge—tips, tricks, insights, and experiences—to its two-thousand trainers and educators scattered throughout the world (Davernport, De Long, and Beers, 1998).

FEL members have consistently noted that though databases or knowledge bases have come into popular use, their deployment within communities of practice requires that they function as a management tool, not as a mere information process. This means that the data must be stored and accessed with ease. The data must also be specific; if it is too generic, it will have little practical use. FEL members acknowledged that usable databases with specific content also require greater security to ensure confidentiality.

Action Science

Action science is a work-based intervention strategy for helping learners increase their effectiveness in social situations through heightened awareness of their action and interaction assumptions. Although initially aimed at the individual level of experience, action science is ultimately concerned with improving the level of public discourse both in groups and in organizations. Individuals' mental models—the images, assumptions, and stories carried inside our minds about ourselves and about others—are often untested and unexamined and, consequently, often erroneous. In action science, these mental models are brought into consciousness in such a way that new models are formed that may serve us better (Senge, 1994).

Action science thus calls for the deliberate questioning of existing perspectives and interpretations, referred to by Argyris and Schön (1978) as "double-loop" learning (see Chapter 2). When a mismatch occurs between our values and our actions, most of us attempt to narrow the gap by trial-and-error learning. We also prefer to maintain a sense of control over the situation, over ourselves, and over others. In double-loop learning we subject even our governing values to critical reflection, resulting in free and informed choice, valid information, and high internal commitment to any new behavior attempted.

Robert Putnam (forthcoming) sees the goal of action science as improving social discourse in at least two important ways. First, it can improve discourse in the moment so that the people involved can engage with each other in a more productive way. They may be able to do this by themselves, but typically they will require the assistance of a facilitator. Second, action science can invoke the deeper causal factors that lead people to interact as they do. In order to bring about fundamental and lasting improvement in the quality of discourse, people need to reflect upon and alter the assumptions embedded in their behavior and reasoning patterns. While some of this can occur in the midst of practical conversation, Putnam believes that it more likely requires planned learning sessions.

Donald Schön (1983) preferred the term "reflection-in-action" to characterize the rethinking process of action science, which attempts to discover how what one did contributed to an unexpected or expected outcome. In order to engage in reflection-in-action, a practitioner might start by offering a frame of the situation at hand. Then, if in a group situation, he or she might inquire how others see it. After receiving feedback, the individual and subsequently the whole group might collectively reflect upon these frames and begin to surface and test their underlying assumptions and respective reasoning processes. The ultimate aim is to narrow inconsistencies between one's espoused theories and theories-in-use. Espoused theories are those characterizing what we say we will do. Theories-in-use describe how we *actually* behave, although their revision of our espoused values is often tacit. The goal of action science is to uncover theories-in-use, in particular to distinguish between those that inhibit and those that promote learning.

Framing and subsequent communication in action science correspond to Habermas's views of knowledge and human interest, which, in turn, shape human discourse (Habermas, 1971). Technical knowledge involves predictions about observable events, physical or social. This type of knowledge may result in empirical or theoretical discourse, in which claims to truth may be validated by empirical tests. Empirical discourse relies upon hypothetico-deductive logic developed in applied science.

The second type of knowledge is what Habermas refers to as "practical," which entails social norms, ideals, values, and moral decisions. Practical or rational discourse, in the absence of empirical tests, may call upon tradition and authority but preferably uses consensus based upon a dialogue over contested meanings. Learning through metaphors—understanding one kind of thing in terms of another—may be a useful method (Lakoff and Johnson, 1980, p. 5) to help resolve contradictions or inconsistencies between concepts and contexts or to allow expression of particularly indeterminate practices (Bateson, 1972). Ultimately, practical discourse will search for meaning rather than attempt to delineate causality (Wolff, 1975).

Habermas's third type of knowledge, emancipatory, is gained through critical self-reflection of our taken-for-granted assumptions and feelings. Reflective discourse is used in this instance to determine whether the premises for our interpretation or understanding are themselves valid. The concept of third-order learning (Bateson, 1972), described in Chapter 2, represents this level of discourse. There is some dispute whether reflective discourse should or should not also incorporate such critical dimensions as questioning wider social, political, and cultural practices, including the issues of power, vested interests, and control. Most practitioners of action science believe that they can be most effective improving reflective discourse within the organization.

A critical difference between practical and reflective discourse, to which Habermas has not devoted much attention (Burrell, 1994), is the distinction between perceiving and feeling experience. The latter refers to the explicit referencing of emotional reactions that are often denied or dismissed, be they defensive reactions, embarrassment, or general anxiety (Vince and Martin 1993). Action science allows social relationships to form in a group but, unlike conventional work environments, also encourages the surfacing, in the safe presence of trusting peers, of these emotional reactions that might be blocking effective interactions.

Action science essentially creates an on-line learning environment that permits and encourages learners to engage in emancipatory discourse, thus testing their mental models, especially their inferences and assumptions about others and about their own behavior. Coworkers come to understand the embedded cultural myths that underlie their felt needs and wants expressed in their relations with others.

Action scientists also make direct comparisons between individual and organizational learning. Argyris and Schön (1974) find that people tend to learn and, in fact, are socially conditioned to use a cognitive model referred to as "Model I." Mostly concerned with detecting errors in our problem solving, Model I is unfortunately characterized by a need to control, maximize winning, suppress emotions, and be rational. Its consequences tend to be defensive behavior, miscommunication, and in actuality, the escalation rather than the reduction of error (Argyris, 1982). Model II behavior, on the other hand, is based on directly observable data and requires that people support their advocacy of positions with illustration and with inquiry into others' views. Accordingly, Model II practitioners tend more reliably to produce intended consequences and thus increase learning.

Individuals using Model I will create Model I organizational systems. Unfortunately, such systems, characterized by minimal learning capability, are difficult to change because of self-fulfilling processes and defensive reasoning strategies that individuals become unaware of using. Such systems, in turn, reinforce individuals to continue to act in ways characterized by Model I. On the other hand, Model II attempts to test and make explicit individuals' assumptions about the dynamics going on within their organization. Action strategies reflecting Model II values will serve to create organizations with Model II attributes, most prominently, the ability to learn at an emancipatory level of knowledge.

There are many techniques, such as projective visualization and Socratic dialogue, that can be used in small group settings to elicit and challenge psycho-cultural assumptions behind habituated ways of perceiving, thinking, feeling, and behaving (Mezirow, 1981). One relatively new and intriguing method to help learners either individually or in groups reflect critically on concepts and their interrelationships and, in addition, search for alternative ways of interpreting these same or allied concepts is known as "concept mapping" (Trochim, 1989).

Concept maps are visualized representations of problem situations that can help teams make sense out of a predicament (Eden, 1988; Hofman, 1997). Huff (1990) suggests that groups involved in cognitive mapping need to make three choices: (1) which territory the map should cover (individual or group perceptions); (2) which form of data collection should be used as input (post-hoc analysis or interactive generation of the data); and (3) which purpose the map should serve (direct product or a tool). In action science, teams are typically interested in representing their individual and collective mental models in a here-and-now setting. Hence cognitive maps may be used as a tool to facilitate this representation process. Although there are a variety of methods of cognitive mapping in use today, three will be described here.

Peter Checkland has developed a learning approach known as soft systems methodology (SMM) (Checkland, 1985). SSM compares pure models of purposeful action with perceptions of what is going on in a real-world problem situation. Using a seven-stage process, SSM teases out and then calls for testing via debate the complex assumptions underlying our actions, including relevant myths and meanings as well as facts and logic.

Strategic Options Development and Analysis (SODA) was designed by Colin Eden (1989) to help consultants work with clients on messy problems, especially during strategy formulation processes. Using interviews with participants, individual cognitive maps are created and then merged into a collective model. In SODA, it is critical that each member of the group be allowed his or her personal subjective view of the "real" problem. During the merging stage, a process of negotiation permits the aggregation of data without participants feeling that they have lost any of the richness and detail of their own cognitive maps.

A third mapping technique, based explicitly on action science design, is known as data mapping and was introduced in the graduate program in human resource development at the University of Texas (Watkins and Shindell, 1994). After going through a series of workshops on action science techniques, learning teams are formed in groups of four to six participants. Once in the teams, participants continue to study action science concepts while building trust with one another. They subsequently bring to the group personal cases from their lives as a means to help them become more effective in their human interactions. The cases are representative of incidents that the presenter would classify as demonstrating interpersonal or strategic ineffectiveness. The process is publicly reflective as team members learn to challenge tacit assumptions, whether they belong to the case presenter or to the observers.

As part of an on-line case experience, data mapping would be introduced to extend the action science problem-solving model of diagnosing a problem, inventing action strategies to solve it, producing action to enact the strategies, and evaluating the results. The data map assumes the format of an "if-then" statement, incorporating the following components (see Table 5.1):

> When ___ (contextual cue or triggering event) _____ happens, I ____ (make the following assumptions about what I should do) _____, so I implement the following ___ (action strategies) ___, which guarantees that the following _____ (consequences in the behavioral world of learning) _____ will occur.

With the help of the team, the case presenter progressively revises the case to determine if he or she can invent an alternative approach more in line with a Model II action strategy. Using action science methods, the presenters learn to develop strategies that can reduce the inhibiting condition of defensive routines in the workplace and replace them with models that encourage mutual learning.

The action science methods discussed here extend the lesson of action learning that, at the level of practical discourse, is more concerned with meaning making—helping participants enhance their sensitivity to the ways others perceive or react to them. Whereas action learning seeks to contextualize learning, action science decontextualizes practice so that learners can become more critical of their behavior and explore the very premises of their beliefs.

Table 5.1
An Action Science Data Map

Model Components	Model I Map	Model II Map
Contextural Cue or Triggering Condition	"When given a task by my boss to delegate to one of my staff—a task that is inappropriate to delegate	"When given a task by my boss to delegate to one of my staff—a task that is inappropriate to delegate
Underlying Assumptions	I should do it anyway	I should trust my instincts and tell my boss what it is I am concerned about
Action Strategies	So I implement my boss's unreasonable request	So, I bring up my concern to my boss and share why I believe the task shouldn't be delegated and then ask if my boss agrees
Consequences in the Behavioral World for Learning	Which guarantees not pleasing anyone."	Which predisposes us to an outcome that may please both of us."

Keen (1975, pp. 37–40) has provided language to help us decontextualize our practice. He proposes a three-step process. First, we engage in *phenomenological reduction*. This means that we must try to let whatever we encounter be what it is, apart from our perception of it. As a human being, it is virtually impossible not to attempt to impute meaning to a phenomenon. In this first step, however, we must try to open ourselves to the situation while holding our preconceived notions to a minimum. For example, when we start up with a new group, we all have a tendency to want to size up each member's contribution even before anyone speaks. Can we learn to be open to each person's potential so as to allow our perception to evolve with experience?

Keen's second step is known as *imaginative variation*. Here we play with all the contingencies in a situation, combining and recombining them in conventional and in unconventional ways. Again human instinct forces us to use familiar categories to organize our perception. Keen is asking us to consider multiple combinations of perceptual organization to release the phenomenon from our habitual modes of control.

The third step is the more familiar *interpretation* wherein we assess the desirability of various scenarios. Although in interpretation we arrive where we may have started, Keen's process helps us consciously and reflectively work through our perceptions of phenomena and our inferences of others so that our mental models become more understandable and coherent to us.

The assumption-challenging process of action science is akin to lateral thinking placed into a public arena. Now part of our common language, lateral thinking was invented by Edward de Bono in his lifelong quest to inspire us to think about our thinking. His work in this domain is remarkably consistent with the broad view of learning advocated in this book. Acknowledging the value of our brain to create and use patterns in helping us make sense of our world, de Bono (1994) nevertheless suggests that at times we need to change and to keep on changing our familiar patterns and routines, be it through accident, mistake, humor, or practice. In the latter instance, we can use a variety of approaches within our work groups to help us suspend judgment and through exploration gather new insight. This form of thinking tends to be more difficult in the West, where we prize the clash of opinions or dialectical methods over mind expansion devices. Yet we can be trained in lateral thinking and may experiment with techniques to help us consider problems and relationships "out of the box."

Craig Johnson, who is with the firm VCB Ltd. in Bradford, England, has reported on the use of a familiar de Bono technique known as the Six Thinking Hats (de Bono 1986). This technique can help participants apply different modes of thinking, especially in regard to Keen's imaginative variation stage of decontextualizing practice. As a problem or issue is being discussed, participants metaphorically put on six different hats, which they focus on in turn:

White: Hard facts, figures, statistics, etc.

Black: What can go wrong with the problem, what is the worst case.

Yellow: Optimistic, what is going to go right.

Green: Generative, new ideas to investigate.

Blue: Can't remember . . . sorry!

Red: Emotions, anger, anguish, stress.

Chris Argyris (1982) and his associates Robert Putnam and Diana Smith (1985) have developed a number of unique techniques to surface mental models, including the popular "ladder of inference." This technique is often used in an action science group in which the facilitator helps a member examine his or her inferences regarding a project situation or worksite problem. It can also be used to help members reframe how they currently are working with one another. The ladder of inference is based on an action model, wherein given the context of the (business) situation we are in and our stock of knowledge we frame how we view ourselves and others in the situation. Based on our framing, we then take action. Unfortunately, since as human beings we don't typically have the time to be totally informed about every situation we encounter and cannot redesign every action we take, we respond using models that we have counted on in many prior situations in our lives. By reusing these tried-and-true models, we are able to act fairly expeditiously and do not have to reason through each and every new situation we encounter. To do otherwise would virtually hamstring our ability to act spontaneously.

Unfortunately, by acting instinctively without occasional reframing, we become disconnected from our reasoning processes and even become unaware that we are unaware of our theories-in-use (Argyris, 1983). Using the ladder of inference, we learn to reframe or alter our spontaneous understanding of a particular situation, which can lead to new ways of seeing ourself and others and thus can also lead to new actions that might accomplish our goals more effectively.

Consider how the ladder of inference might be deployed. As shown in Figure 5.1, our action model is invoked whenever we place ourselves in a situation containing observable data. Let's say that you recently convened a staff meeting and engaged in an interaction that you subsequently wish to process in your action science group. The exchange was between you and a colleague named Paul and occurred during a short break.

Paul began the exchange by saying that the way you handled Rebecca during the meeting was "interesting." Rebecca was going off on one of her tangents about the team's unwillingness to consider a reengineering of the payroll function and you had to cut her off by saying, "Thanks, Rebecca; now let's hear what Paul has to say." (Having attended a process-reengineering seminar, Rebecca was convinced that we could have saved valuable resources by farming out payroll to a reliable contractor, even though you told her repeatedly that you wanted to keep our tradition intact of never firing anyone who was doing a good job because of corporate restructuring.) Paul's comment that your way of handling Rebecca was "interesting" invoked an immediate and tacit response. For you, the word *interesting* is a red-flag word that connotes disapproval. However, if Paul wasn't going to explain what he meant by the word, you weren't going to tolerate his ambiguity. Hence your response was merely to thank him for his approval and move on to other matters.

Now back in your action science group meeting, you want to probe whether you handled the exchange with Paul in an effective manner. You have an uncomfortable feeling that more could have been uncovered from your brief exchange with Paul, but you also believe that little can be done with someone who is so cryptic and unclear all the time.

The action science facilitator can demonstrate, using the ladder of inference, how from all the available data having to do with your exchanges with Paul and with Rebecca, you moved up the ladder by selecting out his one comment about your managing her as having been "interesting." In doing so, you invoked some fundamental assumptions. Primary was the assumption that when an observer says someone has made an "interesting" intervention, that means that the intervenor has made an inappropriate comment. You then further interpreted what Paul said by making an attribution that he was being indirect or off-handed. From this interpretation, you leapt to a higher rung of the ladder when you concluded that when faced with indirectness, your only option is to respond in kind. However, it was the action from this inference that you are now questioning as being potentially ineffective.

Opening up the ladder of inference, the facilitator can work with you at each rung to show you, first, how you selected just one piece of data (Paul's comment that your intervention was "interesting") from an entire conversation. From there, you made an assumption that Paul disapproved of you but, in turn, you attributed to him the

Figure 5.1
The Ladder of Inference

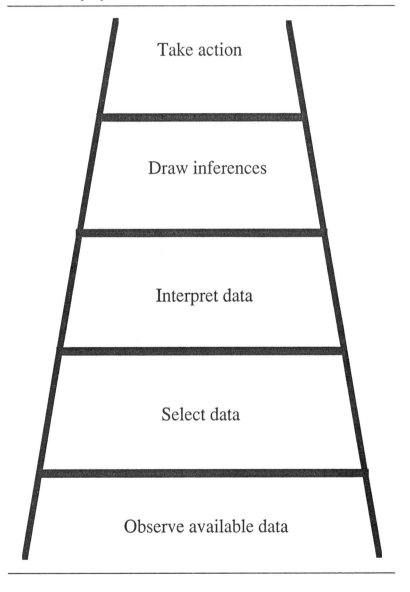

ineffectual practice of being indirect. Looking at the data, you could have also focused on any number of other interpretations. For example, you could have considered why Rebecca seems to be repeatedly bringing up the subject of reengineering. You could have examined whether there might really be a problem in payroll. As for your attribution of the instant comment from Paul, you could have made a series of alternative interpretations, among which might have been that Paul was afraid of approaching you directly because of past suppressive behavior on your part, or that he actually might have approved in part of how you handled Rebecca though he was interested in questioning why and when you resort to this approach. Opening up the ladder of inference in this way could have produced not only different conclusions but alternative actions, which might have led to more effective behavior not only in this one instance but as a convenor of other staff meetings. Essentially, this type of action science intervention can produce a reframing that alters our reasoning and action models to be more consistent with our values and intentions.

Although action science as a pedagogy tends to work on one individual at a time, its practitioners gradually expect to increase the level of public discourse in the organization in order for people to feel free to voice their opinions and shape outcomes according to mutual decision making. An example of this contagion of action science principles occurred in the late 1980s at Knight-Ridder, the Miami-based newspaper chain, when it undertook a project called 25/43 to increase readership among persons between the ages specified in the label, 25 and 43. The impetus for the project was the company's newspapers' recorded drop in readership among young adults. The project sought to change newspaper design to attract readers in the target age group. However, changing the design potentially conflicted with the mental models used by the chain's journalists, who viewed themselves as first-class writers. Was quality going to be sacrificed to produce more relevance for the less appreciated age group?

According to Wishart, Elam, and Robey (1996), Knight-Ridder's executives exhibited a high degree of learning and reflection as they worked through the contradictions embedded in the 25/43 project. First, they listened to the journalists and encouraged them to surface their mental models regarding their work preferences and identity. Then they turned their attention to their readers by conducting market research and focus groups with their target audience. In time, the 25/43 process became an institutionalized method of assessing consumer opinion at Knight-Ridder, expanding to other "at risk" groups beyond baby boomers. Throughout the process the company kept dialogue alive by trying to uncover underlying assumptions and to engage in reflective discourse.

Motorola Inc., perhaps one of the best exemplars in the United States of employee development and learning, believes that it is critical to have individuals aside from top management continuously raise questions about new products, markets, and business processes. Although the ideal is to have every employee act in this way, Motorola actually has assigned 44 individuals the role of scout or trailblazer. The education center of the company, its Motorola University, tracks the dialogue between these scouts and their organizational contacts to capture key lessons for the company. The lessons are reviewed by a Planning Evaluation and Alliance Group, which comprises Motorola's business leaders from around the world whose units might have been directly affected by the findings. The view taken at Motorola University is that as the strategic horizon of the company continues to shrink, techniques of this nature are needed to extend the boundaries of known behavior (Baldwin, Danielson, and Wiggenhorn, 1997).

6

Public Reflection as the Basis of Work-Based Learning

The range of what we think and do is limited by what we fail to notice, and because we fail to notice that we fail to notice, there is little we can do to change, until we notice how failing to notice shapes our thoughts and deeds.

—Ronald Laing

I have referred frequently in this book to the process of reflection, initially as an explicit individual learning type, but also as a collective property. It is the latter sense that distinguishes work-based learning from standard classroom practices. Through public reflection we may create a collective identity as a community of inquiry. In this short chapter, we examine the process of public reflection, known also as reflective practice, in greater detail. In the following chapter, we will look at four explicit reflective practices.

Reflective Practice: What Is It?

Reflection is the practice of periodically stepping back to ponder the meaning to self and to others in one's immediate environment about what has recently transpired. It illuminates what has been experienced by both self and others, providing a basis for future action. In its public form, it is typically associated with learning dialogues. These types of discussions, rather than constitute an exchange of statements of points of view, surface in the safe presence of trusting peers the social, political, and emotional data that arise from direct experience with one another. Often these data are precisely those that might be blocking operating effectiveness. Learning dialogues also are concerned with creating mutual caring relationships. However, they can reveal, but with permission, a person's solitude and mystery.

Reflective practice tends to probe to a deeper level than trial-and-error experience. It typically is concerned with forms of learning I have already referred to as double-loop and triple-loop, learning that seeks to inquire about the most fundamental assumptions and premises behind our practices. David Hardy, of the Institute for Learning at the Bank of Montreal and a FEL member, explains it as a thinking about our thinking. We noted in the last chapter, for example, that what makes a work team a learning team is its interest in clarifying its thought before and after action. David likes to point out that our brain, as a sophisticated information processing organ, can handle some fifty thousand to sixty thousand thoughts per day. Unfortunately, as we encounter problems in our work, we tend to go no further than to consult our "solution database" (as depicted in Figure 6.1) to find an answer.

In thinking about thinking, we are actually able to reflect together about our solution databases and add to them or alter them entirely. The reflection referred to here is more than "navel" reflection—reflection that is private and introspective. Reflective practice occurs in the midst of practice but is also produced in the presence of

Figure 6.1
Our Normal Problem-Solving Pattern

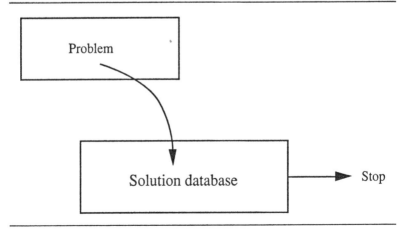

others. Taylor (1997) goes even further in his insistence that without the medium of relationships, critical reflection can be impotent and hollow, lacking the genuine discourse necessary for thoughtful and in-depth reflection.

Plato had the idea of relationships in mind when he remarked that "the unexamined life isn't worth living." This phrase has often been misinterpreted as a call for additional introspection by people. Although this might be useful, the actual meaning is that we need to include others in the examination of experience in our life. Plato's idea resonated with Aristotle, who recognized that human beings are social animals whose good is bound up with the good of the polis. Underpinned by these Greek roots, the egalitarian tradition in Western thought has long since recognized that the dignity of human persons is achieved only in community with others (Hollenbach, 1998). Jürgen Habermas (1984), referred to as a "late" modernist, sees the reconciliation between individual and society through intersubjective recognition based on mutual understanding and free cognition about disputed claims. It is through communicative action that we are able to realize ourselves within a civic community. We must subject our entire experience to criticism, even our tacit understanding. For Habermas, then, the Enlightenment project of modernity can be saved through open, public dialogue.

Reflective practice with others or public reflectiveness is fundamental to the learning process described in this book. There are a number of reasons why reflection must be brought out in the open.

1. Managers not only need to be aware of their own actions but at times need to move from a position of unawareness to awareness. Oftentimes, we are simply unaware of the consequences of our behavior. To complicate matters, our unawareness occasionally does not allow us to be open to new data or information to help us learn from our actions. We may even be unaware that the questions we ask might be producing defensiveness in others, closing off the possibility of generating new information, even new questions. It is often only through the support of and feedback from others that we can become receptive to alternative ways of reasoning and behaving. For example, an executive may see herself as having an open-door policy, but she may be unaware that she "kills" nearly every idea brought to her attention by some of her associates.

2. There is an unfortunate gap between what many of us say

we will do and what we actually do. Recall how action science refers to this gap: an inconsistency between our "espoused theories" and our "theories-in-use" (Argyris and Schön, 1974; Raelin, 1993a). We are simply all guilty of deceiving ourselves that we can practice what we preach, though what we preach may be very difficult to accomplish in particular organizational cultures. For example, managers are often pressured to produce reports without sufficient time to get all the facts. Under these circumstances, though one might believe in and espouse the value of participative processes, one might be unaware that he or she has begun to order people to come up with subsidiary reports. Once the pressure has subsided, the same manager might still fail to notice that his or her behavior has persisted.

3. Most of us are biased in how we obtain information, which, in turn, produces "errors" in our perceptions of reality. According to Bright (1996), errors constitute such practices as collecting data superficially, ignoring certain pieces of information, making assumptions about data rather than investigating them, or using self-confirming reasoning. However, if we are interested in improving our managerial practices, we have to become aware of these so-called errors. Such an awareness is extremely difficult to awaken without the involvement of peers who can detect the use of untested assumptions and raw biases.

4. Although past practices can give us very cogent clues in deciphering future situations, oftentimes the new situation presents itself in a different context. Prior solutions may not fit, even if the situations appear alike. We tend to look, however, for the similarities between the situations rather than their differences. This type of normal cognitive processing can play tricks on us. Even when we consult a repertoire of available responses (recall the solution database), we may not find one that fits the new situation. Consider a scenario in which an executive exudes great confidence in making an acquisition, having successfully acquired a firm in a prior year. In a year's time, however, the environment may have changed, be it as a result of economic or political conditions. The target may have little resemblance to the recently acquired firm, perhaps due as much to elusive cultural and personal contingen-

cies as to financial considerations. It is only through reflective practice exercised in the presence of critical and even disinterested peers that such an executive can distinguish that part of his reasoning that is measured and critical from that which might be self-fulfilling and self-justificatory.

Reflection and Experience

Although I have been using the notion of experience in this book as representing the identity of practice, experience also carriers the meaning of preparation for practice. Research by Ferry and Ross-Gordon (1998) suggests that experience in the second sense may *not* be sufficient to explain practitioners' use of reflective practices; rather, it is how one uses experience that is critical to understanding why some individuals use reflection to grow in their professional learning. Reflective practitioners "reinvest" in learning by participating in continuing education, by seeking out greater challenges in their work, and by tackling more complex representations of recurrent problems (Bereiter and Scardamalia, 1993). As a consequence of their learning reinvestment, reflective practitioners engage in problem posing as much as problem solving, continually expand their solution database rather than select the first solution that works, view inconsistencies as opportunities rather than inconveniences, and enjoy reflecting back on their decision making rather than sealing off debate. Of most relevance to work-based learning, reflective practitioners also seek to involve others in their search for new solutions (Schön, 1983; Terry and Ross-Gordon, 1998).

When experience is viewed as representing the world of practice it becomes coterminous with public reflectiveness. Consider that when people in interpersonal transactions sometimes pause for a moment to catch their breath and reflect, the process of reflection does not end once one resumes the conversation. Reflection continues on into the engagement as one becomes absorbed in practice. So, consistent with prior formulations about work-based learning, reflection is mixed up with practice. Our experience with others informs us, pulls us, and even transforms us. As Wenger (1998) suggests, we create ways of learning in practice in the very process of contributing to making that practice what it is.

In addition, the social and political setting of our experience can contribute significantly to our reflection. We tend to assume that everyone has the psychological and even physical security of reflecting with others, but in fact this may not be the case for marginalized groups in particular settings. Although not well researched, it is also likely that cultural background may play an important role in the encouragement or discouragement of reflective practices (Taylor, 1997).

In our everyday work activity, although we may be learning, we may not be subjecting that "learning" to conscious activity. Such concentration might indeed disturb our performance. We Western positivists tend to think of learning as that time when we stop our performance, assess how we're doing, and then determine how we can improve. We may choose at that point not to change anything. But when we stop and reflect, we at best capture what we had already learned tacitly in the past. Our learning may be continuing beyond that point of capture.

The stopping, however, is important, if not to help us figure out what we had learned, then at least to help others learn what we have done well (or poorly). Work-based learning is concerned with what we can do collectively during this stop-and-reflect period. How might we observe and experiment with our own collective tacit processes in action? One way to think about the reflective process in action is through the metaphor of the self-guided tour bus, the kind that allows you to hop on and off to explore some areas of the city on foot. If you choose never to get off the bus, your experience is broad but perhaps superficial. Stopping gives you the chance to see more deeply what is being experienced. It gives you, in the words of Isabel Rimanóczy (1998) of LIM Ltd., an opportunity to "lean over" an event and even to melt inside the situation, becoming part of the scene. Note also that once you've completed the excursion on foot, you normally have the option of reboarding the bus to continue the general tour.

Consider as a more practical example the instance of time-outs or adjournments in meetings used to give us time for private reflection on the transactions that took place, thus helping us prepare for the next meeting. In fact, this version of reality may be oversimplified and even misplaced. Private reflection does occur and may well help us prepare for the meeting, but any subsequent communication during the meeting extends that reflection because the meaning derived from that interaction is as much social as it is an internal activity (Vygotsky, 1988; Holman et al., 1997). In other words, we may be just beginning our reflection when we do it in private. Our thoughts are constantly reshaped when converted into language and brought out in the presence of others. Indeed, as we use language to persuade others about our points of view, we may notice that in our very process of argumentation, we begin to reframe our position.

Furthermore, most of us find that we may change our viewpoints slightly or even a great deal as the conversation ensues.

There are other qualities that tie reflective practice to experience and to work-based learning. For example, practitioners are sometimes called upon to improvise on-the-job. Often, the use of real-time improvisation is enhanced through conscious moments of reflection. Beyond improvisation, however, is the need for managers to question the contradictory forces that often impinge on their decision making (Wilmott, 1994). How does one respond, for instance, when asked by one's executive supervisor to "bury" an expense in order to show a positive quarterly result? What if one becomes aware of unsanitary practices in a plant owned by the company? It is one thing to speak about how one would redress these ethical issues; it is another to "practice" taking authentic action in one's work-based learning project and then reflect upon that practice.

Reflection also considers the affect experienced by the practitioner. Often overlooked, emotions can play a significant role in enhancing or in distorting the facts within a situation. Since emotions may not work in concert with rational behavior, public reflection can act as a validity check against decisions made in haste or in the spirit of the moment. Emotions arising from interpersonal relationships can also contribute or detract from learning experiences. Such subjective elements as trust, friendship, and support tend to enhance learning resulting from interpersonal reflective processes.

Finally, we need to continue to experiment with ways to bring reflective practice to management education. Management is truly a messy, interactive, and typically tacit activity. We tend to treat instruction at an absurdly low level of complexity, akin to single-loop learning, using the latest tools and recipes. MBA education seems to reinforce the application of tools and techniques instead of reflective engagement. Should we be relying exclusively on clean tools, such as cases, when dealing with people who wish to engage? We need to devise new ways to help managers work through real-world problems. We need to elicit the contribution of a reflective practice.

The Practicality of Reflection

One wonders, nevertheless, whether reflective practice is possible or practical in this age of the busy corporate executive who is virtually socialized to be a person of action, not of reflection. Nor are CEOs, according to some fatalistic observers, prone to inspire reflection in others. They want an answer rather than a question; they are looking for solutions rather than problems. They want to take credit for successes rather than be part of the "team" (Jackall, 1983).

We may wish to recall here from Chapter 2 the questions asked of executives who participate in the exercise known as "Actors and Reflectors."

- What is the quality of your work and personal experience?
- What are others at work saying about the intense pace of the workplace?
- What is your desire for personal reflection time?
- Do you desire more genuine conversation in a group or with a colleague?
- What is the community saying it needs from business?
- What is the Earth saying in her painful cry?

By examining questions such as these, we begin to see the shortsightedness of pure action as a worldview. Lee Bolman and Terrence Deal (1997) believe that action without reflection—or without "reframing," as they call it—can be fatal to corporate success. The decline of Sears in the face of its stronger competitor, Wal-Mart, or the precipitous decline in market share of General Motors can be attributed, in their view, to an inability to use reframing. For example, Roger Smith, upon assuming the role as CEO of GM, killed a design for a new small car to compete with the high-quality compact cars from Japan. It was thought that his commitment to rational thinking and financial logic got in the way of his mobilizing his company to undertake the necessary visionary strategy that would have been necessary to compete with the Japanese car manufacturers throughout the 1980s. As Bolman and Deal suggest, Smith's inability to reframe comprehensively kept him from seeing in a new light the problems confronting his company. In other words, he was unable to question the fundamental assumptions of his business sufficiently to generate creative responses to cope with the treacherous environment characterizing his industry.

The authors go on to suggest that managers consider at least four different frames or perspectives as they work through critical business decisions.

- The *structural* frame emphasizes goals, specialized roles, and formal relationships.
- The *human resource* frame sees an organization as an extended family, inhabited by individuals who have needs, feelings, prejudices, skills, and limitations that must be

attended to.

- The *political* frame sees organizations as arenas in which different interests compete for power and scarce resources.
- The *symbolic* frame treats organizations as cultures, propelled more by rituals, ceremonies, and myths than by rules or managerial authority.

Some members of the FEL community like to think of CEOs as guerrillas who believe more in rugged individualism than in learning, and tout individual performance over collaboration. Whatever else one might say about them, they seem to get performance and growth out of their company. Other FEL participants question this view of executive control. Learning and reflection cannot just happen at the middle level. It needs to be made known as a corporate-wide phenomenon.

Corina Holmes pointed out that her company, BT (British Telecommunications plc), is team-based and reflective in its outlook. She reported at one point that a "late-night group" was created where executives pretended that they were the board members and their task was to discover the profile of the executive best able to steer the company into the twenty-first century. Once they decided on this profile, they developed a competency model that was implemented on a collaborative basis by all senior managers in the company and integrated through all human resource policies and processes. The model was incorporated into a card that people carried and against which they questioned their everyday actions.

In our turbulent global environment, it appears almost definitional that we need executives who can inspire reflection to the extent of generating new ways of coping with change. There is a natural inertia that seems to accompany size and structure in organizations. A reflective culture is one that makes it possible for people to constantly challenge things without fear of retaliation. Hammer and Stanton (1997) believe that of all the tasks involved in the reflective process, breaking assumptions is the most critical. In their view, businesses operate on fundamental assumptions, for example

We are and always will be the low-cost producer.

Every new product we develop must be unique.

Our people are the best and brightest in the industry.

We are known for being the first to bring out new models.

Although these assumptions are necessary, they must be subject to review and revision as change occurs. Yet this almost natural step is the most difficult to undertake since change requires having people in control lose their grip on the status quo.

FEL members have described an assumption-breaking culture as one that deliberately keeps a company off-center. Executives also need to determine ways to make reflection and learning contagious within their organization. Perhaps one indicator of whether executives are prepared to accept reflective practices is the extent to which they themselves are receptive to feedback—the extent to which they can allow others to have an effect over them.

In fact, inspiring reflective practice in an organization does not have to be an onerous task for executives. Although managers are by definition people of action, they are also people who, when given a hospitable environment, like to share their experiences and, moreover, to help one another. Unfortunately, any formal reflective sharing that is made available to managers typically arises through discussion at training events or on strategic plans already formulated. However, managers are almost always working on challenges and puzzles in their daily work that would benefit from public dialogue. Many come to realize that they do not have a monopoly on good ideas and solutions. They might even crave the opportunity to share their experiences, insights, questions, and even failures with others if given the right climate—a climate receptive to open discourse. Indeed, they might appreciate an opportunity to replay their plans and actions in front of like-minded colleagues who are not assembled to take advantage politically of their faults, but who want to help because they realize that they, too, need the understanding of others.

In this age of strategic planning, it is also important to note that reflective practice is not equivalent to planning. Planning, be it determining one's strategic advantage, gathering competitive intelligence, or exploiting one's strategic competencies, constitutes reflection at a somewhat superficial level. It takes for granted the goals we are working on in solving our problems. Higher levels of reflection, noted earlier as process and premise reflection, examine not only the assumptions and procedures in use but the very presuppositions attending to the problem to begin with.

Reflection of this order requires an institutionalized capacity to rethink the nature of the business including its strategic goals. To truly shape organizational learning, reflective practices should also occur simultaneously with knowledge sharing so that new meaning and methods can be accessed by organizational members and partners. Shared meaning often gives way to new plans as well as to new or renewed action. Whether the action produced from reflection is new or renewed, it tends to be more coordinated than before since it has presumably engaged everyone involved in a publicly reflective process. Action then precipitates more reflection and the process begins again.

Finally, is public reflection a practice that should be reserved for those unpredictable times in corporate life when we have to reason our way out of turbulence? In fact, there isn't much routine in organizational practices among most organizations these days, but if there were to be, it might be the perfect time to engage in reflective behavior in order to reengineer taken-for-granted processes.

Why Reflection Leads to a Better World

Most of us accept the view that, especially under stress, we human beings do not behave that well. That is, we become defensive, mean, combative, sullen. Jensen (1997) refers to our behaviors in this mode as our pain avoidance model. Compatible with a learning style that Chris Argyris has called Model I (in contrast to Model II, discussed in Chapter 5), under pain avoidance, we tend to avoid personal error, remain in control, maximize winning and avoid losing, act as "rational" as possible, cling to our theories of the world and our view of self, and suppress negative feelings. These reactions are more often than not nonproductive for us today, though as automatic responses programmed through our brain, in particular our amygdala, they were helpful to us some four hundred thousand years ago. Now as we have become more populous, have created more of a global society, and have devised organizations as a basis for working and even living in society, we need to adopt a different pattern of response, one characterized by learning. However, this pattern may be invoked only through a process of reflection. It is reflection, for example, that will allow us to search for truths even if they are unpleasant to us, to take personal causal responsibility for problems, and to allow us to accept some pain in order to learn how to become a better societal participant.

Recalling our initial thoughts in this chapter, the reflection we are talking about is public more than introspective. Private reflection affords us the chance to cool down and come back with a presumably more rational response. However, walking away to reflect might rob not just ourselves but those in our immediate— perhaps intimate—environment of a potentially productive, albeit highly charged, moment. In the *Drama of Leadership,* Pitcher (1997) cautions us that emotion can impair judgment but its absence can result in even worse judgment.

So we return to the need for learning dialogues that encourage reflection even after one of our temporary rages, in the presence of trusting others. That way we don't have to walk away; we can work with others to help us make productive use of our emotional energy, and we can do so in a way that is sensitive to others, if not always perfectly pleasant. The reflection in this instance may not only be about our statements, but about our thoughts, feelings, and actions. The dialogue might also extend to what was not said or done. Hence, even under the grip of emotion and tension, we can develop the discipline of acknowledging our feelings and inquiring about the feelings of others, at least to the extent that we can understand the frames or meanings afforded by our statements and actions.

Sigmund Freud understood the value of inquiry and dialogue even on his deathbed. There is a story that one of his students approached him and, seeing how much pain he was in due to an afflictive mouth cancer, sheepishly uttered, "I presume your illness is so serious that you won't be interested in talking about the tenets of psychology." Freud immediately retorted, "My illness is fatal but not serious."

Reflective practice addresses two fundamental dilemmas posed by Giddens (1991) underlying the very process of reflection. Giddens referred to the "unification versus fragmentation" of ourselves and our being in the world. In the unification dilemma, there is the danger of becoming so enmeshed in self-consciousness that questions of collective morality become lost from view. In fragmentation, one becomes so imbued in a social context that one's self becomes dependent and invisible.

The first dilemma is addressed in reflective practice as people show a willingness to confront themselves and ongoingly create alternative interpretations of their own constructed reality in the company of trusting others. They become receptive to what Gouldner (1970) once referred to as "hostile information," or data that run contrary to their comfortable stance. They submit to the critical gaze of others (Weil, Romm, and Flood, 1997). But one can only accomplish a collective morality when, in Giddens's (1991) terms, one "does not just live for oneself, but develops meaning through relationship with others and through a feeling of wholeness with the earth's ecosystems."

As for the second dilemma, reflective practice encourages individuals to distinguish themselves from their social context. They are willing to be challenged on their interpretations but they also have the courage to posit constructions that might not be accepted in their community. They become willing to face the utter isolation that may come from ostracism from the group. Most of us have been in situations in which someone has asked for a second look at a proposal. In so doing, that person faces the stern rebuke from nearly everyone in the room. Do we have to go over this one more time? Yet how often does the second review lead to new critical insights? Are we not better off encouraging voice, or at least having a public debate about it, than suppressing it?

Reflective practice, then, considers data beyond our personal and interpersonal taken-for-granted assumptions. It is just as interested in exploring historical and social processes that go even beyond the individualistic notion of "learning-to-learn." As Giroux (1981) advocates, reflection can help us understand how knowledge has been constructed and managed and how what is deemed to be relevant or even common sense has been arrived at. Critical theorists, such as Freire (1970), are also concerned with how we consciously or unconsciously use power, privilege, and voice to exert influence and suppress dissent. We need to examine whose interests are served by the forms of knowing in popular use, be they instructional methods, curricula, or classroom technologies. Lectures and case studies provide the means for control to remain securely in the hands of the instructor. Dialogue, on the other hand, encourages learner voice because it attempts to develop critical consciousness by engaging learners in desocializing discovery and linking experience with text. Dialogue ensures that multiple points of view are heard, leading to new ways of thinking and ultimately of acting. Learners enter the conversation knowing that it will produce something totally new to each one of them. Dialogic practice, then, moves from an instructor-identified beginning point through numerous, subsequent rounds of interaction. Questions are raised by both learners and instructor as a given theme is explored (Shor, 1992; Boyce, 1996; McMasters, 1996).

Critical consciousness enhanced through public reflection recognizes the connection between individual problems and the social context within which they are embedded. Once this connection is made, learners can participate in educational projects that may transform their world by their very participation in it. Consider the case of Mark Twain's Huckleberry Finn, who believed he was committing a moral sin because he was harboring a slave, his friend Jim (Twain, 1948). Huck eventually gave up on his morality because of his feelings for his friend. Most of us can agree that acting on his feelings was correct, since turning in a slave who also happens to be your friend is bad morality to begin with. However, Huck did make one error. He did not question the underlying values behind the morality of the day. In public reflection one learns to criticize even societal norms and values by surfacing one's own beliefs, and in Huck's case, one's own tacit wisdom. By engaging in civic dialogue, wherein we take others' points of view into consideration but in which we also advocate and illustrate our own viewpoints as well as surface our underlying assumptions, we advance the cause of community. We mobilize to create a true community of practice and thus a better world.

7

Reflective Practices

*If I continue to believe as I have always
believed, I will continue to act as I have always
acted; and if I continue to act as I have always
acted, I will continue to get what I have always
gotten.*

—Marilyn Ferguson

Having laid out the rationale for public reflection as the critical component of work-based learning, I would like to turn our attention in
this chapter to four explicit reflective practices: learning teams, the
journal, developmental planning, and developmental relationships.
They can be deployed individually or in combination. Each represents
a distinct method for integrating public reflection into the workplace
as a basis for learning.

Learning Teams

In most work-based learning programs, but especially in action learning, participants work on projects with assistance from other participants as well as from qualified facilitators or advisors who help them
make sense of their project experiences in light of relevant theory.
This feedback feature principally occurs in learning teams or sets.

During the learning team sessions, participants discuss not
only the practical dilemmas arising from actions in their work settings
but also the application or misapplication of concepts and theories
to these actions. The rationale for the learning team structure is
simply that people engaged in similar work will tend to encounter

similar difficulties and hence will be likely to offer practical suggestions to one another and, through this process, learn how to manage their own problems. J. R. Mercer (1990), who wrote about his experiences in an action learning set, put it this way.

> To my surprise I found that they [the other set members] could often look at my problem from an entirely different perspective to me and yet arrive at the same conclusion.

The typical conversational device in most learning teams is questioning rather than advice-giving. Through apposite questioning, the problem solver is led to reflect on a problem from different perspectives. The type of question used in an action learning team matters in that questions are not designed to (1) place the focal person on the defensive; or (2) illustrate the cleverness of the questioner. Rather, questions are designed to open up the focal person's own view of the situation. They should keep the focus on the focal person and not on the questioner. Questions tend to be open-ended rather than closed (requiring a "yes" or "no" answer); tend to ask for specifics; and, when asked in a "why" format, are typically applied to future actions rather than past actions. The idea is to create an environment for exploration rather than rationalization (Beaty, Bourner, and Frost, 1993). As the process unfolds, the questioners might themselves come to appreciate, through the very process of inquiry, particular nuances that affect their own problems and environments.

Frank (1998b) suggests a number of conditions that make for what he calls "good questions." A good or nondefensive question

- is based on human curiosity or knowledge gathering;
- does not presume that the questioner already knows the right answer;
- is received in a constructive way;
- is not stopped by the fear that in questioning, one is ignorant;
- does not cut off further inquiry;
- is not based on the assumption that a past answer will be the best answer.

Ultimately, a good question leads to possible changes in action as one is led to challenge the assumptions of practice. In an in-service program for teachers using a community of practice approach, Lauriala (1998) reports how one teacher in her own words experienced her learning team's inquiry process:

> I felt my own teaching at that moment, when I started to compare it

to this (inquiry-led) system, quite absurd. When I was looking at that system, I started to question myself how could teaching be carried out otherwise.

In addition to asking nondefensive questions, learning team members also need to practice active listening wherein they can demonstrate to the focal person their interest in listening with such undivided attention that they truly understand both the content and feelings of the message. Active listening is a difficult skill to learn; most of the time, rather than deeply listening, we use our listening time to prepare our next response. To practice active listening, team members might occasionally try paraphrasing, which, rather than asking a question, makes a statement or expression that shows the focal person that they understand the meaning of what he or she has just said. They might also use perception checking, which makes a statement or expression that shows the focal person that they understand the feelings behind what he or she has just expressed. Active listening, when used effectively, conveys a sense of empathy, which, according to Beaty, Bourner, and Frost (1993) is the most important attitude to cultivate as a learning team member. Using empathy, listeners try to feel what it might be like to be "that person with the problem."

Consequently, rather than give advice, listeners try to open up cognitive avenues to help the focal person solve his or her own problem. No one is a better expert on a problem than the person with the problem, so advice may not only be naive from the focal person's point of view but it may even be counterproductive to learning. There are countless factors, both known and unknown, in the focal person's environment that impinge on the problem, and it is the focal person's prerogative to choose what to share. Focal members of the team have autonomy to choose how to use the other members as mutual helpers in the design of solutions to their problems. For example, they might choose to focus on events that recently occurred in their project and/or they might prefer to focus on plans for future actions.

The aforementioned concern regarding empathy also has implications for feedback in the learning team. Feedback should report on specific, observable actions without placing value judgments on them as good or bad, right or wrong. But team members are hard-pressed to report on actions that the focal person chooses not to disclose or chooses to avoid or keep hidden. This consideration is depicted vividly in the well-known JoHari Window (Figure 7.1), developed by Joe Luft and Harry Ingram (Luft, 1969).

According to the model, four quadrants are displayed, representing different aspects of a team member's experience in the group.

Figure 7.1
The JoHari Window

SELF

	Known	Not known
Known	**1** **Open**	**2** **Blind**
Not known	**3** **Hidden**	**4** **Unknown**

(left axis label: O T H E R S)

Source: From *Group Processes: An Introduction to Group Dynamics, Third Edition* by Joseph Luft. Copyright ©1984, 1970, 1963 by Joseph Luft. Reprinted by permission of Mayfield Publishing Company.

Some behaviors and feelings are known only to the individual, which he or she may choose or not choose to disclose. Other feelings and reactions to the focal person are known only to the team members, which they may choose or not choose to reveal.

Quadrant 1 is the open area, known to self and to others. Everyone in the team can notice such things as each other's height or eye color, but teams are unlikely to operate well unless more critical behaviors and feelings are revealed.

Quadrant 2 is the blind "spot," representing mannerisms and other personality characteristics observed by others but not revealed to the focal person. For example, someone might believe himself to be calm, unaware that he gets easily perturbed.

Quadrant 3 is the hidden quadrant, also known as the facade, which represents things about ourselves that we prefer to keep to ourselves. Perhaps, for example, we don't wish to reveal prior negative reactions we have had toward other members.

Quadrant 4 is the unknown domain, representing behaviors and feelings that lie below the surface and thus are hidden from our conscious awareness and also not known to others.

When it comes to interactions between members in the learning team as well as to the group's overall development, it is advisable to enlarge the open area of Quadrant 1 in the JoHari Window. (In the aftermath of the T-Group movement of the 1960s and 1970s, some might suggest that Quadrant 1, however, should never be completely opened for fear of overexposing the self.) The way to enlarge the open quadrant is to move the line dividing the "others" axis down and the line dividing the "self" axis to the right. This would mean having the focal person disclose more of himself or herself and having other team members provide more and more feedback to the focal person. However, members of the learning team typically take cues from the focal person regarding whether, when, and how to provide critical feedback. Initially, it might be important for whomever volunteers on the first focal person to ask for feedback. That individual also has the opportunity to ask for information of a certain type to keep the focus on his or her issues. Not every comment from the team can be absorbed by the focal person—nor is it necessary to debate every point.

On the other hand, it is equally important to disclose more and more of oneself to show a receptiveness to open feedback. Beaty, Bourner, and Frost (1993) talk about learning how to receive as follows:

> It is important to really hear the questions that are asked and the comments that are made. It is easy to keep the blinkers on our own ideas and sometimes hard to accept that there may be other ways of doing things. If you decide to reject the ideas you hear, then your own ideas will have been strengthened by having considered alternatives.

In order to encourage feedback from others, it is also helpful to let down one's guard a little. It is not exhibiting weakness to demonstrate a need for support and encouragement. In this way, empathy works both sides of the street. An appreciation of empathy from others breeds more empathy from them and, perhaps later, by you to them. As is demonstrated in the JoHari Window model, one has to learn to both give and receive interpersonal attention if the learning team is to function at its optimal level.

The support generated among members in a learning team establishes close bonds, which subsequently may account for dramatic expressions of teamwork and encouragement, one member to another. In a learning set organized through the Britvic Soft Drinks Developing to Lead action learning program, the following anonymous quote was recorded by the company's training manager (Meehan and Jarvis, 1996):

> I was seriously considering defaulting. I sent Jane an e-mail, just saying the word "help." She responded immediately: "We cannot complete without you, we all do it together or not at all. Don't give up now, we are so close. Where can I help you most?"

In a typical action learning team, members will be seen listening, posing questions, and offering suggestions to another team member whose project is under scrutiny. Occasionally, the focal individual might listen as the other set members brainstorm ideas regarding his or her issue or project. Participants often decide to experiment with new approaches in light of the group discussion, leading to new theories or ideas to be tested in action during the intervening periods between set meetings. The results are then brought up at subsequent set meetings.

Since the pattern of the meeting tends to be sequential, moving from one member to the next, sufficient time is required to give each member a chance to develop his or her project situation. Hence meetings require a minimum of two hours and in some cases even up to a full day to give every member a chance to present. If meeting times are relatively short, they should be scheduled at frequent intervals, perhaps every two weeks, so that members who have not had a turn get a chance to air their project or team concerns. In any event, learning teams should meet as often as monthly in order to sustain momentum and to give members a chance to bring up issues before they become stale or are forgotten.

The matter of where and when to meet is not a trivial issue. Many a learning team has become stuck when it is time to take out one's calendar and schedule meetings. Weinstein (1995) advises learning teams to meet away from the participants' workplaces to reduce the likelihood of members being called away for on-site emergencies. As for meeting times, it is typically useful to schedule a full slate of meetings at the very first session. That way, dates can become fixed for nearly all members, aside from prior commitments or unexpected emergencies.

An important programmatic issue for learning teams is whether to staff them with in-company or mixed-company members. It should not be assumed that the familiarity of in-company membership makes the process easier. One still has to deal with the admixture of expertise, background, role, and level in the same-company format. In fact, in-company teams can occasionally produce political repercussions, leading some work-based learning exponents to advise programs not to constitute a team with direct supervisors present. On the other hand, staffing teams with diagonal hierarchical levels provides a unique opportunity to see how the other levels "think," giving participants a chance to dislodge their assumptions and biases. Staffing teams with in-company members representing diverse functions also gives participants a unique networking opportunity. Such teams also tend to create a sense of community as participants discover how things are done in other parts of the organization. It is not unusual for teams to lead to contacts that can last for years. Finally, when in-company teams reach a critical mass, they can become infectious as a learning vehicle or approach that can extend throughout the entire organization.

Mixed-company learning teams offer their own distinct set of advantages. They expose members to ways other organizations may look at comparable problems. For example, there are advantages to seeing how participants from other industries, sectors, or from organizations of very different sizes address particular issues. Members also tend to report feeling freer to disclose sensitive matters, especially as they enter the team with others' having fewer preconceived notions about their position and responsibilities. Hence they might feel that they can start their participation with a cleaner slate, giving them a chance to try out new roles and behaviors. Finally, mixed-company teams constitute the only work-based learning method for senior executives to communicate with their peers.

Perhaps the most critical concern regarding learning team membership is to provide for some diversity of background and ways of knowing to avoid having the team begin with an entrenched mental model that inhibits divergent thinking. It is thus advisable that members display variety in their learning and cognitive styles. In that way, members can enjoy the opportunity to work with others who have different ways of learning and thinking in order to improve the quality of sharing within the team.

Beyond the contribution of learning teams to project operations, some teams provide feedback to members to help them assess their effectiveness in a group setting. As we shall see, participants may also develop personal agendas or development plans for individual and managerial change and share these with the rest of the group. Team members then discuss each others' plans, identify potential pitfalls, and suggest improvements. Occasionally, participants may even be called back together six to eight months later to report on the successes and frustrations in implementing their personal development plans.

Learning teams thus provide many opportunities for members to develop their interpersonal and managerial skills. Learning tends to be enhanced because, compared to other teams, the learning team explicitly focuses on member development. Among the lessons available to members are such managerial practices as providing and accepting positive and negative feedback, negotiating with others, dealing with internal and external politics, testing publicly one's espoused values and beliefs, fielding a new strategy, and managing change. The experience is designed to encourage the participant to challenge his or her own actions and consider novel views and processes. At the same time, participants are encouraged to be critical of academic theories placed into their use. The experience also leaves ample room for making mistakes, provided that participants learn from them.

Weinstein (1995) and Mumford (1996) have identified a number of other skill opportunities available to members:

- time and space for reflection
- support in setting goals and time scales
- insights and inquiries from others
- different perspectives of others
- knowledge, expertise, and experience of others
- sharing of ideas, confusion, and successes with others
- support from others, especially to try out new behaviors and actions
- challenge by others
- confidence from hearing oneself be helpful
- opportunity to hear oneself think—and respond
- learning how to manage oneself in a group and to manage the overall group process and group learning
- space to experiment with new ways of behaving in order to become more effective in interpersonal situations
- opportunity to be "out of role"

Learning teams also develop a social culture in their own right, which presents participants with lessons regarding group dynamics. As such, they are not unlike other groups that must confront the inevitable processes of their own development (Schein, 1967). As learning teams, however, there tends to be explicit focus, in this case, on group learning. Hence, learning teams, as a special form of team, might reflect a different set of norms compared to performance or task teams. Although each learning team is unique, the following norms would not be unusual:

- We should strive to become more and more open and honest with each other.
- We try to be supportive of one another; we are concerned about each other.
- We actively listen to one another.
- We are interested in giving and receiving constructive feedback from one another.
- As our main purpose is learning, we are committed to reviewing our individual and group learning processes.
- We commit to distribute our work load equally.
- We arrive fully prepared for our meetings.
- We are as committed to each other's and the group's agendas as our own.
- We act in complete confidence and never reveal our deliberations outside the group unless we receive permission to do so from respective members.
- We are committed to learn how to develop deep trust in one another; that is, we don't have to "stand on ceremony" or be an authority. We can at times be tentative and even vulnerable.
- We agree to accommodate our team schedule and make all meetings unless there is an emergency that we must attend to.
- We try to have fun.

It goes without saying that for development of the learning team to proceed, it is critical that it not change its membership on any regular basis. The team is designed for team members and team members alone. However, visitors may certainly be invited from time to time, especially if they can offer some expertise unavailable from any of the members. Clients may also be invited to the team to provide some perspective on perhaps a vexing issue within a project.

As a method of reflective practice, learning teams allow participants to engage in critical reflection of the assumptions underlying actions in their own organizations. Some organizations, though sponsors of work-based learning interventions, are not always hospitable to the probing that characterizes the dynamics of this form of learning. Hence, participants appreciate the opportunity to try out their ideas and examine their values and assumptions in the learning team. With the help and encouragement of their team members, especially their facilitator, they can also try out some new interpersonal skills or managerial competencies based on "reframed" assumptions derived from public reflection within the team (Dixon, 1990). After rehearsal, they can bring their new ideas and competencies into the organization with renewed confidence. There is no better experience in learning about a new idea (or even a personal competency) and its practicality than by attempting to use it in a work environment where it may initially be considered unworkable.

The Journal

It may seem contradictory to include journal writing as a *publicly* reflective learning practice. After all, the journal is completed in private and is not necessarily shared with other persons. In fact, the journal is arguably the most endemic technique we have to enhance our self-reflection. Yet, often used as an introspective tool for personal growth, it can also serve as an aid to bring together the inner and outer parts of our lives. It offers a lens to view experience—be it before, during, or after the event under scrutiny—and it even allows further reflection on the journal entries themselves.

Given that most people bring their journal insights into public dialogue, the journal has a direct bearing on the work-based learning principles discussed in this book. Therefore, it is a potent vehicle for reflecting on experience, for clarifying our assumptions and behavior, for improving our powers of observation, and for promoting consistency between our beliefs and our practices (Raelin, 1993a). Journal writing also requires support from a variety of sources, such as from peers, mentors, or supervisors, to provide feedback and encouragement to continue the writer's self-development through reflection (Rigano and Edwards, 1998).

One of the most influential writers in the domain of journal writing was Ira Progoff (1975), whose approach, referred to as the intensive journal process, was designed to bring people back to critical events in their lives and give them a chance to relive them and make decisions based upon them. Within this overall approach, Progoff formulated three main methods:

1. *dialogues*, in which conversations with people from the past or present, from literature or history, or even with

oneself are held in order to confront events, ideas, images, assumptions, and even unconscious motivations;
2. *depth dimension*, in which creative forces are used to explore hidden meanings, as when journal writers free-associate using dreams, metaphors, unsent letters, and images;
3. *life study*, in which the writer becomes a "trustee" for another person's life by writing a journal as that person, looking at the world through that person, thus intensively empathizing with him or her.

In work-based learning settings, journals can be useful in helping participants reflect on experiences, be they in their learning team, in their projects, or just in everyday life. The journal can serve as a vehicle to integrate information and experiences that run counter to preexisting viewpoints. It can also help participants more deeply understand their current reasoning and associated behavior or spur their consideration of new methods or skills introduced in the program. A participant in a professional self-development program offered through James Cook University in Australia, sponsored by professors Donna Rigano and John Edwards (1998), produced the following journal entry regarding workshop skills he was hoping to incorporate into his work practice:

> I notice that I automatically started to use the small range of lateral thinking techniques that I found interesting over the last six months. I consciously realized when I was "black-hatting" (see the reference to de Bono in Chapter 5). These techniques definitely helped as the bank of normal personal ideas ran out. I must spend time reviewing, reflecting on, and practicing these techniques, as they appear to work.

Newcomers to journal writing might wish to begin with some express questions to help them work through interpretations of their experience (Kemmis and Carr, 1983; Boud, Keough, and Walker 1985):

1. How have you processed the particular experience? Note your thoughts, reactions, and judgments (though try not to prejudge your or others' behavior). Be aware of the context surrounding the experience and try to recall the sequence of events.
2. What were your feelings attending to the experience? Try to understand the range and depth of your feelings emerging both at the time of the experience and subsequent to it. Be aware of feelings that may hinder your learning or that may distort your recollection of what happened. Include positive as well as neg-

ative feelings. Recall incidents when you felt similarly. Be prepared to check with others about your affective reactions.

3. How do you now evaluate the experience? What new insights or information have been revealed? Perhaps you might relate the incident to other experiences or compare it to your personal beliefs and attitudes. After this process of association, be prepared to integrate the data to see if they form any coherent or complete whole. Once you have a sense of the new knowledge that has been generated, subject it to tests of validity by asking whether the integrated information squares with reality as you know it. Check whether the new knowledge has internal consistency—that it remains consistent with other experiences as well as values in your life. Try also to visualize how the new knowledge would apply to new experiences that might arise. Be prepared to actualize the new knowledge into current and future practices and thereupon reflect again on its utility.

Associates participating in Leeds Metropolitan University's Company Associate Partnership Scheme (CAPS) complete learning logs, dividing them into three sections: (1) they are encouraged to identify and reflect on any significant event or experience and to write a full description of what occurred; (2) they attempt to list so-called "learning points" that show what was gained from the experience; and (3) they are asked to select one of the learning points and use it to generate an action plan regarding how they can institutionalize their learning (Ahmed et al., 1995).

McKernan (1991) suggests that if participants make the commitment to use a journal, they should attend to it on a regular basis; otherwise, key events or observations might be forgotten if left for completion later on. Further, it is through practice that participants might progress to higher levels of reasoning and to reflection that begins to analyze data from multiple perspectives. Persistency in journal writing (along with skilled support from the work-based learning program) can help participants overcome the frustration of acquiring unfamiliar skills, especially when these skills reflect back on the self.

Once participants develop some comfort with the journal-writing process, they will likely develop their own style. In addition, it may be useful to consult methodologies offered by other authorities. Below are suggestions from the work of Progoff (1975), Ranier (1978), Fulwiler (1987), Lukinsky (1990), and McKernan (1991):

1. *Logs* or reports represent factual accounts of specific experiences.

2. *Lists* represent clusters of ideas on a topic (e.g., my ten pet peeves, a table of contents of the person I am at this moment).

3. *Portraits* are descriptions of people who are admired or disliked. They help one learn more about oneself as portraits of others are developed.

4. *Memoirs* are personal accounts of oneself that are written to be objective, perhaps as might be told to others, and that include the landscape of events swirling around the writer.

5. *Catalogue of feelings* lists what the writer likes or does not like about particular experiences, ideas, or people.

6. *Intimate accounts* set down personal notes and logs rich in personal sentiments, even confessions. These represent the most personal of the journal types.

7. *Dialogues* entail the writing of both sides of a conversation to obtain insight into multiple points of view and perspective.

8. *Conceptual understanding* represents an attempt to write about a new or existing theory in which one may not have had much exposure or prior appreciation.

9. *Applications* take relevant concepts and attempt to apply them into practice, normally with commentary as to their potential or worthwhileness.

10. *Social histories* record consensual and conflicting ideas between various individuals and groups.

11. *Maps of consciousness* are drawings that capture the writer's feelings or state of mind at a given moment.

12. *Guided imagery* constitutes a meditated frame of reference, which could include the recording of daydreams or the development of dream images into the waking state (as in "imagine yourself in a forest" or "imagine yourself taking the last shot in a tied game").

13. *Altered point of view* has oneself writing about oneself in the third person or about someone else in the first person in order to gain empathy, to experience something painful, or just to imagine oneself in a different place or in a different time.

14. *Contradictions* and dilemmas compare aspirations and reality or reveal decisions around competing values.
15. *Inconsistencies* pick up on differences between what one or others espouse and actual behavior.
16. *Surprises* note differences between what one expected to occur and what ultimately did occur or between the expected behavior of people and how they actually behaved.
17. *Unsent letters* express to someone what one couldn't say in real life, perhaps to a loved one or to someone deceased.

Developmental Planning

Developmental planning is often done in conjunction with executive education and thus represents a practical form of reflective practice. Its principal rationale is to allow participants to anticipate their learning needs prior to or concurrent with any management development program under the assumption that the self-generation of personal and professional objectives will provide a substantial incentive for learning.

The responsibility for developmental planning devolves to two principal constituents: the organization and the individual. The organization has the responsibility for providing opportunities and resources to the individual in order that he or she may plan developmental goals and meet personal and professional needs in concert with the organization's strategy. The individual needs to take responsibility for his or her own growth and development. The organizing principles underlying developmental planning include the valuing of feedback, in particular, encouraging employees to solicit feedback from as many sources as possible; the interpretation of any job assignment as a potential opportunity for development; and the seeking of job and relationship experiences that might provide opportunities for stretching and learning.

As for the nature of planning, there are many approaches to choose from, but a popular one to precipitate the process and that is also easy to remember asks five principal questions: who, will do what, when, under what conditions, and to what extent. Let's consider each of these five questions in turn. First, the participant identifies himself or herself (for example, by role) and then develops some challenging and specific objectives, which though difficult are nonetheless attainable. Through objective setting, the participant is able to more objectively and precisely track progress toward predetermined development goals. As the goals are revisited throughout the feedback process, they can be changed since they are not rigid quotas to be met.

The "what" question needs to be prepared in as specific a language as possible in order that progress be measured. Objectives can be qualitative as well as quantitative. For example, a participant may desire to improve her working rapport with another member of the staff with whom she has had a rocky relationship in the past. Perhaps this person reminds her of people with whom she has had difficulty. Objectives should also tie in, to the extent practical, with both organization and unit goals. Although some objectives may be of a personal or professional nature, and thus specific to individual development perhaps within one's field, it also makes sense to tie some objectives to work tasks and resultant needs within one's department or within the company as a whole. Objectives should also be set in conjunction with one's program sponsor, mentor, buddy, or perhaps work supervisor. Developmental programs may vary in regard to who serves as the advisor to the participant. Although the development plan is a personal document, its learning potential is enhanced as it is made public both within a learning team and with a personal confidant who can reflect on the participant's plans and progress.

The next question, the "when," is determined by specifying a timetable with milestones to assist in establishing some temporal parameters for accomplishing the objectives. Although the time horizon should be kept flexible, it seems best to plan for shorter than longer cycles to enhance the feedback process. If the objective is considerable in terms of time to accomplishment, it may be useful to break down the objective into sub-goals that might be accomplished within shorter time frames.

The conditions establish the legitimate constraints that need to be overcome or actions to be undertaken in order to succeed. The participant, therefore, might specify how particular resources or experiences in the company might be necessary to develop the necessary competencies to accomplish particular objectives. Other conditions might include particular people to interview, textual resources to consult, educational opportunities to take advantage of, feedback from certain individuals to solicit, senior staff to consider as mentors.

Finally, developmental objectives need to incorporate measures to assess accomplishment—that is, criteria that would indicate how the participant as well as his or her sponsors would know that he or she achieved the goals. Participants can learn to become quite creative in establishing useful performance criteria. They might develop so-called unobtrusive measures that are less obvious indicators of performance but nevertheless are quite useful. For example, if a participant wants to develop his listening ability, he might practice certain techniques, such as perception checking, which could be assessed using a standard "fill in the blank" test or by receiving direct feedback from learning team members. However, a more interesting, unobtrusive measure might be to have him tally how many times during the course of a week associates have sought him out to share their personal or work concerns. Increased listening acuity often begets more trust and contact from subordinates or associates.

Once the plan is written, it should be reviewed on a periodic basis. It is also useful to recurrently measure results from the ongoing developmental activities to be sure that the participant is learning what he or she planned to achieve. Perhaps a given activity has not been sufficient or needs to be replaced with another method to exemplify the competency under consideration.

Sponsors and mentors play a number of critical roles in the development process. Sponsors can assist participants in diagnosing their learning needs, in writing their objectives, and in assessing progress toward the achievement of the objectives. Although others will also be detailed in the next main section, I list here some additional responsibilities for sponsors and mentors (Lawton and Ernesti, 1998):

- clarifying how the learner plans to learn
- assisting participants in setting realistic target dates for completion
- helping devise creative measurement techniques
- monitoring the learner's progress toward completion of goals and objectives
- evaluating and renegotiating the development plan as needed
- serving as a resource or even as a role model

Plan Unfolding

Developmental planning may be triggered by the process of reviewing already established objectives. During a consultation with one's sponsor, the participant becomes aware of those areas of performance that are strong and those that require improvement. Although development planning recognizes and builds on areas of strength, it tends to concentrate on performance deficiencies, in particular on the gaps between expected and actual performance. The essence of the development action plan is to identify the types of learning activities that can be undertaken to fill these gaps. Remember that the process is a joint undertaking between participant and sponsor. Often there is considerable discussion and negotiation regarding the appropriate action.

There are a number of activities that can be undertaken to fill gaps in one's knowledge base. These may include:

- on-the-job training
- personal reading and videotape viewing
- planned task rotation
- formal training courses
- coaching
- shadowing
- volunteering
- special assignments
- task force membership
- community service

Plans may lead to experiments in participants' managerial behavior. As part of a middle management program at Ford, sponsored by the University of Michigan, participants work on leadership development plans during a six-month interim between the initial course at the university and a two-day follow-up meeting at Ford's Executive Development Center. Tim Gilberg, a supervisor in Ford's vehicle operations unit, having received feedback from coworkers on the need to develop his interpersonal skills, chose as one of his development activities to work with each one of his subordinates to develop a personal training plan (Stuller, 1993).

Development plans can also take the form of personal learning goals, goals that are designed purely to benefit the personal life of participants and that may only indirectly improve their work performance. However, in most work-based learning programs, participants such as Tim Gilberg, cited above, are inclined to derive goals that are managerial in character or that affect their communication and leadership competencies. Some of the goals that I have observed include improving listening skills so that others are not cut off when speaking; asserting oneself within one's work team; knowing when to stop talking to give others a chance to speak; allowing subordinates to complete a delegated assignment without premature interference; learning to speak more effectively and with more confidence in public; attempting to diversify one's leadership style with different staff; or aligning one's body language with one's verbal communication.

It is one thing to construct a goal, it is another to nurture it throughout the course of a program and commit to it even after the program's conclusion. Goal construction and evolution are taken most seriously when the program devotes time to the goal development process. Participants need to be given a chance to publicly state their goals and say how they plan to achieve them. The program also needs to provide time for review of each participant's progress toward goal accomplishment. For example, a specific time on the agenda might be allocated for the participants to receive feedback from each member of their learning team regarding how other members see their progress.

Whatever their form, personal development plans need to be viewed as a flexible, living agreement. Hence, all parties need to acknowledge that unanticipated events create changes in how one looks at particular phenomena. Participants change their views as they learn. They encounter different experiences and people as their projects evolve. Lex Dilworth has posed a number of questions to help participants develop their personal learning plan once it is initially formulated (Dilworth, 1998). He believes that by giving people space for personal self-examination, the surface layers of the original goal can be peeled back to reveal a more fundamental goal of potentially greater importance. He asks participants to consider such questions as:

- What motivates this goal? Do I really care about it?
- What specific incidents in my life have led me to it?
- Will the goal help me avoid mistakes that I often make in my life?
- How will I benefit if I make the change specified?
- How will I know whether I am successful?

The goal-setting and development processes are comparable to journal writing in that they promote a personal reflective experience that the participant can choose to bring out into public view as desired. Personal developmental planning arises from a philosophy that sees personal growth as arising from personal reflection on one's achievements and from one's mistakes. As people engage in personal dialogue or "self-talk," they may establish a personal vision of where they want to go and how they can make it a reality (Dilworth, 1998).

On the other hand, developmental planning need not take place in a vacuum. Most work-based learning programs provide opportunities for the sharing of personal learning goals. Teammates in learning teams, for example, are available to provide feedback on one's accomplishments or even on one's lack of progress. Participants may also seek out mentors or coaches to assist in the developmental process, as the next section on developmental relationships will expand upon.

Participants often find that the process of developmental planning can be even more rewarding than the achievement of the goals themselves. For many managers, personal development planning may represent the first explicit opportunity for reflection afforded them within their work environment. Work is often construed as a place for doing, not for reflecting, especially with others. The simple idea of stepping back in order to move forward is so often overlooked in cultures of action and progress.

Corporate Examples

Developmental plans tend to be quite varied across companies. Some plans involve a sponsor as well as the participant's supervisor, thus taking the form of a contract or agreement about the work to be accomplished in a project. Developmental planning holds a critical role in Britvic's Developing to Lead (DTL) action learning program (Meehan and Jarvis, 1996). Even before being accepted into the program, candidates need to demonstrate their developmental potential in a written statement, endorsed by their line manager. After a rigorous assessment procedure, a developmental profile is prepared for each candidate. Those accepted into the program draft a learning log that translates their development profile into a personal development plan.

While working on their action learning projects, DTL participants each identify four problems or opportunities for change. These are presented as part of their learning team activity. Updates are given so that their peers can assess progress on developmental plans. At the end of the program, participants prepare a written report on the final outcome of their plan, which is formally assessed not only by the facilitator but by each member of their learning team.

At Xerox, employees prepare Learning Action Plans (LAPs) to assist in their growth both personally and professionally within the company. What is unusual about the LAP is that though individuals set traditional learning objectives for development in both their current and potential jobs, they also expressly work on contributions they can make on behalf of others. This type of developmental objective emphasizes the benefit of teaching and learning among peers and reinforces the corporate value of working as a team.

Many companies are using multi-rater or 360-degree feedback assessments to support the developmental planning function. Under this format, the participants or focal persons compare their perceptions of their own knowledge, skills, and abilities (KSAs) against feedback from their supervisors, subordinates, peers, and customers, each of whom can provide a unique perspective on their performance and potential. There are a myriad of assessment instruments that can be developed or purchased "off-the-shelf" from training suppliers. For example, some assessments reflect KSAs based on one's job, on a set of competencies associated with categories of performance, or on strategic plans (Nowack, 1993). Some companies even offer PC-based access to 360-degree tools and include self-directed workbooks to guide participants through a personal development planning process. However, the effectiveness of these tools seems to rest on the availability of coaches to help explain the feedback from the assessment instrument and plan both strategic and personal activities to overcome any noted deficiencies (Dalton, 1998). Futhermore, for developmental planning purposes, it is preferable to build assessments mutually with participants who normally have a good sense of the KSAs needed to develop their own effectiveness and potential. Hence participants might very well participate in the construction of any instrument and in the selection of relevant appraisers. Assessments should also be given more than once, perhaps semiannually or annually.

After the assessment instrument is administered, feedback can be provided to the focal person using a number of methods. For example, scoring can be presented as a comparison to peers, or participants can choose to compare their own scores over time, using the first set of results as a baseline. It is important for coaches, mentors, and sponsors to participate in interpreting and applying the results of the assessments as a basis for supporting the development plan. Furthermore, as the assessments tend to be sensitive documents, the feedback associated with them needs to be delivered in a constructive manner. For instance, coaching tends to be far more effective when it emphasizes the behavior of the participant under scrutiny as opposed to the individual's personality dimensions. Other skills that coaches might incorporate in working with feedback assessments include active listening; focused interviewing; dealing with feelings, especially from unexpected negative appraisal; targeting improvement areas; helping shape the development of new behaviors; setting specific goals and action plans; and follow-up (Antonioni, 1996).

In Dupont's Leadership for Growth program, participants receive a 360-degree assessment during the very first week of the program. Responsibility for following up on the assessment is less structured than at Britvic in that participants may choose or not choose to share the results of their feedback with their project teams and coach.

Those who do tend to be interested in obtaining feedback from their associates to help them develop competencies cited in their assessment as "needing improvement."

The Career Development Process of United Parcel Service (UPS) constitutes a development approach that is closely tied to the company's strategic planning process (Leibowitz et al., 1994). The program is initiated by managers who, before meeting with their subordinate supervisors, first analyze the KSAs required by their work teams to meet current and anticipated business needs. After the team assessment, attention is devoted to individual team members. They complete self-assessment exercises and develop personal action plans. In meeting with individual team members, the managers share performance appraisal data and at the same time discuss the various business challenges facing their unit, including their analysis of the team's competency needs. The supervisors incorporate their units' needs in preparing their personal career and development goals. The plan is operationalized through such learning strategies as lateral career moves or growth-in-place job assignments.

There is an attempt through this process to merge the employees' desired career goals and developmental needs with the identified business conditions facing UPS. The process is repeated at the division and district levels. For example, division-wide meetings are held at which managers report on their teams' developmental needs against their capabilities. As the process makes its way up the managerial ranks, a master plan is gradually put into place that coordinates staffing and developmental requirements with corporate strategic challenges.

Developmental Relationships

Another option in work-based learning programs using reflective practice is the formal or informal organization of developmental relationships. Typically, this option is referred to under the familiar labels of coaching or mentorship programs. The labels, however, become confusing as the terms become intertwined. For example, some authors refer to coaching as outside advisement and mentoring as internal advisement. On the other hand, professional mentorships sometimes evolve by taking advantage of people from outside organizations.

Using work-based learning precepts, we avoid stumbling on these unnecessary distinctions by merely suggesting that one's learning at work can be facilitated through the advisement of one or more significant individuals with whom to engage in a reflective process about one's thoughts and behaviors. This clarification does not require that the advisor be a peer, a senior member of staff, or an outside practitioner; that the purpose be remedial or enriching; that the content be substantive or therapeutic; nor does it insist that the adviser give advice or merely actively listen. Developmental relationships evolve under various memberships and using a variety of styles and can occur frequently without formal organization. In fact, group mentorships have been proposed wherein a senior colleague can meet simultaneously with several junior protégés (Kaye and Jacobson, 1995). What makes each relationship unique as a work-based learning approach is the parties' interest in mutual reflection and learning. Recall that in the last chapter I suggested that developmental relationships entail dialogue, meaning that the parties are committed to surfacing those social, political, and even emotional reactions that might be blocking their own operating effectiveness.

The parties consciously reflect on experience and even upon their own problem-solving processes and communication patterns. Otherwise confidential issues, be they working relationships with other managers, strategic business issues, or the participant's own growth and development, are given a forum for open consideration. Individuals get a rare opportunity to think out loud and receive constructive feedback on critical and even undiscussable problems (Witherspoon and White, 1996). In fact, the coaching discussion might even discern ways to make what has been heretofore undiscussable, discussable.

Developmental relationships often tie to the developmental planning process described in the prior section. At Arthur Andersen, for example, an action learning program features coaches who work with participants to create learning agendas and action plans. In programs of this nature, participants receive the added resource of a coach, who, in addition to their supervisor or sponsor, can provide feedback on progress in accomplishing their developmental goals. The coach, however, offers the benefit of not representing formal line authority, most likely making it easier for the participant to share confidences.

The intent of the developmental relationship is for both parties to learn and to further their own self-development. Hence they need not be one-way. There is as much for the coach to learn as the apprentice. Developing others can be considered a critical managerial competency, especially in an age when team structures and two-way communication have become commonplace. Coaches and mentors might also find that the unique perspective of a protégé can actually enhance their own performance. They might even obtain organizational recognition from the success of their protégé (Kram, 1985). Aside from its career implications, development can also be a source of great personal accomplishment. Mentors report an exhilaration from the fresh energy provided by protégés (Allen et al., 1997).

There is a built-in check on the effectiveness of these relationships. In reflective practice the parties "check in" with each other as a matter of course to assess their ongoing value to one another. Developmental relationships thus entail situated learning in the sense that the parties do not rely upon preexisting knowledge but develop their learning as they go and as they adjust to the challenges of their own practice. In commenting on the one-on-one mentoring program at Lex Service, the automotive group in the United Kingdom, the director of management development, Nick Holley, points out that "Management development is not about giving people answers. It is about challenging them and helping them to meet people and find the answers for themselves" (Houlder, 1997).

Developmental relationships are not didactic in the form of master instructing apprentice but rather allow for the progressive accumulation of values and skills as they are applied to real problems. Participants in a coaching relationship are encouraged to consult with a variety of knowledge resources to develop an appreciation of how expertise and insight are distributed within an organization (Collins et al., 1989). Such exposure helps them understand that managerial tasks can be confronted in multiple ways and that no one individual embodies all the necessary expertise. Learners need to be encouraged to view all their associates as mutual learners who can offer insight into their personal and organizational performance. In this way, they begin to appreciate learning as a progressive process. Coaches, however, can help them establish benchmarks to measure their own progress.

Some of the mentoring literature suggests that the relationship may be used to create and sustain an organization's competitive advantage (Aryee et al., 1996; Russell and Adams, 1997). Bell (1996), for example, believes that mentors can equip organizations with strategic leaders. He further points out that our future organizations will encounter greater competitive challenges, making their success dependent upon their adaptability and resourcefulness. These organizational characteristics will be furthered through internal programs such as mentorships that reward learning and experimentation.

Evidence from the Field

There are a few lessons from research on mentoring and coaching that can guide the creation and operation of successful development relationships. A program called LeaderLab, sponsored by the Center for Creative Leadership, conducted an evaluation of three of their developmental roles: the process advisor (PA), represented by a staff professional; an in-course change partner, represented by a peer in the program; and a back-home change partner, represented by a peer back at the work site (Young and Dixon, 1996). The evaluation found the PA role to be the most critical feature of the program. The PA represented an ongoing link between the program and the individual, tailoring the activities of LeaderLab to the participant's needs. The evaluation found that participants valued their PAs more for their process concern than for their substantive expertise. It was not the PAs' intimate knowledge of the participant's job or industry that was valuable; rather it was the encouragement they provided that, in turn, was based upon knowledge of change and developmental processes as well as their closeness to the individual. Two typical comments made in this regard by participants were:

> My PA acted as a mirror for myself so I could see patterns, maintain consistency.

> The PA challenged me to explore my feelings and develop different strategies.

Finally, PAs were also found to be especially useful in ameliorating some of the stress that most participants were experiencing in their back-home environment. It was thought, for example, that PAs provided a positive influence on participants' self-efficacy by expressing confidence in the participant's ability to overcome hardship.

With regard to the change partner roles in LeaderLab, especially the back-home partner, the results of the evaluation were mixed. There were two critical ingredients to enhancing these roles. First, the participant needed to be open in sharing and accepting feedback from the change partner. Second, the change partner needed to be seen as trustworthy, discreet, committed, and available.

Clearly, for development relationships to work, learners need someone who can be committed to them and who can afford the time for the relationship to evolve. There is no point in having a mentor, for example, in name only. Nor do you want to have a relationship of this caliber with someone who might be competing with you or who might be "looking over your shoulder" in a controlling sense. Accordingly, some supervisors make for good coaches; others do not. Not all bosses are inherently good at developing others nor, unfortunately, is development always rewarded in the corporate culture.

In an intensive study of 27 mentors by Allen, Poteet, and Burroughs (1997), the most critical organizational factor that facilitated mentoring was organizational support for employee learning and development. This factor, represented by such comments as "it is important to have a learning environment system where people are encouraged to teach and learn from each other," was followed by mentorship training, manager/coworker support, and a team approach to work. It is interesting to note that by far the most inhibiting factor to mentoring was time and work demands, a quality that I have earlier cited as stifling reflective practices. In fact, the study also found time requirements to constitute the overwhelming response to a query regarding the negative consequences of mentoring.

Although most individuals are lucky to have one good mentor during their entire career, there is something to be said for attempting to develop more than one mentor at any given time. Different mentors can serve different needs. One might be helpful in interpreting office politics; another might understand corporate strategy (Lancaster, 1996). This perhaps presupposes that mentors are widely available, and in fact, there are companies whose mentorship program founders on the lack of participation by potential mentors. In the late 1980s, Motorola University created the Application Consulting Team (ACT), a program staffed by managers with 20-plus years of experience. Rather than continue their traditional management responsibilities, ACT managers serve as mentors or coaches in the workplace to help transfer knowledge gained from Motorola courses (Fulmer, 1997). In work-based learning programs, a good source of mentors is the recruitment of past participants. Having experienced the benefits and challenges of work-based learning involving reflective practices, past participants are in an expedient position to sensitize with current participants.

The deployment of past participants brings up the consideration of "peer mentoring" as a viable developmental relationship. Indeed, the opportunity for mutual learning can be great in this setting and can be propitious, especially in an era of corporate delayering, wherein the number of managers in the hierarchy is being reduced, and at a time when horizontal ties between peers are replacing vertical ties as channels of communication (Kanter, 1989). On the other hand, a peer can become resistant to an exchange that may threaten his or her security. The secret is to build a relationship that honors the equality that exists between the parties and develops their mutual wisdom. A study by McDougall and Beattie (1997) found that individuals were more likely to discuss personal feelings and insecurities with their peer mentor than with a hierarchical mentor, although the latter was thought to be more effective in providing insight into organizational politics.

A program known as the International Masters Program in Practicing Management (IMPM), sponsored by McGill University, Hitotsubashi University, the Indian Institute of Management, INSEAD, and Lancaster University, has come up with an interesting peer-mentoring approach. After developing participant observation techniques, participants from different cultures and industries pair up and spend a week visiting, observing, and reflecting on each other's daily work. The guest shadows his or her host for the better part of the week, and then prepares a draft report on the experience. The report is shared with the host, who then responds with a brief report. The experience is then repeated in reverse at the guest's home site.

A variant of the peer mentoring approach is the supportive relationship that may evolve between a manager and an external consultant. This may occur when the consultant and manager work collaboratively and incrementally over the course of time to design innovative interventions in the organization, which may not only effect change but which may also encourage learning. Robert Schaffer reported one such instance at MVE, Inc., a Bloomington, Minnesota manufacturer (Schaffer, 1998). Karen Prasch, a customer service manager responsible for processing international orders, worked closely with a consultant who had been hired to improve the company's order processing problems. Not only did the consultant's interventions solve the immediate problem, but the effort grew into a program of continuous improvement, which Ms. Prasch extended to her own peers. The learning generated was as much competency-based as functional. In particular, Prasch and her order processing group developed a repertoire of new process redesign and leadership skills, and, in the meantime, doubled their order-processing capacity, reduced order-entry time, improved freight quote accuracy, and reduced the number of missed shipping dates.

Of all the qualities necessary to develop a relationship that can be constructive and inductive of healthy reflection, it is most critical to find someone who respects the learner as an individual and can work with him or her in a supportive and nonjudgmental way. Second, it is helpful to have a mentor who understands the organizational culture and can interpret how the individual's behavior matches with that culture. It is also important to have a mentor who is willing to reassess the mentoring relationship, after a period of time has elapsed, to ensure its ongoing value. Lynda McDermott (1996), in a survey of senior-level professionals, offers these other qualities to describe an ideal coach:

- creates a relationship that isn't forced or contrived
- is comfortable and secure—lets people grow
- provides goals and honest information
- takes time to develop relationship by showing a personal interest in the employee's development
- displays empathy for personal and professional issues
- provides specific guidance, where possible, on substantive issues
- leads by example—works at improving his or her own "needs development" areas
- doesn't force his or her own goals on employees—doesn't push his or her own agenda through employees
- paints the big picture
- talks with employees, not to them
- provide informal feedback, not just a checklist
- provides specific performance criteria
- helps employees plan for improvement

To keep it short, Bell (1996) used the mnemonic SAGE to help mentors remember the key qualities in the developmental relationship:

> Surrendering—mentors are capable of yielding the process to the protégé rather than controlling it, which otherwise would result in depriving the parties of the freedom needed to foster discovery.
>
> Accepting—mentors try to rid themselves of bias, preconceived judgments, and human labeling; they embrace rather than evaluate or judge.
>
> Gifting—mentors are committed to bestowing something of value without expecting anything in return, and the gifts they bestow they give abundantly and unconditionally.
>
> Extending—mentors push the developmental relationship beyond expected boundaries in the interest of seeking alternative ways to foster learning and growth.

Although these items are behaviors, suggesting that mentoring can be learned, the behaviors may derive from key personality traits that may predispose certain individuals to becoming effective in developmental relationships. In particular, mentors have been characterized as having the attributes of high sociability, high openness, but low dominance (Bell, 1996). Hence effective mentors tend to build rapport and lead individuals into dialogue with relative ease. They like to be open and candid about themselves, giving protégés the encouragement to do likewise. Finally, they have no trouble giving up control to others and work hard to listen rather than to talk.

Since developmental relationships are two-way, there are also qualities that might characterize the predisposing behavior and attitude of the protégé. Peters (1996) suggests that to benefit from coaching, the person being coached needs to be interested and able to

- change;
- ask for help;
- share feedback;
- learn from shortcomings, not hide them;
- examine ways to improve;
- try out new and different approaches;
- listen openly, not defensively.

The study by Allen, Poteet, and Burroughs (1997), cited earlier, pointed out a number of characteristics that mentors looked for in particular protégés. Most important was the openness and willingness to learn, followed by the actual ability of the protégé. Mentors looked for people who would be "willing to work hard," who were self-starters, and who had "the drive to succeed." Mentors also sought individuals who were people-oriented and who had high integrity. Finally, it was important that protégés display a willingness to accept constructive feedback.

The Coaching Session

What does a session with a coach look like? There is no prescribed format, but we might be able to provide a sense of some popular practices (Judge and Cowell, 1997). Most coaches are willing to provide a familiarization session with the participant to set the parameters for their subsequent work together, including their respective roles, anticipated results, and the amount of time to be invested. A contract may also be worked out for a certain number of sessions over a given period of time. Monthly or twice-monthly sessions for a period of 6 to 18 months are common. Coaches also offer "check-up" service between scheduled meetings often consisting of telephone conversations or an exchange of e-mail.

The first formal session typically involves some kind of assessment of current practice. Many coaches now recommend 360-degree assessments, which, as pointed out in the prior section on developmental planning, entail survey or interview feedback from the participant's subordinates, bosses, and peers. Self-assessment data are sometimes included as well as input from customers and suppliers. The coach initially reviews the feedback from the assessments with the participant, occasionally even with the rater present. Once these data are understood and integrated, the participant is next encouraged to work on a plan for improving particular behaviors identified in the assessments or cited as a matter of personal or professional preference. Working in a manner consistent with developmental planning, the coach then encourages the participant to plan workplace interventions to try out these new behaviors. At subsequent sessions these actions in the workplace would be subject to reflection on their effectiveness, both in terms of consistency with the participant's original plan and intentions and in terms of their accomplishment of personal or professional goals in the workplace. For example, the participant might be interested in learning how to build a sense of teamwork in his or her unit, how to increase the level of trust, how to relate better with certain "difficult" members of the staff, and so forth. Problems of this nature would be addressed until both parties felt that sufficient progress had been made to allow the participant to proceed without the need for explicit coaching.

Good coaches emphasize the need for ongoing reflection and inquiry. As participants attempt to use new knowledge in practice, which may lead to novel actions or interventions, they will need to reflect on their progress introspectively but also with their peers and with their coach. Journal writing, as disclosed earlier in this chapter, can be emphasized as a particularly helpful tool to reinforce the discipline of reflective practice.

Coaches might also expose participants to learning that involves both explicit and tacit forms of knowledge. For example, one participant might benefit from reading selected literature on team building. He or she might also take advantage of training resources offered through the company or be advised about organizational policies and practices in team development. These explicit sources of knowledge, however, would need to be supplemented by implicit strategies (call them "hints" or "tips") that could be addressed directly in conversation or surmised from observation, experimentation, and, subsequently, from reflection and dialogue (Dovey, 1997). For example, a coach might suggest that a particular director prefers to read supporting documentation before sitting down to meet with staff. In this instance, the participant might learn the contextual value of waiting.

As for the dynamics of each session, naturally the coaching process will vary, but good coaches will tend to use a lot of probing into delicate issues, be they blind spots, biases, or unfounded assumptions. Hutcheson (1996) recommends that coaches pay as much attention to what is not being said as to what they hear. Probing should also be as open-ended as possible in order not to come off as an inquisition. As opposed to a question such as "Why would you do that?" the coach might lead with "Tell me a little more about your thinking behind that." This type of open-ended query tends to produce more expansive thinking such that both parties feel free to explore new information or test unfounded assumptions. In a similar vein, the coach might guide the participant to his or her own solution rather than offer unsolicited advice. The idea is to facilitate the reflective process, asking about likely consequences attending to a particular alternative rather than condemning the viewpoint as naive or ill-advised. Another critical goal in coaching is to help participants come to realize how others might be reacting to their behavior.

As the relationship evolves, the coach might try to uncover the individual's defenses, especially where they may be blocking useful interpersonal and managerial relationships. New skills or new perspectives might also be introduced to help the individual plan and implement workplace changes. In instances where changes in behavior are likely to be difficult to make, the coach and participant might prepare scripts and role-play possible scenarios. Waldroop and Butler (1996) suggest the technique of setting microgoals, which represent successive approximations to the ultimate goal. For example, if the participating manager wishes to become more approachable, successive microgoals might call for asking a staff member how his or her weekend went or soliciting other people's opinion about a decision and following up with them afterward. Among the issues that appear to really test participants is the establishment of useful boundaries between family and work life as well as between personal and professional relationships.

There are abundant variations of the coaching format. Some coaches do not necessarily believe that workplace problems need to become the substantive focus of the relationship; nor does the coaching session have to follow any planned format. CEO Roger Enrico of PepsiCo reports that one of his earliest mentorships was hardly conventional though it was vital to his development (Sherman, 1995). For a couple of hours in the middle of the workday, Enrico would meet informally with then CEO of PepsiCo, Don Kendall. Kendall would close the door and hold all calls. Enrico recalls showing up the first time with a three-hundred-page fact book and a flip-book of charts, but Kendall spent the meeting talking about opera. Subsequently, they moved on to a wide range of other subjects and never viewed Enrico's slides. Instead, Kendall kept the focus on what Enrico would later consider the perspectives of good leadership.

Robert Krim (1988) described an interesting process of mentorship in helping him work through some difficult projects as Assistant Director of Personnel for a large city government. Krim had the benefit of two mentors—one a consultant for the city, the other a university faculty member. He was encouraged to tape-record his reflections of critical incidents in his work, both before and after they occurred. In the recordings taped prior to the incident, he might reflect upon his intentions before attending a meeting. In his tapings after the incident, he would address whether his intentions were actually practiced and what the outcomes were. Krim also used the tapes to record his ongoing personal feelings throughout the process. Finally, his mentors also encouraged him to rehearse publicly with them particular scenarios that might evolve. They would then provide feedback on how they saw his proposed behavior and what likely effects may occur. Through this process, he not only was able to practice new behaviors, but he developed a greater self-consciousness of his own performance as well as the impact of that performance on others (Torbert, 1983, 1987).

In particular, Krim learned that in the work environment, he came across as manipulative because his style was so self-effacing. His mentors felt that his instincts were on the right track but that he should act on them, not suppress them when under pressure. As a result of this developmental experience, Krim created a set of working rules that helped him through many subsequent crises, including learning to state a view clearly and when challenged aggressively by others, to listen, to come to terms with one's feelings, and then to respond by challenging back.

8

Facilitation in Work-Based Learning

*There is no human problem which could not
be solved if people would simply do as I advise.*

—Gore Vidal

In the last chapter, the practice of learning teams was depicted as the principal means of supplying work-based learning program participants with feedback on their planned and unplanned actions or interventions in their work environment. As a critical technology in the arsenal of strategies to implement work-based learning, it requires the skillfulness and artfulness of a trained facilitator. I devote my attention in this chapter to the practice of facilitation. Please note that some of the ideas introduced here can be applied to other work-based learning practices besides learning team facilitation, such as project teams and group mentorships.

Facilitation Methods

Unfortunately, there is no one method that can be isolated as the proper one to facilitate teams in work-based learning. Other than the common functions of helping the group achieve its purpose and improve how members work together, facilitation methods diverge. On the other hand, trained facilitators tend to be comfortable using diverse methods depending upon the needs, pace, and comfort level of the group.

It is considered axiomatic that facilitators not impose their will on a group; after all, the name "facilitator" suggests that the role is to

146

help the group help itself, not to provide "right and wrong" answers. In fact, the Organization Development and Change Division of the Academy of Management specifies in its competency guidelines that facilitation in inquiring into individual and group processes ensures that clients "maintain ownership of the issue, increase their capacity for reflection on the consequences of their behaviors and actions, and develop a sense of increased control and ability" (Varney, 1998).

Facilitators thus tend to rely on the group members themselves to offer recommendations to one another rather than solve their problems for them. However, facilitators do provide resource suggestions and advice on learning how to learn. We have referred to this level of learning as "second-order learning," which is learning that takes the learner out of a context or frame of reference. Instead of teaching about finance (in which the facilitator may not even have expertise), the facilitator offers ways of learning how to learn finance. Participants also learn how to use third-order learning, in which case they might challenge existing assumptions and beliefs in order to come up with new theories about financial systems (Cunningham, 1990). Facilitators also encourage participants to question their own values and assumptions. Finally, facilitators can provide alternative ways to frame the subjects of inquiry—in other words, ways to look at things differently. They encourage a group to maintain a healthy appraisal of alternatives, thus avoiding the dreaded groupthink, made famous by Janis's (1971) account of the Bay of Pigs fiasco.

In practice, some facilitators find it difficult to stay clear of directing the group. In some action learning settings, for example, it has often been found that the more active the facilitator, the better the project outcomes on the part of the participants. Yet there is a paradox in this view of project outcomes. Admittedly, the facilitator's advanced technical knowledge might lead to a better "economic" outcome, but at the same time it may deprive the project team of some less tangible benefits or competencies, such as learning-to-learn, use of judgment, deployment of balance and perspective, and the handling and creation of change. Task achievement may also come at the expense of personal development. Moreover, prestructuring by a facilitator may also deprive the problem of creative solutions generated by a more participative project team. FEL member Kevin Wheeler brought up an example of a project group assigned to a CFO sponsor who charged them with coming up with a system to help one of his units close its books faster. Unfortunately, the facilitator and team prestructured the problem by looking at what was realistic given their prior experience. In Kevin's view, they might have come up with a better process had they set a seemingly unrealistic goal of 24 hours as the time frame for closing the books rather than working toward the more realistic one, which they had selected as 3 days.

Malcolm Knowles (1975), famed adult educator, distinguished between andragogy—participant-directed learning—and pedagogy—teacher-directed learning. In andragogy, participants are allowed to be more autonomous in their actions, more reliable in their assessment of their own capacities and developmental needs, and more capable of accepting greater levels of responsibility for their own and others' actions. According to andragogical practice, then, facilitators need to model such behaviors in the group as tolerance of ambiguity, openness and frankness, patience and suspension of judgment, empathy and unconditional postive regard, and commitment to learning. Eventually, group members will begin to adopt some of these same behaviors, thus all the more limiting the pro-activity of the facilitator. Some other andragogical facilitator skills discussed in the literature include:

- listening and attending
- clarifying goals, agendas, and norms
- promoting airing of problems from diverse viewpoints
- reflecting back and inquiring
- openly but sensitively confronting conflict or disagreement
- looking at the underlying assumptions operating in a situation
- revealing one's own assumptions and inferences
- disclosing, asserting, and illustrating
- giving feedback in a nondefensive way
- soliciting and receiving feedback from others
- reflecting on self and on the process of the group
- taking note of group dynamics to help the group with its own development
- encouraging the group to take responsibility for and owner-ship of group processes and outcomes
- reinforcing an open and participative environment
- engaging in time management

There is a subtle difference between actual intervention in a group, on the part of the facilitator, and the orchestration of actions by others. Reason and Rowan (1981) discuss a number of methods that facilitators could adopt to encourage the development of member involvement and team leadership.

1. One or more members could be charged with keeping a diary of events and experiences for later examination.
2. Members could be invited to visit others in their work settings to observe them as they experiment with new behaviors and practices. Later, during a team meeting, feedback could be given to those who were observed.
3. Questionnaires and other assessments could be introduced from time to time to evaluate the group's or particular individuals' styles, experiences, progress.
4. Members could be encouraged to interview each other and bring results to the entire group.
5. The facilitator could interview members of the group and develop a descriptive model of team behavior to be shared with the entire group once together.
6. Members with a creative flare could be asked to make drawings or other expressive works to tap both conscious and unconscious aspects of experience.

A related issue in work-based learning contexts is whether the project team is better off with a facilitator who is a subject specialist or with one who is strategically ignorant of the project's technical environment. In the latter sense, ignorance implies a need to ask difficult questions that participants might find useful in framing problems. In terms of acquiring team performance competencies, especially those that induce a process of inquiry within the group, the answer to this question is clear. More learning of such "meta-competencies" will likely result if the facilitator is more of an expert in group process than in the technical domains of the project. As such, the facilitator can comment on such process concerns as the distribution of workload responsibilities, group member participation, the management of deviance or isolation of particular members, the expected mood swings in the group from early excitement to subsequent discouragement, and so forth. Nor should project domain ignorance cause the facilitator to refrain from sharing his or her knowledge of the organizational culture that envelops the project. Facilitators are often experienced practitioners and may know a fair amount about the norms of practice in the units affected by the project. For example, they may be able to guide participants to the best people to speak to or they may have a good hunch of how best to obtain data in the unit, be it by survey, interview, or observation. In sum, there are different ways facilitators can share their expertise other than by providing technical direction.

Ultimately, the facilitator has to tread a fine line between offering direction or discretion in shaping the development of the group. Especially in the early phases of group development, if the facilitator comes across as too discretionary, group members may ramble from subject to subject or from content to process in a way that may overly frustrate particular members. On the other hand, if the facilitator comes across as being too directive about the content and process of the group, many of its members may become overly dependent on the continued supervision of the facilitator. Part of the craft of facilitation is knowing when to offer counsel to help the group overcome obstacles and when to hold back to allow group members to assume leadership roles critical to the group's internal development.

The facilitator is thus depicted as eclectic in the use of intervention strategies. The art of facilitation is knowing when to use which. Heron (1989) offers six types of interventions to choose from.

1. *Prescriptive* interventions deliberately offer advice and direction.
2. *Informative* interventions offer leads or ideas about how to proceed on a given matter (e.g., where to find an appropriate resource to contribute to a project).
3. *Confronting* interventions directly challenge members of the team on such issues as their current process, evolving relationships within the team, restricted intellectual frameworks.
4. *Cathartic* interventions address emotional undercurrents and seek to release tension (e.g., by prompting the expression of grief or anger).
5. *Catalytic* interventions provide a structure or framework to encourage the development of an idea or to remove a blockage (e.g., suggesting that a member stop, reflect, and write down her thoughts, asking someone to role-play an individual with whom a member is reporting to have difficulty).
6. *Supportive* interventions display care and attention and offer empathy.

The dexterous facilitator knows when to use each of these styles and activities, including when to use them in sequence or even in combination. For example, cathartic and catalytic interventions might be used concurrently; a confronting intervention might be followed up with a number of supportive gestures. Whatever style is chosen at a given point, the underlying philosophy of most facilitation in a work-based learning setting is to allow the participant ample room for self-discovery and personal learning.

Charles Donaghue (1992) describes four sets of interconnected activities, including intervention, that should preoccupy the facilitator. Note that his work expands the domain of facilitation to incorporate some responsibility for brokering relationships between learning teams and the organizations to which members are affiliated.

1. *Understanding*—having a good sense of the membership of the learning team, their backgrounds, their jobs, their frames of reference, and the nature of their projects.
2. *Intervening*—knowing how and when to act to influence the team, given the facilitator's understanding of each member, his or her project, and the group as a whole.
3. *Reviewing*—providing feedback to the team on its original intentions, commitments, and plans as well as to individual members on their learning plans and personal development.
4. *Integrating*—establishing a link between the members and their projects to the client system or organization in order to establish sound working relationships.

To these four activities of facilitators, Donaghue adds four dimensions or issues that need to be managed along predictable, even developmental, lines, suggesting a role for the facilitator as mobilizer of the group from one dimension to the next. The first dimension to be tackled by the group is that of *administration*, which entails such procedures as the frequency and duration of meetings, logistics, and the relationship of the learning and project teams (if they are not one and the same) to the sponsoring organization. After the basic security or hygiene needs of the team are satisfied, groups typically transition into a *content* dimension. During this period, there tends to be a focus on task achievement related to members' projects, especially their diagnosis, planning, and operation. During the next phase, the *process* dimension, the group becomes interested in processes underlying their surface content, considering such group and interpersonal issues as communication, leadership and authority, group norms, and group development (Schein, 1967). The fourth dimension is the *feelings* domain, wherein affect and interpersonal relationships are dealt with openly and honestly as members acknowledge their importance not only to their learning but to the team's performance.

Weaver and Farrell (1997) suggest fairly concrete roles for facilitators, at least during the early phases of group development. At the outset, for example, they recommend that the facilitator work with the group to establish both a charge and a charter. The charge or mission entails the group's overall assignment; hence it defines the scope of work and the results expected. The charter details the group's specific goals, roles, and procedures. The goals clarify what must be done to fulfill the mission, such as who will do what, when, and how. Roles characterize the skills, knowledge, and abilities that individual members will offer to the group to help it achieve its purpose. Finally, the procedures or norms establish the ground rules that will be necessary to keep the group on track and may include such items as the nature of group meetings, guidelines for communication, making decisions, experiencing conflict, and introducing new members.

Facilitation and Group Development

Part of the role of the facilitator is to raise awareness of the natural dynamics of groups so that members realize the challenge but also the benefit of developing their team. Some writers have used developmental theory to propose specific styles of intervention to move groups through their natural stages of development. There is not unanimous concurrence that all groups go through the same stages since such variables as purpose of the group, constitution, duration, and organizational context will cause a fair degree of diversity. Yet the classic study of Tuckman (1965), with its rhyming stages, has gained a great deal of credibility among "team-building" aficionados.

In Tuckman's model, there are four stages that groups must contend with in their life cycle. A group will achieve greater effectiveness to the extent it can manage the unique challenges attending to each stage. In the *forming* stage, members begin to determine what is acceptable behavior within the group and how to approach their task at hand. As they orient to the task, they begin to establish some group rules, yet they tend to become dependent on the designated leader or authority figure (if there is one). They also begin to test their individual styles and personality to see if they will be accepted by others.

During the *storming* stage, as the group redefines its task and members try to agree on objectives and strategy, conflict inevitably results. Members find that their styles do not coincide; in addition, they may differ in the amount of time they want to commit to a particular task, the priority they may assign to it, or even the means they might use to accomplish it. As a result, this tends to be a time of high emotionality and tension. Members may compete to establish their personal preferences for the group and to achieve their desired position or status.

It is during the third *norming* stage that members begin to come together as a coordinated unit. The jockeying behaviors of the storming stage now begin to give way to a precarious balancing of forces. Members begin to resolve their differences by exchanging their interpretations and opinions about group operations and, as a result, begin to act more cohesively. Team norms and roles also become accepted at this juncture as members display an increased willingness to listen and to contribute to the team. However, for some members, holding the group together may take precedence over successfully working on the group's tasks.

By the fourth stage of group development, the *performing* stage, the integration begun in the prior norming stage is completed. Members not only dedicate themselves to the tasks of the group but do so as they simultaneously support one another. There is also energy for developing ways for the group to continuously improve and renew itself. The group structure becomes stable yet fluid, disagreements are handled in creative ways, and members become motivated by group goals. Further, members understand their individual and collective responsibilities to other units in the wider organizational environment.

If the role of the facilitator is to help a learning team move through its natural stages, then some behaviors may be specified for each of the four stages indicated here. Among the models of group leadership, the situational leadership model developed by Hersey and Blanchard (1988), although initially created for one-on-one manager-subordinate interaction, can be instructive when applied to group development. Revising the original situational leadership model, Carew, Parisi-Carew, and Blanchard (1990) designed the group development model illustrated in Figure 8.1. Accordingly, facilitators might deploy different degrees of two principal behaviors in their work in groups. Directive behavior, related to task functions, is depicted as being directive about member roles and assignments and about what the group needs to do. Supportive behavior, akin to maintenance functions, is concerned with providing support and encouragement to group members, facilitating their interaction, and involving them in decision making.

The situational leadership model is based on the notion that leaders can adapt their style to fit the situation. Hence a proper combination of directive and supportive behaviors is advised depending upon the stage of development of the learning team in question.

Essentially, the facilitator can help move a group through the four stages previously described. Note that in the model the four stages are also depicted in terms of the amount of work expected from each stage as well as the morale or socio-emotional tone of the group. In the Carew et al. model, the amount of work accomplished steadily increases through the stages. On the other hand, morale starts out high during the forming stage but then takes a dip during the storming stage as the expectations of the members confront the stern reality of trying to reach a high level of task performance without having worked through the requisite maintenance functions. As norms are discussed and begun to be defined in this and the subsequent norming stage, morale begins to pick up until it reaches a high level in the performing stage.

As can be seen in Figure 8.1, *"directing"* behavior is most appropriate at the forming stage of group development as the learning team struggles to clarify its task and to set realistic and attainable goals. Directing provides for a modest amount of supportive behavior at least to establish a climate for member acceptance of one another and to initially introduce the process goals of open communication and shared leadership.

By the storming stage, the facilitator is seen as having to increase the level of supportive behavior to balance task provision. Essentially, *"coaching"* behavior is called for as the facilitator trains learning team members in the skills and knowledge associated with task and group process while engaging in more active listening, acknowledging difficulties, and focusing on building supportive member relationships and group cohesion. The goal at this stage is to work toward less dependency on the facilitator and more self-sufficiency within the group.

"Supporting" behavior aligns with the norming stage as the facilitator diminishes emphasis on task and goal clarification. The facilitator at this stage can be seen as encouraging group members to assume more and more of the task and maintenance functions that were once his or her province. As this stage evolves, the facilitator can even begin to lessen his or her supportive behavior since group members will be seen as assuming more of the process work. However, the facilitator needs to be alert to an inclination on the part of some members to avoid conflict and disagreement for fear of losing their new-found cohesion. The facilitator needs to encourage continued free expression and valuing of differences among members.

In the last performing stage, the facilitator uses *"delegating"* behavior as the group itself can begin to take responsibility for task

Figure 8.1
Situational Leadership and Group Development

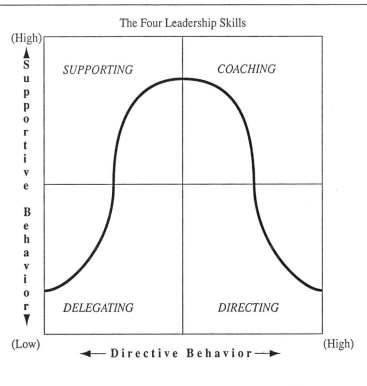

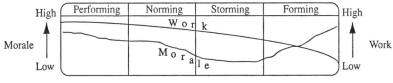

Source: Adapted from Carew, D., Parisi-Carew, E., and Blanchard, K. (1990). *Group Development and Situational Leadership II*. Escondido, CA: Blanchard Training and Development.

and maintenance functions. Although the facilitator continues to monitor the goals and performance of the group, he or she can become more of a resource for individuals and the group as a whole—for example, in providing technical support for members' projects. The facilitator also has to be aware of the need, as the occasion arises, to bring back supportive and directive behaviors as conditions in the team change—for example, if new members were to enter or if a crisis, such as the loss of a sponsor, were to occur.

Facilitation and Change

Just as there are natural rhythms in group development, there are some relative constancies, oddly enough, in the world of change. Work-based learning is by nature about change, so participants—by subscribing to this form of learning—need to accept change as an inevitable course of events. Certainly the learning team is a vehicle for individual and group change, as was demonstrated earlier in our discussion of group development. However, it is also the case that participants undertaking an action project (to be discussed in more detail in the next chapter) become themselves agents of change in their organizations. Facilitators of learning teams can play an important role in helping participants understand some of the dynamics of change when the participants come together to reflect on their actions in their sponsoring organization(s).

Weaver and Farrell (1997) suggest that facilitators first help participants understand the forces for stability and the forces for change that likely exist in their company. Some of these forces will be very influential, whereas others will have little impact on the course of change. Assessing the strength of each force as well as determining whether the force facilitates or resists the change in question are critical diagnostic points for the change agent. For example, a project might be undertaken in the area of mergers and acquisitions. Particular departments might be very much in favor of an acquisition because of the synergies it might bring. Perhaps the new partner might offer a product that will significantly complement the company's product line. On the other hand, other departments might resist the change for fear of losing staff, resources, or prestige. Perhaps the new company has a comparable staff, which will cause redundancies once the acquisition is completed. Kurt Lewin (1951) originally characterized the balance of forces depicted here as a force-field and their diagnosis as a force-field analysis. It can be graphically displayed, as in Figure 8.2.

As can be seen from the diagram, each force has a strength or intensity depicted by the length of its vector. In order to move toward a changed or new state, one has a choice of increasing the strength of the facilitating forces or reducing the strength of the resisting forces. Lewin was clear that it is preferable to try the latter

Figure 8.2
Force-Field Analysis

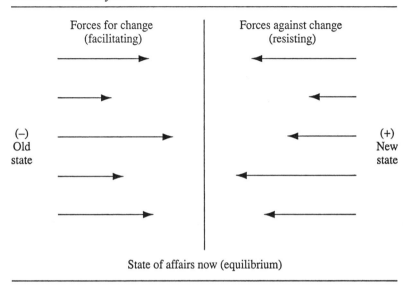

State of affairs now (equilibrium)

since increasing the strength of the facilitating forces can often produce unintended counterreactions. Continuing the previous example, perhaps the manager of the department fearing layoffs from redundancies as a result of the acquisition could have his or her fears allayed by a promise that natural attrition would be used to reduce head count, followed by a commitment to reassign all other redundant staff.

It may also be important to help members of a learning team who are involved in change projects learn the natural effects on people from experiencing transitions brought about by the change process. Change inevitably translates into letting go of the old and embracing the new. However, people and groups respond differently to the transition process, often depending upon their psychological security from experiencing change. The most important lesson is that during change, people need time to adjust. Helping people overcome the losses typically associated with change can serve as an important contribution on the part of change agents. Scott and Jaffe (1989) indicate five types of losses that employees might experience when facing a change:

1. *Security.* They may not feel in control or may no longer feel that they know where they stand.
2. *Competence.* They may not know what to do or how to do it, which in turn may cause them considerable embarrassment.
3. *Relationships.* They may fear the loss of old customers, coworkers, or managers, which in turn may affect their sense of belonging to a group or an organization.
4. *Sense of direction.* They may lose a sense of where they are going and why.
5. *Territory.* They may fear that they may lose the area that used to belong to them, such as a work space or job assignments.

Transitions are also characterized as moving through some fairly predictable stages. Each stage may require a different strategy to help people make a positive transition. Again in learning teams, facilitators can help participants understand these stages so that appropriate interventions can be made in their project work. Reflective discourse in the team can also help participants understand if they've correctly diagnosed where their company or unit might be in the transition process. In the following section, again using the work of Scott and Jaffe (1989), four stages of change are characterized with a brief description as well as suggestions for some appropriate change agent interventions.

Phase One: Denial

Denial, which may also be characterized by numbness or confusion, is often a manifestation of an unconscious unwillingness to accept change. Those endorsing the change may miss the intensity of this stage since it is not always behaviorally visible. But by trying to move too fast, they may miss the natural need to mourn and unwittingly push the next phase, resistance, underground.

During denial, change agents should equip all individuals with ample information to help them understand what to expect. They need to give them time to let things sink in and schedule forums to allow them to talk things over.

Phase Two: Resistance

Resistance occurs when people, having gone through the denial stage, begin to focus on how the change impacts them. At this time, they may experience self-doubt, anger, depression, or any number of manifestations of anxiety. Some people may engage in nonproductive behavior by converting their energy elsewhere, perhaps by trying to obtain another job. Others may become counterproductive and begin to take out their frustrations on the company, perhaps by reducing their output or by staying out of work.

Change agents, acknowledging the natural resistance stage, need to allow people to express their feelings and share their experience. It is important that concerns about the prospective change be aired in the open so that they can be addressed in a forthright manner. It is also comforting to learn through a sharing process that others in the organization feel the same way.

Phase Three: Exploration

During exploration, people finally begin to accept the idea of the change and can begin to focus their attention on the future. Things are still unsettled, though, as they attempt to determine what their new responsibilities may be, how they may have to change in relating to one another, and what the form of the new organization may look like.

Since this phase can still be confusing, change agents can assist organizational members by trying to get management to conduct brainstorming, visioning, and planning sessions. The organization needs to set priorities and goals, follow up on current projects, and provide resources to help people make any necessary transitions in their knowledge and skills.

Phase Four: Commitment

By the commitment phase, people become willing to refocus on the new mission and build action plans to make it work. They have renegotiated their roles and expectations and have realigned their values and actions to commit to a new era of productivity.

This is the phase for building teams and aligning the entire organization toward a mission and long-term goals. The change agent can help management design development and reward systems to keep the organization in a learning mode that will also help it cope with future events.

Facilitator Training

The practice of facilitation is not necessarily natural for most people. Facilitators themselves often require some form of facilitator training to try out the skills until they become second nature. Through facilitator training, novices not only increase their proficiency in facilitation tools but enhance their confidence in handling challenging groups, difficult group members, and outside circumstances. Often, training will also link any facilitation strategy to the stage of development of the group and to the particular needs of given teams.

A critical issue in work-based learning that impacts facilitator training is the fallout expected from both participants and facilitators in transforming learning from a planned approach, typical in conventional training, to the emergent or reflective basis characterizing work-based learning. Participants unaccustomed to directing their own learning or who separate learning from work might resist this approach. They might find reflective practices to be "soft" or too emotional and become defensive if forced to face their own practice assumptions or explore their own inferences about self and others. They often attend training programs to get answers, not to create questions. They don't intend to "look bad" or not in control in front of their peers. And even if they find the experience useful, they may find little invitation to use reflective skills when they return to their regular job, especially if the learning experience has occurred off-site.

Meanwhile, facilitators, accustomed to contented reactions from participants as the former take over the learning process, may ironically find it threatening to hand over the responsibility for learning to the learners. They may unwittingly collude with participants to return to a planned, control approach under the guise of reflective practice. For example, without sufficient practice in inquiry processes, some facilitators might use probing to get participants to arrive at preplanned responses or solutions.

Facilitator training might well include a segment, therefore, that acknowledges the resistance anticipated on the part of both participant and facilitator. The comfort level of the group and of particular group members with regard to emergent learning and reflective practices will predetermine how fast facilitators can move in turning the learning over to the group itself. Facilitators need to be sure that they will have sufficient time to create a team climate for self-examination and self-development. Relinquishing control too quickly might expose group members to unproductive anxiety. Participants might experience the attendant lack of structure as an abdication of responsibility by the facilitator. Having the courage to face one's full range of behavior, including one's reasoning processes, takes time, patience, and above all, skill. Facilitators need to acquire a practical artistry that can guide them in knowing when they can gradually yield control of the group to the members themselves.

Considering more formally the content of facilitator training programs, a few constants seem to emerge. Typically, there is a didactic component on basic group dynamics, including such topics as group process, group roles and norms, stages of development, and intervention methods. Trainees then are given time to practice facilitation in small groups. Often, videotaping is available to help them see their own actions and the verbal and nonverbal responses of group members. A key to the process is the opportunity for immediate feedback from the other trainees as well as from an instructor regarding the effectiveness of various intervention approaches and styles. Some training programs also form learning teams to help support novices as they try out experiments in facilitation in their back-home settings. In the learning teams, trainees can also practice the tools and skills introduced in the classroom segments.

Training approaches might align with the ideology represented by the respective work-based learning approach. Action learning purists would most likely suggest that immersion in learning team experiences is the best device to learn how to become a set advisor. The question is whether there are definitive skills that need to be learned ahead of time by facilitators in order for them to be effective in their teams. David Hardy of The Institute for Learning (IFL) at the Bank of Montreal and a FEL member believes that advanced training can be extremely helpful to team facilitators but with some additions. The IFL program assembles the facilitators for personalized training but then invites their intact teams to join them in the training process. David then takes the full team through a rigorous creative process. Perhaps most critical is the first step, in which he has them work on framing the problem. This provides an architecture for action; facilitator and team need to know the parameters of the problem before plunging into action. For example, they discuss with their teams whether their project involves improving an existing product or process or inventing a new one. Will the project operate within an existing paradigm or can it be revolutionary? Will it require implementation or will it be acceptable to come up with a plan for action? What are the boundaries within which the team must operate? Once framing has been accomplished, then and only then does the team move onto familiar problem-solving steps, such as issue redefinition, idea generation, and implementation planning.

Facilitator Differences

Beyond the constants of basic facilitator behavior, differences across work-based learning approaches may call for differences in facilitator styles. As examples, let's consider some differences in facilitation between action learning and action science methods.

In classic action learning the facilitator's role is, by most accounts, more passive than in action science. Revans conceived of the role as that of a "mirror" to merely illustrate conditions in the set such that participants learn by themselves and from each other. Hence, facilitators need to display a good deal of patience in order to permit member skills in insight and inquiry to evolve. Naturally, some early modeling of active reflection might be required. Facilitators, however, are not to forget a critical precept of action learning to make the learner the center of the experience.

Although action science facilitators would subscribe to the action learning tenet that eventually the group assume the management of the experience, action science skills require more practice and development. It is difficult to learn how to surface inconsistencies between a participant's governing values and action strategies. Besides modeling, the facilitator needs to spend time actually teaching and demonstrating Model II learning skills. In working through individual and interpersonal problems, learners at times may have to reveal their defenses, placing them at given moments in a personally vulnerable position. Facilitators thus need to be not only adequately trained but also quite active in helping the group member or members work through their feelings. Eventually, as the membership of the group gains confidence in using action science skills, learners can serve as co-facilitators and even begin to challenge the facilitator's action strategies. At this point, the facilitator and the membership can transform themselves into a collaborative learning community.

Level of Discourse

One way to view facilitator differences is to consider whether an intervention is to entail a practical or emancipatory level of discourse. The practical level, most associated with action learning, solicits inquiry regarding how others see someone who has been or is currently engaged in action. Action science, by using emancipatory discourse, takes the intervention into another perhaps sequential level. It becomes permissible to challenge not only the actor's theories-in-use but the questioner's perceptions and inferences to the point of questioning the entire system's frame of reference. For many participants, and even for the system under scrutiny, action science intervention can be threatening because it has the potential to cause an entire reframing of the practice world. Even participants in responsible positions may not have sufficient authority or independence of action to challenge their cultures at the level of exposure sanctioned by action science.

Consider how the respective processes might work. Action learning focuses more on problems arising from the handling or mis-handling of on-the-job project interventions. Although these problems might be recent, they are not necessarily here-and-now issues arising from ongoing interactions among members of the set. Occasionally, interpersonal issues are surfaced, but their elicitation is designed more to increase the communication effectiveness among set members than to probe into individual members' mental models. When the action learning set is functioning smoothly, feedback to individuals tends to be open, direct, and unburdened by hidden agendas.

Action science process, meanwhile, may work on workplace problems but is just as likely to focus on here-and-now interactions occurring among members of the learning team. Where workplace problems are chosen, the group process is not necessarily designed to improve the work activity directly. Rather, the selection of the problem is merely a means to help participants learn to appreciate their reasoning processes better. Facilitators are also just as likely to create on-line experiments (perhaps using other members as role players) to help participants focus on their mental models. For example, they might elicit the attributions and evaluations the participants are making about themselves, about others, or about the situation being depicted, or they might have the participants slow down and, using the ladder of inference, reflect upon the inferential steps taken in leaping from data to conclusions.

Detailed Example

Consider the case[1] of a vice-president of a retailer of lumber and hardware products who is concerned about the lack of commitment to the business on the part of the chain's part-time checkout clerks. He has undertaken a project to assess their concerns to see if he can determine why their motivation is lower than their full-time counterparts. In an action learning set, the facilitator might start by having this member, call him Joe, describe his project and anticipated intervention in clinical detail. In a fairly well-developed set, members may join in by probing these details and the underlying assumptions of his plans and actions. For example, Joe might determine that the best way to obtain data from the part-time clerks would be to conduct "focus groups" in groups of three or four corresponding to their work shifts. A group member in the set might challenge the focus group method-

---

[1] This case is adapted from Raelin, J. A. (1997). Action learning and action science: Are they different? *Organizational Dynamics*, 26(1): 23–25.

ology as too intimidating to obtain reliable information, suggesting that Joe would be better off interviewing select clerks individually or even having someone else less senior in the company interview them. Joe would then reflect on his intervention approach and decide whether he might change his plan of action. Other questions might attempt to ascertain why Joe has chosen this project over others. Is this one that the president has a particular interest in, or is it a genuine concern of Joe's?

In some action learning sets, questions and responses of this nature might ensue for the entire duration of the meeting. Notice that the focus tends to be on this one member alone, at least until time is allocated to another member or to the set as a whole. There is a lot of probing going on, and it tends to focus on the member's plans and actions that are typically taking place or about to take place in the work setting. When the focus shifts to the set itself, attention is directed to how to make the group more effective as a learning vehicle for its membership. This might require learning how to engage in active listening and offer feedback more effectively, how to check on one's assumptions about others, how to apply classroom theories in practice, and so on.

An action science group in probing the underlying reasoning processes used by individuals in the group has a different texture. It might start by focusing on Joe's problem with his part-time checkout clerks. But rather than spend time planning and offering suggestions to him regarding useful interventions, the facilitator and group members will focus a lot more on Joe and his organization.

For example, the facilitator might start out by asking Joe why this problem has been standing around looking for a solution. Joe might answer that it's because it hasn't been a high priority item and that the managers assumed that the demotivation of the part-time staff couldn't be helped. The facilitator might then ask Joe if he feels the same way as "management." Joe might answer that he has always been concerned but didn't feel that the president considered it a priority. At this point, the facilitator might ask whether Joe, as a rule, disavows those issues with which he believes the president won't agree. Joe explains that not only does he monitor what he says but that others in management do the same. No one, including himself, wants to be seen as contradictory. In action science terms Joe has not only offered an observation but has provided an inference regarding his perception of the behavior of others.

Although it might be possible to stop here, most action science facilitators would inquire whether Joe would like to pursue the issue further. Assuming he would, the facilitation could proceed using a number of different methods. For example, Joe's inferences could be drawn out more by asking what he assumes drives the president's behavior. The facilitator and group might also ask what makes Joe and his colleagues so reluctant to bring up so-called "contradictory" issues with the president. Another technique might be to have Joe prepare a case in which he recounts a conversation he might have with the president about a controversial issue. In the margin or on one side of the page adjoining the narrative, he would indicate what he and the president were thinking when they responded in particular ways. A data map might also be drawn wherein Joe compares his action strategies using Model I and Model II learning approaches. Joe might be invited to role-play a conversation with the president, played by another group member, wherein he might practice a Model II action strategy. Further "on-line" conversations might be constructed whereby members of the group agree to role-play certain key figures in this scenario to demonstrate Joe's cognitive and behavioral responses. Whatever method is chosen, the ultimate purpose is to surface defensive or inhibiting behaviors that might be blocking Joe and/or his colleagues from engaging in a productive dialogue, one that permits them to achieve useful and just outcomes.

The case suggests that facilitators may need to clarify ahead of time whether they will be pursuing action learning or action science change. Participants need to know in advance whether anticipated changes will arise from frequent questioning of their action interventions, common in action learning, or from in-depth exploration of their reasoning processes, more typical of action science. Likewise, organizational sponsors need to know whether they'll get a completed project of significance in addition to prospectively more effective interventionists, or an organizational culture in which there is far more consistency, even under stressful conditions, between what people say they will do and what in fact they do.

Distress Facilitation

As groups develop in work-based learning, it is likely that facilitators might have to confront the emergence of emotional reactions on the part of team members. A domain that has not been sufficiently addressed in group facilitation, social power relations and emotions associated with differences among people represent facts of life for groups that can either be sidestepped or faced directly (Vince and Martin, 1993). Learning teams clearly evoke more than just rational behavior among members. Although typically left within the unconscious, feelings develop almost immediately among members, and some might come out in the normal course of dialogue. Craig Johnson, a former set member enrolled in the action learning program at the University of Huddersfield in the United Kingdom, noting his reactions from the experience, quipped: "(Such programs) should perhaps come with a health warning on the back of the books. Becoming aware of the depth of one's own ignorance and being reminded of one's own weaknesses is not a particularly palatable process at times."

It is unclear whether deeply held emotions should be brought out in a learning team or whether they should be denied or avoided. Many of our emotions are simply not accessible to us, having been safely placed into our unconscious. They remain there unless solicited or pointed out by others in the group. Since learning teams are by no means therapy groups, it is important to know the role emotions should play in the deliberations and process of the team. Should the facilitator encourage the release of affective content?

Facilitators have to keep in mind that members of learning teams typically come from organizations that are built on the bureaucratic principle that rationality should govern at the expense of emotions (Goleman, 1996). Emotions are seen as an interference in an organization's functional purposes. Yet most of us in organizations also recognize that we respond to phenomena emotionally, oftentimes without conscious awareness. From a work-based learning perspective, facilitators need to consider a number of delicate issues that might have a considerable impact on learning itself, namely:

1. Teams need not focus only on pleasant feelings. There are times when learning requires the surfacing of unpleasant feelings and memories. People arrive at their learning team with their life issues, and some of these are uplifting while others are unpleasant.

2. There are typically certain emotions that are not only encouraged but indulged in organizations (e.g., pride in being first, bearing up in the face of adversity). On the other hand, there might be emotions otherwise proscribed that might be bottled up in individuals, keeping them from performing their best work (e.g., a resentment toward a coworker who is thought to have stolen one's ideas).

3. Human beings find themselves in difficult emotional states in the course of their lives, be it fear, guilt, depression, rage. Although it is not the job of a manager or of

one's associates to alleviate these states, they may deserve attention to the extent that they significantly affect on-the-job performance.

4. Personal development is a legitimate topic for learning. For some people, the struggle for self-realization requires the need to uncover and work through the sources of their fears and anxiety. Members of a learning team might also choose to try out new ways of behaving in order to attempt to alter ineffectual patterns in their existing behavior.

5. There are instances when employees are manipulated in their work through seduction or coercion. Although "victims" may initially be unaware of such manipulation, they may need encouragement to face the conditions of manipulation, be it by acknowledging the circumstances, changing their environment, or even confronting the perpetrator.

Höpfl and Linstead (1997) contend that there are two dimensions of emotions at work that are legitimate for learning teams to address—learning to feel and feeling to learn.

Learning to Feel. How do we recognize the emotional learning that is taking place, to know what we feel, to discuss which of our feelings are problematic, to become sensitive to the feelings of others?

Feeling to Learn. How do we transfer a threatening and oppressive atmosphere in the workplace to one that is relaxed and supportive?

Although the treatment of emotions within the workplace and within learning teams per se is a controversial subject, I believe that facilitators need to endorse the communication of emotions. Feelings can either expedite or block our learning. Perhaps the most eloquent spokesperson in behalf of this perspective is Peter Reason, whose action strategy, known as "cooperative inquiry," explicitly makes room for the management of anxiety that arises as participants examine their world and their practice (Reason, 1994). Cooperative inquiry, however, has other characteristics familiar to the work-based learning approaches already described in this book. In particular, Reason views participants in cooperative inquiry as co-researchers and co-subjects. As co-researchers, participants contribute to generating ideas, designing and managing projects, and drawing conclusions from their experiences. As co-subjects, they willingly participate in the activity that is being researched. As in the case of action learning, participants might choose to work on some kind of action taking place in the outside world; however, cooperative inquiry also makes room for introspective experiences among members, be they examinations of the self or of states of consciousness.

What is most particularistic about cooperative inquiry is the straightforward view that underlying conflicts and distresses among members be explicitly acknowledged and worked through (Reason and Rowan, 1981). Accordingly, Reason suggests that facilitators receive sufficient training in counseling to minimally facilitate the expression and exploration of feelings and emotions, be they within their project experiences or even within the group.

Although I might not wish to go as far as Reason in advocating the use of counseling as a facilitation tool, the exploration of affect strikes me as a useful agenda for learning teams, provided the individual does not become so distraught that he or she loses minimal control within the team environment. In these instances, the facilitator needs to acknowledge that certain members may require additional psychotherapeutic resources to help them work through some of the deeper, troubling sources of their anxiety.

An example might provide some insight into the types of emotional problems that learning teams can safely examine under the watchful eye of a trained facilitator. Vince and Martin (1993) present the case of an individual manager in an action learning set working through some difficulty relating to a member of her staff. One of the members of the set (not the facilitator) suggests that the manager seems to be avoiding her strong competitive feelings toward her associate. The manager's immediate impulse is to deny the competition, but something in what her set colleague has said rings true. Vince and Martin go on to describe what happened:

> [The manager] feels suddenly on the spot, uncertain, as if she would rather be elsewhere. However, because she felt some truth had been acknowledged, she talks about envying her staff member's ability to be liked by the rest of the team and the competitiveness this envy generated. Through their questioning, set members . . . provide her with the insight that her envy is a block to her effectiveness both with the specific individual and with her team. She resolves to undertake some practical actions which she imagines will overcome this particular problem.

This case demonstrates how providing a forum for examining emotional content can also lead to learning. In some cases, it can even lead to a breakthrough that can produce new practices more in sync with our values, intentions, and desires.

Advanced Facilitator Skills in Reflective Practice

In Chapter 6 I brought out the critical nature of reflective practice in work-based learning, and in this chapter we have considered how facilitators can inspire reflection in a group. However, it may be useful to bring some of these ideas together in developing a portfolio of skills for consideration by facilitators. Consistent with my views about group development, these skills may be introduced by facilitators but can gradually be assumed by other facilitating members of the group itself. In the model presented in Figure 8.3, five principal skills are illustrated that my colleague Robert Leaver and I believe represent such a portfolio. The five skills are Being, Speaking, Dramatizing, Testing, and Probing. The skill of Being is central and pervasive, cutting across the other skills, for it represents the facilitator's presence and vulnerability in creating a reflective climate in the group. Recalling the definition of reflection introduced in Chapter 6, reflection is a stepping back to ponder meaning. The first step of reflection is to experience, or even more simply, to be. In accomplishing "being," we try to experience and describe situations, even our own involvement in them, without imputing meaning to them or without evaluating them. If facilitators are successful in modeling or helping team members learn to "be," members can begin to explore differences and diverse experiences together and learn from one another without initial polarization. In this way they learn to explain together (Griffith, forthcoming).

The skill of Being can place one in a vulnerable state in the sense that one does not rely on defending oneself against experience. The focus is rather on opening up to experience and to the interpersonal environment around oneself. This process produces a reflective response which can be characterized by a number of attributes (from Bell, 1998) that are in direct contrast to the defensive posture.

- instead of maintaining unrealistic standards — one sets realistic expectations
- instead of expressing doubt — one displays tolerance
- instead of concentrating on self-expression — one uses listening
- instead of being self-absorbed — one conveys humility
- instead of feeling out of depth — one feels open to learn
- instead of feeling out of context — one becomes open to experience

Figure 8.3
The Five Skills of Reflective Practice

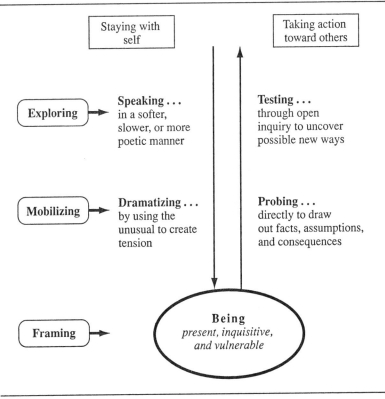

Referring to the dimensions of the model, Being itself occupies the dimension we call "framing." Framing refers to how we think about a situation, more specifically, how we select, name, and organize facts to make a story to ourself about what is going on and what to do in a particular situation. In exploring, we use methods to induce others or the group as a whole to introduce new ideas and questions. In mobilizing, we more directly probe or dramatize, focusing attention on ourselves or on specific individuals to develop and illustrate ideas and actions. The cross dimensions are "staying with self" and "taking action toward others." At times, we make personal contributions to the group or focus attention on ourself. At other times, we extend and dedicate attention to others.

Returning to the skill of Being, as a central skill it may entail staying with oneself or taking action toward others. It is most concerned with exploring differences and diverse experiences apart from members' preconceived notions. The Being skill models an inquisitive, nonjudgmental attitude toward group phenomena. Some of its components include inviting questions and comments, considering one's own positions as hypotheses to be tested, and acknowledging expressions of vulnerability by others. An example of Being might occur in an advertising group about ready to launch a new campaign. Everything seems to be in place, but the group leader (who might also be a facilitator of reflective practices as outlined here), who has actually pushed a particular design, might ask the group to pause with her in a state of vulnerability. She wonders outloud if something has been overlooked and whether the group might take one more look at the design.

The second reflective skill, Speaking, is in the upper-left section of the diagram, signifying that it constitutes an exploring mode that stays with oneself. The purpose of Speaking is to use language to help people slow down and understand one another and to help them explore their processes beyond an immediate agenda. It may entail summarizing the true and full words of a group participant or it may call for reciting a poem to open people's hearts. Facilitators using Speaking like to develop images that may characterize the state of a group at different points. For example, one group never lost the image presented at an earlier time by their facilitator who said the team was operating like "a cargo plane having to make its destination to Istanbul but with one engine knocked out."

In the third skill, Dramatizing, the facilitator stays with oneself but tries to mobilize by building tension in the group and then releasing it. By using drama, the facilitator uses the unusual, thus choosing to be more animated than in the exploring mode. Sometimes it requires gentleness; other times it may startle. Although one can use voice in Dramatizing, as in slowing one's voice down, Dramatizing can deploy nonverbal skills, such as respecting silence when it naturally emerges or asking people to be conscious of their breath. In Dramatizing, some facilitators are skilled at drawing a picture or asking others to help in such a drawing.

Testing, the fourth reflective skill, is an open-ended query, directed toward the group as a whole, that attempts to uncover new ways of thinking and behaving. In using Testing, the facilitator may ask the group to consider its own process or may attempt to explore underlying assumptions previously taken for granted. In Testing, the facilitator is trying to promote a process of collective inquiry. Some of the component skills are asking for a process check, playing devil's advocate, or acting out a scenario to explore an option. As an example, rather than offer another opinion to help a group resolve an impasse, the facilitator might suggest that group members cease defending their positions for a moment and turn to a discussion about ways to resolve the impasse.

Finally, in Probing the facilitator mobilizes the group or a member by making a direct inquiry, typically to one member at a time, to find out the facts, reasons, assumptions, inferences, and possible consequences of a given suggestion or action. For example, Probing might attempt to point out inconsistencies in members' reasoning patterns, perhaps helping them to uncover the assumptions and beliefs behind particular actions. In using Probing, however, the facilitator needs to be careful not to interrogate or make any member feel on-the-spot or defensive. On the other hand, Probing may initially have to make some members uncomfortable if they are asked to consider assumptions that had been hidden even from their own consciousness. To help create a positive climate, facilitators tend to avoid the use of "why" questions, resorting instead to reflexive modes such as "It seems like…could it be that?" As an example, consider a discussion between a salesperson and a buyer team. After presenting the features and benefits of the product, the salesperson (using facilitation skills) probes into the personal dimensions of the prospective sale, inquiring whether the sale might expose the buyers in some negative way or how it would reflect on them. A more personal and productive dialogue ensues.

9

The Action Project

Paddle your own canoe.

—Maurice Kirkpatrick

As readers may have surmised, the technique of the action project is perhaps the most consistent tool associated with work-based learning programs. Whatever theories, competencies, or practices are exposed to participants, the ultimate learning of these subjects may depend upon participants trying them out in actual situations. There is benefit to having participants test their newfound skills in a simulated setting, but ultimately, as has been repeatedly emphasized throughout this book, there can be no substitute for practice in the very midst of real live experience. Only then will participants know whether they can change their assumptions and behaviors on-line. Only then will they know whether a particular conceptual theory might help them wend their way through an operating problem or whether they may need to devise a new and alternative practice theory to help them make sense out of their actual behavior. In the following sections, I discuss a number of elements to be considered in designing the work-based action project.

Project Choice and Operation

In order to replicate real-time conditions, it is normally advised that projects have strategic value to the organization or unit within the organization that is sponsoring the project—that the project contribute meaningfully to, perhaps even challenge, the goals established by the sponsoring unit. The project could entail an assignment that is already being done, but perhaps in a unique or more effective manner. Most projects are experimental in at least two ways: (1) they tend to involve doing something that has never been done before; and (2) there is no known solution to the problem or there are at least different opinions regarding how the problem is to be solved. Another way to look at project choice is to consider problems with solutions that will depend upon any number of unpredictable circumstances and conditions that need to be surfaced during the course of the venture. An ultimate guideline is to consider projects that otherwise might have been contracted to a consultant.

Given this description, there can be no definitive list of project topics; projects need to be tailored to the individual unit sponsoring the endeavor. However, it is possible to list some prototypical topics to give the reader a flavor for the significance of these ventures. Projects, then, have entailed such concerns as:

- developing candidates for a merger or acquisition;
- devising a marketing plan for a new line of business;
- identifying logistical cost savings;
- developing synergies across divisions;
- integrating suppliers into the business plan;
- demonstrating the social and economic trends affecting key markets;
- combating private-label competing products;
- designing an integrated customer database;
- streamlining the customer support process;
- creating a shared business service center;
- developing a knowledge storage and transfer process;
- improving management of a company's patents;
- streamlining an invoice processing and payment system;
- enhancing the work-order process used by facilities management staff;
- creating a strategy for a new business unit;
- developing a plan for revamping or integrating service departments;
- deciding whether to invest in a new technology;
- integrating technology into work design and output;
- engaging in cross-selling across business units;
- fostering integration among business units to improve customer service;

- developing community/corporate partnerships;
- improving the corporate image of a company through a community-wide survey;
- redesigning the human resource function;
- streamlining the delivery schedule of a supplier;
- enhancing company-wide communication using information technologies;
- easing work-life conflicts through a comprehensive benefits package;
- improving customer service through focus groups;
- producing a strategy to improve sales performance;
- enhancing the commitment of temporary workers;
- devising employment alternatives to downsizing;
- developing a balanced scorecard to evaluate an organization's practices.

The logic used by Revans to support the use of a here-and-now project is the opportunity it affords to confront real change (Lessem, 1991). Revans was also concerned that the work be neither too difficult or challenging, nor too easy or unchallenging. Projects should also provide milestones for assessing meaningful progress so that participants can take advantage of the reflective components in work-based learning. A useful approach is to generate action points at appropriate junctures, perhaps at learning team meetings, where the project might be discussed. Beaty, Bourner, and Frost (1993) suggest that action points be clear, specific, and measurable. That way colleagues in the learning team can assess whether, in fact, progress has been made in the interim. For example, if Rhonda were to say that to establish a proper setting to get her project off the ground, she will need to intervene to improve the conduct of her boss, Jim, at staff meetings, that would not be as useful as saying:

> Next Friday, I plan to meet with Jim prior to our staff meeting. I plan to point out to him that though his opinions are always well thought out, he tends to dominate the meeting in terms of air time. Some of us with important contributions never get a chance to get a word in. He seems especially resistant to input from Susan, who seems reduced to a silent observer. After dialoguing with him, we might work out a way to determine if the staff meeting improves in terms of member participation. Perhaps, he might even let me model some of my newfound facilitation skills.

Notice that with this set of statements, members of the learning team will have specific items to follow up on at the next learning team meeting. They and Rhonda will also have qualitative measures to determine her progress: did she meet with Jim; how did he respond; did he change his behavior at the meeting; what did he do that was different; did he include Susan; did he allow Rhonda to facilitate; and if so, what were her interventions and how did other staff respond?

The only way to have this type of productive dialogue is to be engaged in projects that are realistic as opposed to makeshift. Programs typically are designed to give participants the opportunity to learn from live experience, not from simulated experience. It is the confronting of unexpected occurrences consistent with real problems that underlies praxis, that component of epistemology that emphasizes learning through practical application. Consider the example of Brian Caie (1987), writing about his experience in the action learning MBA program sponsored by the International Management Centre in Buckingham, England. Brian had begun the implementation phase of his project, which consisted of introducing the team briefing strategy into his company. He had gotten management committed to the process and had even begun training supervisors in its use. Then, in the space of a few months, his sponsor, the sponsor's boss, and the company president were all transferred out of the division. His new managers, though sympathetic to employee communications, felt uncomfortable supporting the team briefing approach since they played no role in its development.

Brian's project had to return to the drawing board for a subsequent relaunch. Nevertheless, Brian, in retrospect, reported that the crisis in his project led to the greatest learning from the experience. In his own words:

> [the crisis] provided the opportunity to review the system, reflect on its shortcomings, and improve upon the initial approach. The team briefing system ultimately put in place survives to the present day because of the care taken to implement it properly and because of the lessons learned in what became known as the pilot project.

The strategic value of projects cannot be overstated in the sense of their having impact on the direction of the sponsoring unit and, subsequently, systemically across the entire organization. They're also typically linked to a planned or ongoing change effort. Unfortunately, some projects are undertaken as planning or analysis studies. Once the analysis is completed, it is presented to an official who might decide whether to accept it or not. If the decision is "go," another individual or team might be assembled to work on the recommendations of the original project team. This form of project is not an action project, nor does it provide an opportunity for sufficient reflective practice for significant double- and triple-loop learning. Projects in work-based learning are best designed when participants know that their actions are potentially going to have an impact and thus need to be evaluated against normal, difficult operating standards. Planning studies often do not require the level of commitment that might lead to serious self- and public examination.

There is also an element of scope to action projects that requires a good deal of time and concentration. Projects often involve participants in endeavors outside their own department and may require the support and commitment of other colleagues, perhaps to form a team, as a basis for undertaking the project on a useful scale. Some participants, particularly those who have not yet had strategic responsibilities, may not have had experience with projects of significant scope and time. They might be more familiar with projects that can be accomplished quickly or might produce short-term results. Working through the more ambitious action project in a deliberate manner—especially taking the necessary time at the outset to pose the question accurately, frame the problem, and collect data—elicits useful skills in strategic reasoning.

Another key question in project choice centers on whether the participant in the work-based program or the sponsor should ultimately select the project. If the work is to have strategic value, there may be some sympathy in having the executive sponsoring the activity decide which problems need to be addressed or which tasks need to be done. On the other hand, learning is facilitated when it makes most sense to participants; hence there is an argument for letting the participants choose their own projects, admittedly within the constraint that they have real value.

One rationale for allowing flexibility in project selection is to provide an opportunity for participants to experience double- and triple-loop learning, as mentioned previously. If there is not enough flexibility built into the project design, participants, though giving the executive sponsors what they want, may not arrive at a solution that gets at the root of an issue and may not produce much of a learning opportunity for the sponsors themselves or for their organization.

Another argument on behalf of participant choice was presented in our FEL community by Robert Kittrell of Leadership Solutions. He noted, "Those persons directly involved in any learning project, whatever it is, must be directly involved in identifying and articulating what is to be done." Mr. Kittrell offered two reasons for his contention:

> The first one is the most obvious; people pay attention to and follow through on projects they have had a direct say in developing and articulating. This might be known as Ownership or Enlightened Self-Interest.
>
> The second one is known as Personal Responsibility. It comes from our fundamental job as educators to enlighten people so that they are in a position to help themselves. This means challenging those we work with to identify, face, and address those core problems and/or challenges that keep them, or their organization, from advancing toward a worthwhile future goal or mission.
>
> It is working to develop within them the courage to learn not only from what they are doing, but more importantly to question (not why they are doing what they are doing, but) the basis on which they have chosen as they have, and how the projects they selected connect to their hopes and aspirations for the future, be it personally or professionally or organizationally.

Where project choice ensues after the formation of a project/learning team, team members may have to decide on which problem or set of problems in the organization to focus. In this case, there are three questions that the members may wish to consider once they derive a list of possible projects (IFAL, 1996):

1. *"Who knows."* Which members of the team know, not only about the problem, but about the opportunities and inherent difficulties it will present to the team.
2. *"Who cares."* Who among the team and also within the organization feels sufficiently strongly about the issue to do something about it.
3. *"Who can."* The team typically wishes to tackle something that will effect change or progress; hence members need to be allied with senior staff who have both the power and motivation to sponsor and to endorse the change effort.

The issue of project selection raised here is critical in work-based learning, for it poses the question of whether the objectives/benefits of the program extend to the organization or to the individual. The obvious answer is that it needs to be both. The word "learning" in work-based learning does not suggest individual learning alone. Through project work that stretches the boundaries of methods to elicit and then confront organizational problems, the organization learns new ways to examine its fundamental goals and processes. Nevertheless, individuals undertaking the project are not pawns in a system; rather, they are unique individuals who wish to develop and to enrich their own professional and personal lives. Thus, projects require the imprint of human creativity. They should evolve as participants who plan and manage them evolve. They need not be overly predesigned. Morgan and Ramirez (1984) noted that "the more one designs the process in advance, the less opportunity for self-organization according to the insights which emerge."

So the bottom line seems to be this: Keep the executive sponsors involved, make sure the project is of real value to the organization, but build in enough flexibility for not only participants' buy-in but also for their shaping of the project. According to David Ashton, formerly of Cable & Wireless College, this shouldn't be an onerous task since most managers and executives enjoy working on real stretching problems of direct relevance to business success. On the other hand, they do need clear rules and support to surface and reinforce their learning agendas.

Consider some examples. At DuPont, Susan Mazur reported that meaningful results occur when senior executives are involved in but not necessarily sponsoring the projects:

> In our process the senior executive team sets the theme and defines some of the parameters that the projects must include. The leaders of strategic business units and functions submit proposals for projects they are willing to sponsor. A team of about a dozen business unit and function leaders reviews and prioritizes the submissions and sends recommendations to the senior executives, who in turn make the final selection. Six projects are chosen for each class and the class participants then rank order their preferences as the projects are described to them by the sponsors. In our initial class 90 percent of participants were assigned to their first or second choice. Some "tweaking" is done in order to achieve the desired racial, gender, and regional diversity of each project team.

In the PHARE program, referred to in Chapter 5 as a good example of a managerial action learning program, the choice of the project is seen as a two-way process, with the consultant assigned to each action learning project team having a critical bridging function. The CEO or top management team is asked to come up with themes regarding organizational change in the company. The project team must at least show how the project responds to these themes.

Project Presentations

The criticality of project choice and operation is matched by the importance of project presentations at the conclusion of the experience. Having worked on an assignment of value for a significant period, at least in the case of most projects, participants are given an opportunity to present their results. Although there are some cases where participants have lost energy by the conclusion of the project and are no longer motivated to present their findings, the typical scenario finds participants quite eager to make a presentation. The key questions on project presentations tend to be:

1. Who should attend these presentations?
2. How should they be done?

Who should attend: There is little question that the direct sponsors of the project should attend the project presentations, but there is also sympathy for having even higher-ups attend, especially where the project has had a strategic impact on the organization as a whole. There are two constraints in having CEOs present if they are not sponsors. First, the project may not have a direct bearing on their operation and thus they may not be an interested party. Second, executive presence may inhibit the presentation, causing it to look more like a briefing than a learning experience.

How should they be done: Although the presentation of one's project should have a celebratory element to it, it is also best viewed as an opportunity to share one's learning from the experience as well as to present results and make recommendations. It is an opportunity for all members and related stakeholders in the work-based learning program to reflect on the experience as part of a learning community; therefore, there should at least be a balance between "show and substance." What needs to be avoided is glossing over project results that were less than satisfactory for fear of executive retaliation. On the other hand, participants should not completely avoid an element of "sell" in their presentation. After all, they have worked hard on their project and they want it to succeed. Part of the learning in the action project is knowing how to manage the political dynamics in the organization in order to give their project a good chance to move to the next level of full implementation.

In a work-based learning program in a major northeast utility company in the United States, with which I have served as a learning facilitator, senior executives from the division sponsoring the project attend not only the formal project presentations but also sit in on a session devoted to individual and team learning. Executives from other divisions are invited both to the session on learning and to the formal presentations where their area of expertise pertain to the substantive nature of the project.

Susan Mazur from DuPont reported in some depth to our FEL community about project presentations concluding her company's project-based Leadership for Growth offering. The projects are real, substantive business issues sponsored by high-level executives and take place outside of the participants' work area. Susan indicated that presentations became more effective to the extent that the presentation audience was project-specific. The team collaborated with the sponsor to determine the appropriate makeup of the audience. Susan explained:

> Initially, we planned for an audience composed of the project sponsor, one to three members of senior corporate leadership, and four to six global business unit leaders. As it worked out, one member of senior corporate leadership was invited and present at each presentation. Some presentations also included the sponsoring business unit's global leadership team; others included heads of business units likely to have an interest in the project team's recommendations. By getting the right audience, there is motivation to do a credible presentation. In addition, it is clear from the outset that the business unit leader is counting on getting the feedback.

In regard to the nature of the presentation, Susan reported:

> The expectation for both learners and project sponsors is that this work is about *both* learning *and* contributing to real business issues. Since a key part of this development process is about leadership's role in enabling individual and organizational development, honesty, dialogue, and reflection between the presenters and the sponsor (plus others attending the presentations) is essential. If the presentation teams suspect they are merely going through the motions, it will be obvious in the quality and depth of the presentations.

Project Composition

Projects may be initiated as individual ventures or may be staffed by a team of participants from the same company. Even if undertaken as an individual endeavor, the project may inevitably involve other people in the organization or external to the organization (vendors, customers, etc.). Oftentimes project participants will recruit others to form a team to help them work on a project, even though the other members may not be formally participating in the work-based learning program. Microsoft, for example, maintains an expert network that stores knowledge competencies and personal profiles to help teams find individuals with particular expertise necessary for staffing software development projects (Davenport, De Long, and Beers, 1998). Occasionally, the project might be initiated with the help of either internal or external consultants.

Another project variant is to have a team from the program actually engage in the project while also meeting as a learning team. The team may be constituted of employees from the same department or may be entirely cross-departmental or even cross-divisional. Cross-functional teams are encouraged where practical because they expose participants to different ways of thinking and enlighten them to knowledge processes outside their own boundaries. An example of a cross-divisional team was the one organized through the University of Salford among five members from the George & Harding Group of Construction Companies in the United Kingdom. Each member of the team was from a different regional company making up the Harding Group. Meeting for four hours once a month over the course of twelve months, the learning team members not only worked on their own personal development but also came up with many usable ideas for quality improvement in both their individual companies and for the company as a whole (McCrudden, 1998).

It might be noted that if the format is team-based, each individual must take responsibility to ensure that he or she is working on a specific component of the overall group venture. Otherwise, individual initiative and learning may be lost within the team effort. This is why some project exponents believe that individual projects tend to produce greater individual learning as compared to group projects.

I believe there is ultimately no best way to constitute a project team. There is perhaps a natural efficiency in having a team work on a project while also meeting as a learning team. Further, there is a benefit in having team members mutually observe and offer constructive feedback on each other's actual job performance. Reflections on plans, assumptions, and practices can be more spontaneous and immediately contextualized. However, it may not be practical for an organization to release an entire group to work on one project.

The scope of project activity, therefore, must also be considered as a program feature. Not only must an organization decide whether to release a full team to work on a project, but it may need to decide how many projects to have going at any one given time. For example, it is possible to suffer "action project overload" (Tucker and

Taylor, 1997). This can occur if management becomes distracted by the frequent requests for information, interviews, customer visits, and the like, which are associated with project requirements. For example, projects often send out members to obtain information from organizational or unit data banks or directly from top management. Although managerial staff are generally happy to accommodate such requests, there are limits to how much distraction from one's current job one can tolerate. Since projects have been characterized as typically strategic in character, there is also a need to retain sufficient staffing to do the tactical and operating work of the company, especially in instances when projects are being undertaken on a full-time basis. Some of these decisions on project composition will depend on the size of the organization but also on its learning orientation.

A relatively new issue in project composition is the question of constituting "external" action projects, or projects made up of managers from different organizations. Such an approach seems to be very applicable at senior levels where top managers may not have anyone with whom to share personal and confidential problems. There is also a strategic side to external projects that gives top managers an opportunity to discuss business topics of mutual concern, be it marketing strategy, distribution policy, or even mergers and acquisitions. Naturally, such project groups are careful not to put direct competitors together. Nick Holley, director of management development at Lex Service, and Harvey Bennett, manager for senior management development for the Automobile Association (AA) in the United Kingdom, formed what they called an "external action learning set" made up of senior people from companies operating in a range of sectors, including the water, retail, and food industries (Arkin, 1996).

Project Location

A controversial topic in project development is whether the project should be conducted at the participant's very worksite or at a different location, typically in the same organization (there are also experiments in which someone may "volunteer" services for another organization, perhaps a nonprofit agency). Although there tends to be immediate payoff for the work unit if the individual remains at his or her worksite, the opportunity for long-term learning for both individual and organization may be enhanced where the project occurs offsite or minimally alternates between settings. Yet the practicality of having a staff member acquire new skills and ideas in the classroom component of the program and then bring them back simultaneously into one's actual work setting is hard to pass up.

Besides payoff and practicality, there is yet another reason to support project placements within familiar surroundings. This would be the case of staffing projects using different hierarchical levels, although project designers may wish to ensure that supervisors and direct reports not work together. Managers do not necessarily have the opportunity in their daily assignments to work with higher levels of management as equals. Complicated dynamics occur in this setting and can be instructive and even, at times, liberating to disassemble. For example, lower-ranking members might find an immediate impulse to defer decision making to the higher-ranking members, and the latter may be inclined to delegate the "work" to the lower-ranks (Tucker and Taylor, 1997). At times, it is also more challenging to work with peers with whom one is familiar than with strangers with whom one can start fresh with new roles, new expectations, and new assignments. The spirit of the project team should be to allow members to develop their own levels of responsibility and contribution apart from prior duties and ranks. Furthermore, discrepancies in commitment and participation need to be managed, regardless of past reputation or performance.

There are, on the other hand, a number of arguments to be made in favor of alternative or unfamiliar sites. Without the benefit of input from different cultures, we may develop what Hayes and Allinson (1998) refer to as "strategic myopia." This is a form of single-loop learning that goes only so far as correcting the prevailing mental models within the organization. However, we occasionally need to examine our underlying assumptions and principles in order to respond to strategic challenges in a new light. Hence if one considers the places where people work to be "culturally ordered" (Lave 1988), with their own unwritten rules about what's important, then working in a different location can encourage new ways of thinking about otherwise familiar problems and provide breadth of experience. Tyre and von Hippel (1997) found that engineers who went to sites to observe a problem firsthand learned about many unexpected occurrences of problems that they never could have fathomed in their usual site, that is, in the laboratory communicating by phone.

Working in alternative sites may also reveal unexpected insights or provide opportunities to reframe problems as knowledge and experience increase. Alternative sites can also help diffuse the knowledge that is embedded in one site into other parts of the organization. As one thinks about the use of alternative sites, projects can be categorized as performing one's already mastered job responsibilities in the new site or as assuming entirely new duties. In the former instance, the new unit obtains whatever skills and knowledge the participant transfers from his or her prior workplace, while the participant experiences the dynamic of adapting his or her typical job duties or even professional responsibilities to a different culture. The exercise of new duties in a different location offers the potential for literally "unfreezing" all of one's assumptions about work, releasing the participant to a totally new experience, both in terms of task and environment.

Project Administration Issues

Once project groups are formed, program administrators need to decide whether or not they should be funded. Some programs insist that funding should become a constraint on project development like any other constraint that the group has to overcome. If the project is to be considered worthwhile, the team might need to solicit resources from the relevant stakeholders, convincing them of its value. On the other hand, seed money might initially be needed to get the project off the ground. Worthwhile projects inevitably require expenditures, be they for travel, communications, survey work, report preparation, and the like. At Knight-Ridder, Inc., the large U.S. newspaper chain, project teams start out with a budget of between $10,000 and $12,000. Knight-Ridder projects, however, have a six- to-eight-month duration, so there is ample time for teams to solicit additional subsidization (Reed, 1997). Citibank's Team Challenge projects operate with liberal budgets. For example, one project had its team members individually travel all over the world to determine if it made sense for each of Citi's country and business units to maintain a separate treasury to manage their funds. This particular project resulted in Citibank centralizing its treasuries, an outcome that even with the extraordinary travel expenditures, according to CFO Victor Menezes, was "much cheaper than a management consultant" (Reingold and Bongiorno, 1997).

The duration of projects is often debated in the literature, but there is no optimal time frame. Some programs that run over two years can support lengthy projects of six months to a year, as in the case of Knight-Ridder; others can be quite short, as in General Electric's four-week executive development program and Citi's month-long Team Challenge. Avon's Passport Program brings teams together for six weeks but spreads it over an eighteen-month period (Reingold and Bongiorno, 1997). The longer programs tend to provide more conceptual development and in-depth experience but suffer the risk of loss of participant intensity and/or supervisory support.

Projects can also take on a life of their own once the program is over. In fact, full implementation of a project, once it has been completed through the program, may represent the highest form of success. There is an indication that the team's work has been so critical that its effort needs to be institutionalized within the unit or organization. Projects, then, should incorporate within their presentation a plan for full implementation of their findings and recommendations. Citibank's Team Challenge projects, for instance, typically end with a 30/60/90-day schedule. The team proposes some concrete steps that must be taken within these time frames in order to make their project recommendations actionable (Dotlich and Noel, 1998).

Where work-based learning programs are provided apart from academic accreditation, there may be some resistance on the part of participants to commit their learning and substantive outcomes to writing. However, sponsors minimally expect some report of recommendations from project teams. If credit is given for project work as part of an academic qualification, normally a full report is expected that would meet the dual standards of academic rigor and workplace practicality. Besides the recommendations for action steps in the domain of the project, the report may also contain some conventional academic elements, such as a literature review and an accounting of the data collection methods used to undertake any research components. In the Boston College Leadership for Change program, with which I am affiliated, the project accounts for one-half of the qualification of 12 credits awarded upon successful completion of the program. Leadership for Change is described as a graduate level executive development program to enhance participants' individual, organizational, and societal leadership. There are 10 criteria used in assessing the project work. They are presented here as questions posed to the participants to help them prepare their final project report:

1. Was there *a clear statement of the purpose of your work*? (e.g., did you furnish a rationale of the importance of your work to you personally, to your team, to your organization, or even to the broader social environment?)

2. Did you gather and *cite a literature* and other sources giving a background to your project and description of prior work in your area of interest? (e.g., did you attach a bibliography and make reference to it in the body of the writing?)

3. Was your *methodology and/or intervention strategy* appropriate for the task you set for yourself? (e.g., did you carefully describe the interviews you conducted, provide lists of questions asked, show the context for them?)

4. Did you make a *coherent argument* based on the information (data) you gathered? (e.g., do your conclusions follow logically from the evidence? Do your policy recommendations follow directly from evidence?)

5. Did the project make an *impact* on your organization or unit? (e.g., has something really changed as a result of your work? Did you include "bottom line" measures of cost savings or benefits that occurred as a result of project implementation?)

6. Did you use *action learning* in your work? (e.g., have you been a reflective practitioner, allowing what you discover to influence your work and to change you? Have you encouraged others to reflect on their own work, and to change, as well?)

7. Did you *integrate theory and practice?* (e.g., is it clear that you took information from readings and modules and used it in your practice and then, in reflecting on your actions, revised your theories?)

8. Does your project show *innovative thought and expression*? (e.g., does it contain rich concepts and creative, original ways of looking at problems?)

9. Is there strong evidence of your *leadership effort and ability*? (e.g., what obstacles did you overcome? Did you make meaning in a community of practice?)

10. Does the project as a whole make a *contribution to the common good*? (e.g., is there a rationale for your work that follows from, and expands upon, the model of social change we have been developing in this program?)

To prepare participants for the project, the Leadership for Change program also encourages them to prepare a prospectus of their project at its outset. By writing a brief prospectus, participants become more comfortable with the program's expectation about writing, although they are encouraged to journalize throughout the entire experience. In addition, committing the project to a prospectus form tends to make it a reality and gives it the vitality often needed to get it off the ground. The instructions for the initial project prospectus follow:

Instructions for a Project Prospectus

Please prepare and submit the following for your next learning team meeting. You may wish to bring sufficient copies to share with each of your team members. The prospectus should be at least 6 pp. in length.

Provide a *title* and *topic* of your proposed work. Summarize your *research problem* in a sentence or two. Then, elaborate on the *level of analysis* at which your project topic will be focused (individual, group, organizational, societal/global).

Furnish a *rationale* or explanation of the importance of the work to you personally, and if relevant, to your team, to your organization, to the societal/global environment.

If there is any previous research or analysis that has been done on topics related to your project, either within your organization or outside of it, provide a review of *relevant sources*. Don't forget to use sources already examined in prior modules. Say how you are adding to knowledge in your topic area or to the knowledge base from which decisions are made in your organization.

What *concepts, variables*, and/or *indicators* are you using to measure behavior, opinion, or outcomes? How are you defining "success," "meaningful change," and/or "leadership"?

If you will be undertaking an *intervention*, discuss your initial plan for action; the change agent role you might assume as well as the sponsor and target roles; how you plan to overcome resistance to change, including concerns about threat or embarrassment; and how the evaluation is to be conducted.

If applicable to your project, explain your *data collection strategy* (surveys, observation, interviewing, etc.). Describe in detail how you are going to gain access to information and to people. If you need to *sample* some population, how will you draw your sample? What will the *setting* for the research be? How long will it take? How will data be *processed* and analyzed? How much will it *cost* (in money or other resources) to complete your project?

Finally, what will you learn from doing this project? Describe any personal transformation that you hope will occur. What are the benefits to your organization? How are these to be measured?

Virginia Tucker and Maria Taylor (1997), directors of Penn State's executive development programs, recommend that expectations about action projects be communicated at the outset. Besides some of the requirements already discussed, they suggest that the following issues be addressed:

- project deliverables (over and above the report);
- acceptable parameters regarding customer contacts;
- target audience;
- loss of client;
- duration;
- responsibility for implementing recommendations;
- effect on participants' daily responsibilities;
- continuity of the group after the project is completed.

The Challenge of Action Projects

Although projects, if structured well, can have a meaningful impact within the organization, they can, at the same time, cause confusion and resentment. Knowing some of the pitfalls of action projects in advance can help program administrators plan them to achieve salutary ends.

By their very nature, action projects are a challenge to the status quo. All affected management, frequently the entire organization, need to be apprised of their unique nature. Even if well publicized, however, there is an inevitable threat to individuals whose roles or responsibilities might be challenged by the recommendations forthcoming from the project. Hence, it has to be made clear at the outset of any work-based learning program involving projects that although the program will not threaten anyone's employment security, it may result in different ways to organize the work of the organization. Further, most projects are not typically designed to reengineer anyone's current job; rather, they tend to be future and change-oriented activities that affect entire operations and strategies. They are what might be termed "white space" endeavors. Nevertheless, since they look at ways to anticipate and cope with future organizational challenges, they may indeed invoke risks to present operating conditions. In the end, they are designed to help *everyone* in the organization prepare for the future.

This raises a larger question. Work-based learning may become a political undertaking, in that it could very well bear on questions of power and social relationships in the organization as a whole. Are executives capable of making themselves vulnerable to unexpected answers? Do they want the entire organization, including themselves, to be involved in learning? Participants who have experienced work-based learning tend to report having gone through a much deeper and holistic exercise than ever anticipated. In a way, as Weinstein (1995) warns, work-based learning can even be considered subversive within the context of conformist organizations because of what it values:

- It examines everything.
- It stresses listening.
- It emphasizes questioning.
- It fosters courage.
- It incites action.
- It abets reflection.
- It endorses democratic participation.

At the same time, one could argue that projects should be managed in a way that leverages whatever the prevailing culture allows. For instance, in learning how to manage effectively, one needs to learn how to sell a project proposal to both one's peers and to senior management (Peters and Smith 1997). Further, although projects might start off as local ventures, the outcomes of work-based learning flow into the surrounding environment. Participants begin to question things beyond their local context.

Projects, at least if they are to have strategic impact, do not operate in a vacuum. Indeed, work-based learning is not typically designed as a one-time, individual learning opportunity. Most designers see it as having organizational learning implications. In that sense, Weinstein may be correct; it can be subversive in organizations that expect conformity to a party line.

Projects in work-based learning are most effective when participants are given responsibility to pursue and follow through on the problems they confront. Project success, when defined as a learning opportunity for the sponsoring unit or organization, is dependent on releasing the talent and experience on the part of the individual or team involved. Projects gradually take on a life of their own and, at times, even diverge from the question originally posed to the team. What tends to be consequential to participants is a sense that no matter what they discover in their study, they will have the opportunity to see the project through to its natural conclusion, even if it means challenging the status quo. Project recommendations need not be automatically accepted. Team members just need to know that their recommendations will get a fair hearing by their sponsors even when they conflict with existing norms and plans. Work-based action projects, then, virtually require an organizational culture of risk taking and openness that permits occasional surfacing of ineffectual rules and practices. There is no place for reflective practice in a closed culture; work-based learning works best when all organizational members, including those at the top, agree to submit even their governing values to scrutiny.

10

Managing and Evaluating Work-Based Learning

A man found an old shoe ticket in a desk drawer he was cleaning out. He couldn't remember the pair of shoes it represented but it had to be several years old. Out of curiosity, he took the shoe ticket to work and on his way home that night, he stopped by the shoe shop. Without saying a word, he handed the ticket to the old cobbler. The old man studied the ticket for a minute, shuffled into the back room, and soon returned, saying: "They'll be ready next Wednesday."

—business anecdote

Having considered the building blocks of work-based learning, we now need to turn our attention to program management so that we can put these ideas into practice. We must also learn how to measure our performance against our goals in order to establish further goals for mutual learning. In work-based learning, as we know, the practice of learning is continuous.

A Guide for Program Managers

Work-based learning as a management development practice is unlikely to evolve on its own. Normally, it requires some "structure" since it is technically a program. If successful, it might evolve into a standard way of operating within an organization. For example, team or project-based organizations have some of the rudiments already in place of what we might term a work-based learning culture; however, the teams or project groups are typically work teams, as we have defined them, and not also learning teams.

Initiating work-based learning will require the presence of a program manager whose job it is to set up and launch the work-based learning initiative within the organization. The program manager is responsible for recruiting the participants, the learning team facilitators, teachers, if there is an instructional component to the program, and the sponsors of the projects. Teachers and facilitators might be recruited initially from outside providers; however, internal staff could be trained to take on some of these roles, especially facilitation. In fact, facilitators might be drafted and trained from prior cohorts of the program.

I have used the term *sponsor* to refer to the supervisor of the unit within the organization who provides the project and endorses the work of the participant. Some programs, however, refer to this role as that of the "client," whereas the "sponsor" may be the individual's supervisor who enlists the employee for participation in the program. Of course, in instances when the participant works on a project in his or her own work site, these roles are one and the same. I prefer to hold to the definition of sponsor as the role that provides the project. In this case, sponsors and program managers often need to negotiate adjustments in participants' schedules with supervisors, especially in instances when projects require time away from the job or when current job assignments are inevitably affected.

Besides these natural tasks, program managers also coordinate the various assignments and project opportunities attending to the program. They are often involved in negotiating the nature of the project and ensuring that all parties—participants, sponsors, supervisors—are satisfied with its selection and ongoing operation. This can only occur if the parties maintain regular communication with one another. The program manager also needs to be sure that the mutual objectives for the project be supported by all constituencies and that there is an agreement for the scope of the endeavor as well as its time requirements. One guideline that can be used to manage possible disputes between the parties—and in keeping with the overall philosophy endorsed in this book for work-based learning programs—is to remind people that learning is a first priority; hence, the participant needs to have a genuine commitment to the venture as a learning opportunity yet also produce something of value.

In order to engender support from sponsors, Alec Lewis and Wyndham Marsh (1987) developed a contracting process in the program they provided for nearly all field managers of the U.K. Division of the Pruduential Corporation. Before the participants begin their projects, they spend a day with their sponsor, who reviews the participant's project proposal in detail. Critical to the establishment of the informal contract is an agreement that the project is not only real but also potentially beneficial to both the participant and to the district in which it will be carried out. Participants and sponsors also develop an action plan for the first month of the six-month program. Action plans are then revised on a monthly basis after learning team meetings.

Program managers would do well to spend some time with sponsors before the program to ensure that the latter understand the program's mission and methods. Preliminary contact can also generate and/or refine project ideas. The work-based learning program at the utility company that I referred to in the last chapter deeply involves its sponsors. Among the activities which sponsors are asked to undertake are:

- obtaining information and coordinating with senior leaders regarding the projects that they will be sponsoring;
- determining the participants for their team and verifying their availability;
- ensuring that the participants' supervisors understand the program's time and project commitments;
- contacting each participant prior to the program and discussing expectations regarding their participation;
- reinforcing the expectations of balance between project work and learning throughout the course of the experience;
- lending support to the project in the form of resources and commitments;
- meeting with the learning team, facilitators, and other sponsors;
- establishing success criteria for their project, including measurement of project performance as well as individual goal achievement;
- establishing personal learning goals for themselves that will be shared with learning team members and the facilitator.

Program managers need to play a central role in organizing an evaluation of the work-based learning experience. Although I shall elaborate on measurement later in this chapter, some of the critical evaluation components include identifying criteria that can be used in defining program performance, establishing a base of comparison with either other programs or with current conditions prior to the program, and using the evaluation results to improve both the effectiveness and credibility of the program. Program managers also need to ensure that the views of all internal and external constituencies are considered when evaluation criteria are developed (Wholey, 1991).

Perhaps the best way to manage a work-based learning program in which there are multiple stakeholders is to arrange for a partnership in the administrative structure. For example, an advisory board could be set up that represents the various constituencies, all of whom would have a role in designing the critical features of the program. The board would continue to meet throughout the program to advise on policy-related matters as they evolve. For example, how should the program adapt to a sponsoring company being acquired by a company not affiliated with the program? How might the program respond when a program participant leaves or takes an extended absence from the program? How should the program handle a request for a project extension or even a project adaptation that falls outside the original project brief?

Program managers need to ensure that facilitators or set advisers are sufficiently trained to handle the administrative, political, and social challenges confronted within a learning team. They also need to schedule a variety of operating features and support mechanisms during the life of the project, be they ongoing learning team meetings; mentorships or other developmental functions; technical assistance, including occasional workshops or classes; and, of course, final project presentations. Although most programs expect participant teams to provide written recommendations to the sponsor of their project, many also require oral presentations, as I have suggested in the last chapter, and ask that participants talk about their learning from the work-based learning experience as well as about the more substantive outcomes.

Program managers may be involved not only in managing a current cycle of work-based learning programs but also in managing numerous program cycles over a period of years. In such an instance, it is important that current project groups have access to prior endeavors to help them build on past accomplishments as well as to avoid "re-inventing the wheel." Program managers can introduce an important service by creating a projects database that would provide a record of all past projects. Besides including a complete description of the project and its results (or current status if its recommendations are still in the implementation phase), the database should also list the names of key contact persons who would be available to share information with current program participants.

Some work-based learning programs intersect with formal providers, such as action researchers from colleges and universities or management consultants, to help them get started. There are controversial elements in work-based learning when viewed from a pure academic perspective. For example, work-based learning considers managerial problems or performance deficiencies as viable elements of the curriculum. Further, instructional components may be introduced "just-in-time," that is, structured to respond to current managerial needs. Strict academics may also object that work-based learning programs do not provide sufficient breadth of subject coverage and mistakenly rely on business criteria as a basis to assess academic performance (Raelin, 1994). Program managers need to make the case that work-based learning arises from a different intellectual tradition than standard training programs. It questions the view that the field of management can be known in advance using systematic logic. The world of management practice is as much chaotic as ordered, and no matter how hard managers try to apply universal criteria or use advanced analytic techniques, they confront everyday idiosyncrasies that defy categorization. Work-based learning derives from a tradition that values interdependence among diverse stakeholders and perspectives in order to account for the changing circumstances, values, and needs of practicing managers.

Typically, program managers serve as a link between the program and top management and thus carry out the critical role of gaining and sustaining the top team's support of work-based learning practice. In this way, they serve as an ambassador of the logic of learning as a reflective practice and help assimilate this logic or approach within the psyche of the organization itself. Work-based learning projects typically do not provide quick fixes to problems. They might even reveal new ways of approaching particular processes or markets. In this way, they can be potentially threatening to current job incumbents. As has been emphasized throughout this book, work-based learning typically requires a mindset that accepts the inevitability of risk and change within the organization. If the organization has not accepted this mindset, the program manager needs to prepare all parties emotionally as well as strategically for this change in the way things are done, and this includes not just top management but operating management as well.

Lack of support from the top or from supervisors can constitute a recipe for failure. Work-based learning projects should not be designed as "skunkworks" that operate in isolation. By design, they operate in a context—the context of the surrounding culture. That culture and the systems that underlie it need to be at least partially supportive of the ideology represented by work-based learning. As has been demonstrated throughout this book, this ideology is far from a radical agenda. It merely espouses the value of a questioning, democratic form of organization. Participants tend to come out of work-based learning programs more inquisitive, more challenging, more self-confident yet more exposed, and more collaborative than when they went in. Although they may feel freer to challenge organizational goals, they tend to take responsibility for the public discourse that they may evoke. Hence, senior managers should find them willing to make not only their conclusions but also the reasoning behind their conclusions accessible to others in the organization (Dixon, 1998). They also tend to be bold in their leadership behavior, for example, they feel free to engage in upward influence and are interested in second- and third-order learning, which involve change affecting the very governing values of the organization.

It is, therefore, beneficial to have a surrounding culture that endorses experimentation, trust, risk-taking, and an interest in reasoned change from the status quo. Sponsors and operating managers will at times need to relinquish control and risk releasing the potential of program participants, trusting that they will do what is in the best interest of the unit or company (Quinn and Spreitzer, 1997).

What can happen when these conditions are unavailable? For one, department managers, fearing scrutiny of their unit because it could reveal weaknesses, might be reluctant to hand over worthwhile projects, and makeshift work could result. Even if worthwhile projects are initiated and completed, they may never be implemented on any wide scale within the organization if they are seen as threatening the turf of a director. This in turn could have an especially alienative effect on the participants who had tackled the project in good faith with hopes of broad influence.

In addition, program managers, especially those who in the past had been involved in the delivery of training, have to be prepared to face the insecurity and political risks of managing a program whose outcomes are not predictable. Classroom programs, although edifying for students, do not typically foster much internal change within the organization. They are normally dedicated to helping employees do their current jobs better, and this includes the job of management. Work-based learning, as we have seen, has the potential of mobilizing a transformation in organizational structure and operation. Participants begin to perceive how their individual learning may be tied to changes in the wider organizational culture. Hence they may return to their jobs questioning some of the basic values, practices, and power relationships within their unit. This may create tensions within the department, especially when their questioning concerns social, political, ethical, and personal issues as opposed to mere technical matters (Jones and Hendry, 1994). Without sufficient support from peers and superiors, program managers are unlikely to risk their professional careers on a program that, by definition, is about learning and change.

Is there anything a program manager can do to "soften up" reluctant managers or executives to prepare them for work-based learning ideology, perhaps even to the point of gaining their endorsement? If preservation of the status quo is the manager's ultimate modus operandi or if the manager refuses to permit time for reflective practice, there may not be much that can be accomplished. There is no point pushing against a brick wall. However, be aware that we tend as human beings to imagine resistances as firmer than they may be. There are some strategies, therefore, that might work with resisting bosses.

First, try to link some of the components of the program to strategic initiatives to which the boss may be committed. Even further, link the program, where possible, to financial indicators of success, such as metrics of growth, profitability, and performance. Invite well-known people from other organizations or from academia who subscribe to work-based learning approaches to address your organization and speak personally to your executives. Be aware of the comfort zone of your boss and try not to make any proposal that would invade that zone. If possible, arrange to give hesitant executives a preview of the work-based learning experience. For example, FEL member Susan Mazur found that executives became more predisposed to the value of feedback and reflective processes after having experienced 360-degree feedback on their own behavioral practices. Finally, remember to nourish yourself by developing a support base around you with whom you can reflectively practice. Introducing change is tough business from a psychological standpoint. Don Schön (1983) put it this way:

> When a member of a bureaucracy embarks on a course of reflective practice, allowing himself to experience confusion and uncertainty, subjecting his frames and theories to conscious criticism and change, he may increase his capacity to contribute to significant organizational learning, but he also becomes, by the same token, a danger to the stable system of rules and procedures within which he is expected to deliver his technical expertise.

David Pearce (1991) has provided an action manual for action learning program administrators in which he proposes the following steps. With some slight modifications made for our purposes, they seem applicable for managing most work-based learning programs.

- Decide you really want to do it.
- Start explaining why and what you are doing.
- Gain some support and commitment.
- Obtain agreement on the people and problems/opportunities that the program is aimed at.
- Produce a basic outline of the program (e.g., objectives, estimated time and costs, resources activities).
- Present a cost/benefit analysis (in operational and financial terms).
- Produce a prospectus explaining the program.
- Agree on a budget.
- Recruit staff and resources internally and externally.
- Recruit participants and organize projects and learning teams.
- Brief everyone on the program, but particularly participants, sponsors, participants' bosses, your boss(es), top management, colleagues, human resource staff.
- Bring everyone together for an orientation.
- GO.

The Measurement of Work-Based Learning

Standard Performance Indicators

As in any human resource intervention, work-based learning activities need to be measured and evaluated to ensure their ongoing worth. Not only must sponsors be apprised of the outcomes of work-based learning but program managers and facilitators need measures to inform them how effective the ongoing program is. Assessment is thus used as a vehicle for continuous improvement. Like any intervention, work-based learning programs need to change to be responsive to their stakeholders. Once changes are recommended, measurement is also required to ensure that they have been effectively implemented.

There is possible concern that without measurement, work-based learning programs will not be able to sustain the support of chief executives. CEOs tend to notice and support human resource development programs when they demonstrate that they consistently convert learning into improved business performance. CEOs are also reputed to respond most critically to financial performance measures—measures that impact the economic "bottom line." A Conference Board report (Brancato, 1995) disputes this latter claim, arguing that most companies view traditional accounting and financial measures as mainly reporting on the stewardship of money entrusted to management, not charting the strategic direction of the business. Human resource practices, such as work-based learning programs, address the utilization of human and intellectual capital and thus should be viewed as a source of genuine competitive advantage for most corporations (Wintermantel and Mattimore, 1997). Human resource activities thus need to demonstrate how they can alleviate the obstacles to reaching an organization's strategic goals.

Nevertheless, economic benefits that can be traced back to work-based learning programs unequivocally lend them extra credibility. One way of demonstrating the impact of work-based learning would be to establish an intervening effect between the program and its financial results. A method to measure the intervening effect is to measure changes in the participants going through the program. Once those changes are measured, then the second relationship can be demonstrated between the benefits to the participants and financial results. Reflective practices, for example, are known to be essential to group development, especially in helping group members learn to appreciate others' contrary points of view, styles of interaction, varying levels of commitment to the team, and so forth. Effective teams in turn are known to produce consensual decisions leading to implementable and effective actions. The actions—be they more efficient operations processes, reduced downtime, higher quality products— are in turn measurable using standard financial indicators.

An example of this intervening effect is the link that Sears, Roebuck and Company makes between employee behaviors and business success (Boudreau and Ramstad, 1997). At Sears, the first set of measures establish a relationship between leadership development and improved employee attitudes, especially in the area of customer relations such as meeting customers quickly, greeting them with a smile, and calling attention to sales items. The next set of measures show how these customer behaviors have led to customer satisfaction and purchases, which in turn have led to store revenue and profitability.

Measurement systems such as this can go a long way toward convincing skeptical CEOs—insisting on bottom-line results—of worthwhile work-based learning practices. As noted earlier, however, work-based learning-type programs tend to have intermediate rather than strict bottom-line impacts. Profitability measures, for example, derive from the accumulation of improved managerial performances over time. Project results, such as improved customer service, may affect one function but not necessarily the entire organization. The main reason for the difficulty in measuring long-term impact resulting from one change is the chance for moderating effects resulting from counteractive forces elsewhere in the organization. For instance, improved customer service may be counteracted by an outdated or disjointed information system; therefore, program administrators of work-based learning need to caution against their ability to "prove" bottom-line results.

Nevertheless, there are many ways to assess mid-level or intermediate results that can be readily seen as ultimately affecting the bottom line. For example, the careers of program graduates can be tracked to determine if their managerial careers progress at a faster rate than their peers. If so, a connection could be demonstrated between the supply of managerial talent and strategic accomplishment. Similarly, it might be useful to measure attrition rates of participants compared to their non-participating peers under the assumption that program participants might reciprocate for their developmental experience with increased loyalty and commitment (Urban et al., 1985). Once the program recruits a critical mass of managerial talent, organization-wide measurement systems might be installed. A U.S. Department of Labor study (1994) examining a number of firms' valuation levels found that those firms noted for their progressive use of employee development and process management practices had price-to-book valuation ratios significantly higher than their industry peers.

Although not always necessary for organizational purposes, evaluations might be tied to academic research efforts in order to provide a firm empirical basis for the value of work-based learning. Program managers might therefore consider commissioning impact studies using more sophisticated techniques than before-and-after assessments. For example, through time series analyses, evaluators can track outcome trends. Using randomized experiments, evaluators can estimate the extent to which a demonstration project in work-based learning differentiated outcomes between randomly assigned experimental and control groups. Finally, cost-benefit analyses can be conducted to compare program costs with estimates of the economic value of program impacts (Wholey, 1991).

As for specific studies demonstrating the effectiveness of work-based learning programs, there are ample testimonies. Burgoyne and Stuart (1977) found that translation of managerial skills into practice was enhanced when participants were involved in solving real—as opposed to simulated—management problems. Further, Rackham and Morgan (1977) found that skill retention was augmented when managers were asked to perform new skills in specific contexts rather than when they merely acquired them generically to be applied at a later time. Joyce and Showers (1988) also found greater transfer of training when programs provided opportunities for local, factual feedback on trainee performance in actual practice situations. The Reed Travel Group, part of Reed International, has calculated that its project-based action learning programs can generate a return of five to ten times the investment in less than two years (Alder, 1992). Shell Oil Company of the United States has exceeded its goal of a return of 25:1 on its LEAP (Leadership and Performance) action learning program (Brenneman et al., 1998), and Motorola has concluded from its own internal research that targeted (as opposed to general classroom) educational efforts can generate better than a 30:1 return within three years (Fulmer and Vicere, 1996).

Consider the customized five-week program developed by Wharton for a bank holding company. According to the director of program development, Michael Seitchik, it led to a new information system and pricing structure that saved the company an estimated $5 million in consulting fees and was expected to bring in $10 million in additional revenues (Stuller, 1993). At Britvic Soft Drinks, one of England's largest manufacturers of soft drinks and mineral water, an action learning program called Developing to Lead, was reported to have saved in its first year £2.8 million in projects and assignments on an investment of £70,000 (Meehan and Jarvis, 1996). Enderby and Phelan (1994), reporting on an action learning program at a major Australian bank, compared customer perceptions between branches that sponsored action learning groups and those that did not. In every dimension of customer service, customers rated the action learning branches more highly. Perhaps the most revealing outcome of a program was reported by a FEL member who offered the following testimony from a participant whose personal development goals led to a rather dramatic impact on his organization as a whole:

> One participant, the global director of manufacturing for a multi-billion-dollar SBU, attributes a 5 percent increase in global output to his participation in the [program]. He was stifling the leadership development of the team of leaders reporting to him by urging them to rely on him for direction and decision making. By allowing them to shape the five-year manufacturing strategy, the plan was better in quality and implemented with more speed and greater commitment. This SBU will exceed its 1997 profit objectives by 20 percent due in part to this new capability and productivity.

Work-based learning not only produces outcomes that affect individual and organizational learning but can have bottom-line impact on corporate operations through projects that are organization-wide in scope. One FEL member reported that a sponsor in her company made the following observation about the project done in his area: "You have given me millions of dollars worth of consulting. The payback is enormous." Leadership in International Management Ltd. (LIM, 1997) reports that a global truck company, having adopted the company's Action Reflection Learning process, saved a year's production time and earned approximately $7 million from a project team's design of an innovative parts distribution system for their operation in Poland.

There are several levels of measurement that can be recommended in work-based learning. In the tradition of the well-known Kirkpatrick model of evaluation (1975), it is not enough to measure the degree of satisfaction of participants during the program. We are also interested in the knowledge and skills acquired as well as the behavioral changes detected on the job. Most critical, however, are the results or outcomes of the program both in terms of project success and in terms of organizational changes that result from managerial improvement experienced by the participants.

Another way to consider the levels of measurement is through the three criteria of effort, process, and performance. Effort (also referred to as input) measures the resources expended in behalf of the program. Process details what the program did. Performance (or output) measures how well the program achieved its goals and can be evaluated both short-term and long-term.

Consider some more specific measures for each of these three criteria:

Effort

What was the cost of the program?

How many people participated?

How much time did it take (e.g., in terms of participants being away from their job)?

Who sponsored the program and what were their expectations?

Process

What need is the program responding to?

How is the presenting problem being addressed?

What were the distinguishing features of the program and how should they be changed during the next iteration?

What instructional strategies and materials were used to supplement the project phase of the program?

Which projects were chosen and how?

Were learning teams or other reflective practices built into the program?

Performance (short-term)

What competencies were addressed, changed, added?

What were the participants' reactions to the experience?

How did other stakeholders, such as the participants' supervisors, react to the experience?

Did the program meet its cost and time schedules?

Did the project produce a direct beneficial change?

Was the need that inspired the project met?

How were the learning teams received?

Performance (long-term)

Have participants changed their managerial behavior? Did it result in a salutary effect on their unit, organization?

Was there significant transformation in the participants' personal development, values, practices?

Did the program lead to career change or advancement for any participants?

Have there been residual effects from the project in other parts of the organization?

Did the program produce reflective practices not only in participants but in the units to which they were affiliated?

Has the project evolved into a significant venture for the organization?

Did the program change any cultural norms or organizational practices?

Were changes noted in costs, revenues, or other bottom-line results?

Beyond these programmatic measures, specific features of the program need separate measurement and measurers. We wish to know how participants themselves feel about their personal development and achievements in the program, so individual assessment should be built into any evaluation system. In addition, peer assessment has become more common in the human resource field and can be very applicable in work-based learning, especially given that learning team members perhaps know one another better than any other possible assessors. Since project work is built into the process, program management might also seek evaluative data from sponsors and perhaps from the participant's manager or coworkers. Finally, if the program is tied to an academic degree, it may be advisable to use standard academic measures of achievement, which are normally assigned by faculty.

It may be very useful to obtain measures *before* as well as after the program. Such pre-testing, when compared to after-program measures, is thought to achieve greater validity according to academic standards, but can also provide important information to program administrators and to participants. For example, if conditions within the work site change due to program participation, we would be in a better position to credit the program rather than other factors for influencing the change. At the same time, participants should have benchmarks of their personal and managerial performance prior to the program in order to gauge any subsequent change or improvement.

Alternative Substantive Measures

As work-based learning emphasizes reflective processes, it is important to measure results that help members of the entire learning community reflect back on their own learning from the program. It is also useful to communicate these results, even though difficult at times to articulate, to those who have not experienced the process directly (Humphries, 1998). Measuring these substantive results may at times require indicators not typically used in conventional training programs. Work-based learning, as we have seen, encourages individuals and teams to create their own workplace reality through ongoing individual and public reflection. Measures may incorporate, for example, informal or incidental learning that occurs within the workplace itself rather than in the classroom.

There are some general guidelines (Boyett and Conn, 1988; Brancato, 1995) that might develop and foster such substantive measures.

- Use a family of measures rather than rely on one global measure to serve as the ultimate indicator.
- Limit the number of measures.

- Develop team-oriented measures where appropriate and separate them from individual measures of performance.
- Identify measures that are accomplishment or outcome-based as well as process-based.
- Develop some averages to track measures.
- Seek the level of precision sufficient for the purpose (you don't have to reach six-sigma in every project).
- Don't be afraid to change course in midstream.
- Seek to raise standards.

Patricia Inman and Sally Vernon (1997) suggest the development of narratives and dialogic approaches, such as scenarios and process maps, to capture the rich, embedded learning made available through work-based learning. Narratives are comparable to journals but seek to connect the individual's accomplishments to the wider organizational culture. Camcar Textron of Rockford, Illinois, has been using the narrative as a personal assessment tool to examine workplace learning along three dimensions.

1. What knowledge do I bring to the workplace?
2. How does this fit into the context of the organization's strategic plan?
3. What learning project would be most appropriate for my organizational role?

Scenario building and process mapping extend the narrative methodology by engaging participants in planning and consensus-building processes that invite them to reorganize their perceptions about future team/unit development and organizational growth (Inman and Vernon, 1997).

Measuring the substantive outcomes from work-based learning can be grouped into four categories: (1) effects on self, (2) effects on interpersonal and team relationships, (3) effects on managerial behavior, and (4) effects on projects. Self- or personal outcomes refer to changes in one's individual behaviors, dispositions, and organizational standing. Important measures might include gains in self-esteem, increased awareness, commitment to challenge oneself, knowledge of one's preferred learning style, ability to reflect both individually and publicly, proclivity to share more with others, and confidence to present one's vulnerability. The aforementioned outcomes could also, in turn, lead to career advancement within the organization, though it may be difficult to isolate the program as the only cause of career growth. Volvo Concessionaires (VOCS) found that participants who went through its Young Manager Program—an action learning program sponsored by Sundridge Park Management Centre—improved on their performance appraisal ratings and displayed a greater willingness to regard job mobility (lateral moves) as a development opportunity (Branch and Smith, 1992).

The learning team approach of work-based learning affords participants an opportunity to acquire enhanced teamwork or interpersonal skills. Measures of success might incorporate increased awareness of team dynamics, improved performance as a team member, ability to facilitate teams, greater patience with others, improved listening acuity, faculty in communicating one's feelings, greater sensitivity to others, better probing skills, proficiency in challenging others, adeptness in soliciting collective inquiry, and enhanced networking capability.

My own research of three comprehensive executive programs using action learning (Raelin 1997a) verified some of these individual and interpersonal outcomes, which I noted were quite different from conventional executive program results. In particular, the programs developed avid questioners—practitioners who questioned not just their own work or that of their unit, but the governing values of their own organization. Johnson's research (1997) found that action learning produced both breadth of learning, in the sense of the experience touching on everyday work issues, as well as depth, addressing deeply rooted attitudes and beliefs. It also yielded some less conventional individual outcomes, such as:

- the skill of empathetic listening;
- increased self-confidence;
- increased awareness of self and others;
- increased readiness to take responsibility and initiative;
- ability to formulate more informed actions;
- enhanced learning to learn.

Research by Harley Frank (1998a) at Huddersfield University in the United Kingdom disclosed three principal effects on British managers who participated in the university's Masters program based on work-based learning.

1. In working on live issues, the managers began to reframe the problem and even saw themselves as part of the problem they were attempting to deal with.

2. In working through their work-based problem, they ultimately became personally transformed.
3. They experienced double-loop learning.

Consider a case from Professor Frank's work. He described the account of Maggie, a new registrar of a Museum Service in a large British city. The Museum Service comprised four separate museums plus a large art gallery. As registrar, Maggie was given the responsibility to upgrade the Service's collection standards in order to qualify for national registration and receive funding aid. The enhancement of the Service's collections became Maggie's project for the year. In working through this project, Maggie exemplified how a work-based learning student experiences each of the aforementioned outcomes.

1. *She became part of the problem.* Maggie reported that initially she began her project more as a consultant than as a member of the staff. She realized that to be effective she would have to adopt a role in which she would be seen more as "one of them." As she became aware of the gap that existed between herself, a motivated young woman, and the comfortable, settled, middle-aged "men with their cardigans," she began to reframe the situation. She came to think of herself as being a "learning manager" in a "non-learning organization." Thinking of herself in these new terms considerably helped her to formulate new actions she could undertake to positively influence the organization.

2. *She became transformed.* As her project evolved, she began to see that she herself was using ineffectual attributions to characterize her staff. For example, through reflective dialogue in her learning team, she became aware of her observation that her colleagues were unable and unwilling to change, graphically captured in the phrase "Old men in cardigans waiting for retirement." Maggie noted, "Following discussion in my set, I reflected and realized I needed to look again and reinterpret my observations. I found I came to appreciate more clearly the staff's situation."

3. *She experienced double-loop learning.* In double-loop and triple-loop learning, which I first introduced in Chapter 2, participants seek to inquire about the most fundamental assumptions behind their very practices, even the governing values of the systems of which they are a part. One of Maggie's interventions was to initiate an extensive training program for staff, but in order to make it useful, she had to overcome a widely shared perception that training was a "waste of time." Again, through assistance from her learning team, she reformulated training as something more than teaching and instruction; it

could also serve as a tool for community building, bringing together groups and individuals in the Service who had never met. Further, by rotating the training venues among the Service's different museum sites, staff could be given the chance to visit sites in the same city that many had never seen. Better working relationships evolved among the staff and Maggie established vital contacts with both internal and external training providers and other stakeholders throughout the city.

The work-based learning methods described in this book have been applied for the most part to settings involving management and executive development. Thus, programs are designed to have beneficial outcomes on the participant's managerial behavior. One could develop an exhaustive list of managerial competencies evolving from work-based learning programs, but many would be specific to the functional or technical area in which the participant may have chosen to concentrate. Research by Lewis and Marsh (1987) and Weinstein (1995), however, point to some generic indicators that participants who have already gone through a program used as a gauge of their improved managerial ability. Participants report that they have learned:

- how to organize teams better back in their work site;
- how to relate better to their staff, especially to listen and take criticism;
- how to critically question their colleagues on their own problems;
- how to delegate more effectively, in particular to give their staff more responsibility;
- how to be more open with their coworkers;
- how to behave with greater confidence with senior managers;
- how to be more organized;
- how to take initiative in improving conditions at work;
- how to take on more responsibility in their role;
- how to monitor operations more effectively;
- how to effect culture change more effectively within their organization.

Perhaps the most critical feature in a work-based learning program is the project and the effect it has had on the sponsoring work unit. The measures used in this instance should apply to the business function in question and might be derived as business indicators of effort, process, and performance. If the project was to initiate quality processes, to reduce downtime, to improve customer satisfaction, or to save on costs, then the measures should flow from these respective variables. The reason for including the three categories of measurement is to avoid an availability bias resulting from concentrating on only a few measures (Bazerman, 1990). As suggested earlier, it might also be advisable to collect data both before and after the project to demonstrate change and improvement. If the data can be converted to quantitative metrics, the measurement process can proceed in a straightforward manner. Consider as an example a project in the domain of distribution (Kelly, 1993). A new system is to be put in place to cut down on the number of wrong deliveries from a retail distribution warehouse. The costs associated with wrong orders can be quantified using such indicators as:

- cost of picking up the wrong order and redelivering the correct order;
- staff time in stores and at the distribution center reorganizing the order;
- time attributed to sales staff in pacifying angry customers;
- time calculated for the finance staff to reinvoice and issue credit notes.

Using data of this sort can lead to explicit calculations that can demonstrate the benefits from the project; however, less obvious, non-quantitative measures should not be overlooked in the measurement system. Some benefits, such as customer goodwill or staff morale, though not as readily assessed, should be incorporated. There may also be hidden costs in a project of this nature that should be accounted for, such as resistance from critical stakeholders or loss of staff commitment if there is pressure to achieve immediate targets.

A measurement system should be designed initially based upon the goals of the project and then adapted as the project unfolds. Any decision regarding the number of measures should follow the well-known canon that one should measure everything that matters and not much else! The key is to provide project stakeholders with timely and reliable information that would be relevant to the ongoing development of the project. Intangible factors, such as morale and satisfaction, should be included along with standard performance indicators. In some instances, "proxy" indicators or unobtrusive measures will need to be devised in place of the less tangible variables. An example of an unobtrusive measure is growth in resources attached to the project over and above its budgeted expenses. Successful projects generate support that can be measured in the amount of resources, physical and human, that are allocated to it. Another unobtrusive measure is the survival of the project beyond the work-based learning program. This measure suggests that successful projects take on a life of their own. Similarly, in the instance of measuring the overall success of a work-based learning program, one might use the willingness to pay for a repeat performance as an appropriate proxy.

The more direct measures can be divided into the three criteria already presented (effort, process, performance), but let's refer to them using the systems references of input, process, and output. Consider the following example of a project in the domain of order entry (adapted from Kaydos, 1991).

The project was initiated in the order entry department as a result of what appeared to be a growing number of complaints about orders picked up by the customer service department. The participant undertaking the project was asked by the OE manager to find out if, in fact, the number of complaints was accelerating, what the source of these complaints was, and what the implications were. The project unfolded as a research undertaking for the participant, who designed a plan to interview staff, survey customers, assess records, and observe the department in operation. Although the analysis constituted the bulk of the project in this case, a more extensive project or a follow-up to the diagnosis would require the planning and implementation of some specific interventions to solve the problems identified, not only in order entry but also in related departments.

The measures that might be used for the project phase include some of the following:

Input

number of orders changed as a percentage of total orders over a specified monthly period

number of complaints received by product, severity, and reason, (i.e., order incorrect, order incomplete, order damaged on delivery, order unduly delayed)

Process (internal)

number of complaints processed per hour by product, reason, and severity number of orders processed that were considered illegible

a detailed description of the order entry job as it relates to complaint handling as reported by order entry clerks with any variances noted

Process (external)

assessment of phone system downtime/problems based upon records over a monthly period

assessment of mail delivery system over the same monthly period

sales forecast for the month in question

shipping errors occurring during the month in question

Output

cost of complaint handling in terms of time and labor

cost of complaints in terms of refunds, replacements, and lost sales

percentage of complaints not resolved on first inquiry, within 24 hours

customer satisfaction index (from direct mailing to complainants)

It is important to keep in mind that outputs from work-based learning cannot always jibe with standard financial indicators since we are often measuring knowledge, an intangible asset. Intangible assets constitute the difference between the market value of a company and its official net book value. They embody the competence of its employees and their contribution to the success of the organization through such vehicles as R&D, customer and supplier relations, concepts and "know-how," and image. Measuring outputs in knowledge and learning is very possible but requires the development of nonstandard measures of performance. Consider as an example the indicators Sveiby (1997) has developed in the domain of customer relations for some Swedish professional service firms such as Scandia, PLS-Consult, and Celemi. These measures could be adopted as part of project activities, for instance, in the area of market outreach.

Sveiby first recommends that firms categorize customers into such domains as those who can contribute to and extend the firm's image, those who can provide references to other prospective customers, those who provide challenging and growthful assignments, and those who provide learning opportunities for junior staff.

Once customers are so categorized, a number of output measures have been developed beyond the conventional customer satisfaction index, such as:

sales/profitability per customer type

size of customer base

devoted customer ratio

frequency of repeat orders

proportion of junior time spent for competence-enhancing customers.

11

Work-Based Learning Program Applications

Frank Leahy, the legendary football coach of Notre Dame, would occasionally rely on theory to get his point across. At one practice, dissatisfied with the level of play, he picked up an object and said to his players: "All right men, let's return to the fundamentals. Let's say this is a football." One of the linemen, taking notes in the back of the room, yelled out, "Wait a minute, Coach. Not so fast!"

—education anecdote

This last chapter is devoted purely to practical applications of the methods detailed in the book. In particular, for those who wish to undertake a program of work-based learning in their organization, I have prepared a prototype program at the outset of the chapter. I then give a few explicit examples of current work-based learning programs in effect, followed by a catalog of university-sponsored and global programs. I finish with some thoughts about multicultural sensitivity when attempting to apply work-based learning methods abroad.

Prototype Program

I would like to demonstrate a prototypical learning program, combining some of the collective learning types of the model of work-based learning and apply them to the domain of executive education (see Table 11.1). In orientation, which precedes program launch, it is important that the leadership of the firm, as suggested in the last chapter, commit itself to executive development using a work-based learning approach rather than the conventional structured classroom model. The program should also be designed in an environment that supports learning as a basic tenet of the culture. Finally, senior staff should demonstrate their support of the program by being actively involved, whether it be by promoting the value of the program in their communications or by participating as sponsors of projects, mentors, module speakers, instructors, or even participants.

DuPont's Leadership for Growth program has evolved from a culture that represents the organic learning environment that seems conducive to work-based learning. The program emphasizes DuPont's interest in having executives who can use multidimensional and nonlinear thinking, and who can, in the words of our FEL representative from DuPont, "invoke powers of inquiry over quick answers or simple formulae and who in search for insights can create value for all stakeholders rather than perpetually trading off the needs of one against the other."

No two programs need to look alike from one organization to another since the features of work-based learning are dependent on such conditions as the readiness level of the learners, the strengths and preferences of the sponsors and facilitator(s), or the past practices of the sponsoring unit or organization. As a rule of thumb, however, if the learners are uninitiated, it is more threatening to expose them to their tacit assumptions than to have them articulate their explicit beliefs. This is especially the case if the assumptions under review might expose learners to their psychological defenses or to their emotional or personal reactions to others. Hence programs might start by having managers, perhaps through a seminar series, study some novel domains of managerial practice, exposing them to some new skills and competencies that (1) they can immediately put to use in their current job, and (2) they will find helpful in the development of their subsequent work-based learning experiences. For example, they might consider different perspectives of leadership or learn how the company might like to transition to a team-based culture. In support of subsequent modules of the program, participants might study both how to collect and analyze data. This might include a crash course on the use of quantitative and qualitative research methods. Although the discussion at this point might safely begin at the conceptual level, there should also be opportunities for participants to practice some of the new skills introduced, using experiential methods.

Citibank, under senior human resource (HR) executive Larry Phillips, developed a Business Manager Leadership action learning

Table 11.1
A Prototype Work-Based Learning Program for Executive Development

	Orientation	Seminar series	Learning teams	Projects	Community of practice	Presentation
Purpose	Recognition of value of work-based learning philosophy	Exposure to competencies to use on the job and to support work-based projects	Opportunity to try out new theories into practice and obtain the support of a learning team	Practice of leadership concepts in projects that supply strategic value to organization	Merger of learning teams and work teams to undertake worthwhile projects while working toward higher levels of insight and performance	Opportunity for project teams to present findings and learning to sponsors
Approximate time frame	1 day prior to program or through communications	2 hours/week for 6 to 10 weeks	2 hours/week for 6 to 10 weeks	Daily for 2 to 3 weeks or one day/week for 4 to 6 months	Daily for 2 to 3 weeks or one day/week for 4 to 6 months or continuously	1 to 2 days
Sample activities	Communication from senior management to support recruitment into program	Perspectives on leadership, research methods, journal writing, mentorship	Debriefing of real-time experiences, testing of theories-in-use, learning how to publicly reflect	Individuals working in such projects as globalization of HR or IT functions or quality processes, while continuing to meet in learning teams	Current work teams now versed in action learning and action science techniques, complete short- or long-term projects while developing themselves as a high-performing supportive unit	Teams make a presentation of their projects to sponsors and to other interested senior executives, noting challenges, accomplishments, and learning both acquired and yet to be acquired

program that started off with a learning seminar. During this seminar, six skills, thought to be critical in preparing the participating executives for the program, were presented (Dotlich and Noel, 1998):

- strategy
- service quality and handling
- strategic cost management
- risk management
- technology management
- people management

In time, the focus can shift from the experiential level to one in which reflections might be offered regarding the use of the ideas in practice. Participants might even be encouraged to bring in experiences from their own jobs to verify or challenge some of the theories under review. During these components, participants should be encouraged to persistently observe themselves and others in practice and try to become sensitive to why they act in certain ways. In particular, they should try to notice what tacit theories are actually used in practice, how these theories match against the new theories introduced in the program, and whether people actually behave consistently with whatever theories they espouse.

It may be difficult for some participants to engage in the reflective components just described without the assistance of a partner and/or mentor. These "developmental" or "helper" roles can be critical in encouraging participants to try out new workplace behaviors and learn from their experiences. They are particularly helpful where learning teams are not available to participants on any ongoing basis. The "LeaderLab," referred to in Chapter 7, deploys three helper roles; a process advisor (PA), represented by a staff professional who meets with the participants in person and by phone during the three-month experience; in-course change partners who work with one another to experiment with and reflect upon classroom experiences; and back-home change partners who help the participants transfer off-site lessons back into the work site (Burnside and Guthrie, 1992).

Another complementary tool to help participants reflect more on their individual development is the journal (see Chapter 7). Journal writing provides an opportunity for participants to break their habitual ways of thinking and acting through reflective withdrawal and reentry (Lukinsky, 1990). Journals help participants distill lessons from experience and help them track their learning, be it from important lessons, trends, or patterns (Cell, 1984). What makes the journal or log effective is the discipline it imposes on participants to systematically reflect on their experiences. It also has an anticipatory function in that it allows the participant to visualize experiences before embarking on them (Frank, 1996).

Perhaps the most propitious way to engage in public reflection and to assess how effectively new theories are being used in practice is to solicit the support of a learning team. Learning teams or action learning sets give participants a chance to debrief their real-time experiences (Pedler, 1991). The experience of working in learning teams was also described in depth in Chapter 7. Learning teams tend to meet periodically, for example on a monthly basis, and serve as a supporting mechanism for both individual and project development.

Program development can advance to the next collective level of activity in which participants are asked to deliberately work together to practice some of the new ideas introduced. One way to foster this type of learning is to work on action projects in the sponsoring organization. As was detailed in Chapter 9, projects are designed to be challenging, to be experimental, and to have strategic value to their sponsoring unit. The identification of projects can be handled through sponsorship or through self-selection. A learning consortium group made up of six major companies in a large New England city uses a focus group methodology to prioritize the most critical issues for the participating executives to study. Group members come together on a monthly basis to discuss the chosen topic while attempting to carry out changes in their back-home corporate environment precipitated by their learning experience in the group.

Plans and actions undertaken in action projects are subjected to inquiry about their effectiveness. Participants are also typically invited to present their project. Besides a presentation of results, however, participants may be required to prepare a project report detailing the learnings and competencies addressed in the experience as well as any constraints that may have blocked proposed interventions.

General Electric's Executive Development Course is a month-long experience in which promising executives assemble into teams to work on a specific assignment. The assignments vary by topic from year to year, and although sponsors get a completed project at the end of the month, the real issue for GE's Leadership Development Center at Crotonville is the value of the learning experience more than the assignment per se. According to Greco (1997a), half of the month is spent preparing for the project—making contacts, clarifying objectives, and so forth—and the other half is spent doing the field work. At the conclusion of the program, the teams make their recommendations in a presentation to senior leaders and to the sponsors who provided the project.

General Electric's Crotonville has been a pioneer in action learning in the United States. Among its innovations in work-based projects was the preliminary detail it put into project development. Before plunging into any project, participants would receive briefings on pertinent market, customer, and financial information. Crotonville would also lay the foundation for the action projects by providing in the first weeks of the program state-of-the-art concepts in key substantive domains ranging from strategic marketing and financial planning to competitive analysis and organizational change. GE also initiated developmental action planning within the action learning experience through a feedback instrument referred to as the Leadership Effectiveness Survey (LES). Participants would report, however, that it was the initial team-building experiences, including outward-bound activities, that were the most valuable part of the program (Noel and Charan, 1988, 1992).

In Cable & Wireless, Inc.'s Leadership Workshop, participants are drawn from seven countries and diverse functions to work on international projects sponsored by the highest level in the organization, C&W's Executive Management Team. Team members work on their projects over an intensive three-month period while continuing to work on their current jobs. One team investigated how to obtain optimum value from the company's global investment in training and development. Accordingly, they benchmarked C & W's facilities against those of other multinational companies and academic institutions, interviewed Business Unit training and development directors about their needs, and regularly canvassed the views of the company's top executives. Although this and other teams did not have all of their recommendations accepted, Linus Cheung, Chief Executive of Hongkong Telecom (a C & W subsidiary) and a Leadership Workshop team sponsor, noted that even rejected recommendations "were presented in such a way that they triggered informed debates on the issues which allowed us to make decisions on the way forward."[1]

DuPont's Leadership for Growth eight-week program, according to FEL member Susan Mazur, starts with a week devoted mostly to classroom topics but makes room for participants to organize and plan their projects. Week two is spent entirely on project design and data collection and includes meetings with project sponsors. During

---

[1] This paragraph, from a Cable & Wireless newsletter, is provided through the courtesy of David Ashton, former chief executive, The Cable & Wireless College.

weeks three through six, participants are back on their jobs but may spend as much as 50 percent of their time advancing their project work. During week seven, participants reconvene for additional classroom sessions but spend about half the time putting the finishing touches on their project. The last week of the program is spent preparing and presenting their project recommendations to senior leaders and then debriefing the project process. Recently, the program was condensed to a full-time three-week experience in order to reduce travel and program costs. In addition, a business simulation, formerly done in the first week, was canceled as the tools it introduced were found to be brought out more effectively in the action project.

Project groups need not assemble organizational strangers to work on problems outside their work area. Intact work teams can participate in development programs to help them become more of a community of practice. Communities of practice recognize that their very effectiveness rests on their members' ability to learn from one another. Participants in such groups not only learn to observe and experiment with their own collective tacit processes in action but, while doing so, seek to improve their own performance. There are many so-called "team-building" methods available to help intact groups work toward higher levels of insight and performance. Teaching participants how to become process observers of their own interactions can accelerate development by exposing team members to each other's potential contributions as well as to the team's overall needs.

Some companies that are geographically disperse are attempting to create virtual communities of practice. Some functional groups might not be able to meet face-to-face very often but may need to rely on members' mutual expertise to perform their responsibilities. At Cable & Wireless College, a virtual university has been created so that teams of managers in comparable fields can collaborate on-line with one another to ensure cross-fertilization of knowledge. FEL member David Ashton, the College's former chief executive, reports that using on-line communication, groups have been formed to

> share their challenges and experiences. Their outputs have identified competence requirements, which (in principle) the virtual "corporate university" can respond to with "best in class" programs or a rapid program design and delivery loop. A crude measure of the success of this program may be the energy/commitment of the groups—up to 80 inputs a day in one team of 6! Not easy to generate or sustain, but something interesting appears to have been happening.

If the learning community is willing, members can continue to engage their collective consciousness through the process known as action science (Argyris, 1982). More than the other learning types, it calls for the deliberate questioning of existing perspectives and interpretations and thus seeks to make explicit the constituent elements of our assumptive worlds. The practices of action science can vary in personal risk from scenario analysis, wherein participants explore the actions of hypothetical characters, to critical incidents, wherein they have the opportunity to face the assumptions framing their own practice through an analysis of events in their lives that are remembered for their emotional significance (Brookfield, 1992). For example, participants may be asked to describe an event as a manager that made them feel a real "high" of satisfaction and fulfillment and one that made them feel a real "low" of dissatisfaction and disappointment. Repertory grids and metaphor analysis can also be used to help participants bring to the surface their otherwise tacit personal constructs (Kelly, 1955; Deshler, 1985).

At American Express Financial Advisors, the key to the work-based learning approach used with AEFA's sales management group and introduced by FEL member Judy Scoglund, along with Ginny Belden and Marsha Hyatt, is double-loop learning. Forty-five leaders of the company's major market groups have been working in groups of five for two years, and meet three to four times a year given their geographical dispersion. Fundamental to the double-loop approach is the use of questions that help participants develop new assumptions and apply them:

What's been accomplished (the facts)?

What's been energizing/de-energizing?

What have you learned (where the new assumptions come out)?

How will you apply this moving forward?

Judy reported that getting managers to make the transition to double-loop learning has been challenging because, as she puts it:

> the nature of their daily work encourages them to do a lot of "telling" so the idea of reflection and questioning is a very unnatural way to develop individuals. I have to admit, though, that I believe it is probably more exciting to experience it than it is to discuss it (hence like a dream—potentially fantastic as an experience but hard to translate into meaning).

Comprehensive Case Examples

ARAMARK[2]

Let's consider now two examples of work-based learning in action. FEL member Lynn McKee, Director of Human Resources and Executive Education for ARAMARK, provides a comprehensive example from her company. ARAMARK, founded in 1959 as Automation Retailers of America, is today a global managed services company, having core businesses in food and support services, uniform services, and education. It is a partially employee-owned company in that its 150,000 employees own 75 percent of the company. Although the company achieved a unique level of success when it first became employee-owned, revenues and earnings growth were beginning to flatten in the early 1990s.

The executive staff saw its challenge as transforming the company into a growth enterprise. From a human resource perspective, it had to identify the skills and competencies necessary to make this transformation and then infuse them into the organization, starting with its senior leadership.

Accordingly, ARAMARK—in conjunction with the Pennsylvania State University Executive Programs—created an Executive Leadership Institute (ELI) in 1993 to conceive and implement a shared vision for growth for the company and to bring to fruition its executive education initiatives. It divided its efforts into three components: education, personal development, and action projects.

In the education domain, the ELI recruits a world-class faculty to deliver customized courses over a six-month period. The personal development process for each ELI participant features in-depth interviews with a management psychologist; 360-degree feedback from superiors, peers, and subordinates; and the preparation of a development plan based on the results of these processes.

Turning to the action project component, assignments are made during the first class session. Projects are undertaken concurrent with participants' ongoing job duties. Compatible with work-based learning principles, projects deal with real, challenging business issues and provide ample opportunity for professional and personal growth and development. Each ELI cohort is made up of five teams of six participants per team, with the membership being cross-functional and cross-business unit. At the conclusion of the experience, project teams make a presentation complete with strategic recommendations.

---

[2] This section courtesy of Lynn McKee, ARAMARK Corporation.

After the first meeting, project teams schedule their subsequent meetings on their own and decide how they will maintain contact throughout the six-month project period. Lynn reports that they meet on an as-needed basis using whatever communication format is most appropriate. For instance, they might dialogue on-line; they'll use conference calls; or they might meet face-to-face, especially when they can combine it with attendance at regional or national business meetings of the business unit that they happen to be studying.

In terms of project selection, recommendations for project work from line departments first go to a central pool. Selected senior managers review all recommendations, ensuring that there is substantive variety, balance across business units, and minimal redundancy. ELI staff then—in conjunction with business unit managers—prepare a statement of the project, which in many instances is supported by supplemental information, often in the form of a briefing book. Projects are then assigned to select teams. Each team is also assigned a trained coach.

As an example of a typical project, one team was assigned to evaluate critically the strategic and tactical options for the Vending Division route business. As a division of the Business Services Group, ARAMARK's vending services maintain a route-based distribution to its client base, primarily business and industry, hospitals, and universities. The project team began by deciding to reframe vending as the unattended refreshment business. Interviews and surveys were administered to internal and external stakeholders, including competitors. The approach gradually developed by the team was to consider establishing vending as an independent line of business and thus distinct from business services. This would permit other ARAMARK businesses to manage and sell vending services to their existing clients with support from experts in the newly reformulated Vending Division.

The team next recommended that Vending consider consolidating its operation with ARAMARK/Cory Refreshment Services. A route-based distribution business, Cory Refreshment Services focused primarily on small businesses and dealt with white-collar customers as opposed to Vending's solid blue-collar base. The benefits projected by the team, which later came to fruition, were reduction in capital costs—such as the need for fewer vehicles, more efficient distribution, reduction in labor costs as support staff could be shared, and consolidated technology.

Lynn McKee has shared evaluation data from the ELI, revealing remarkable results. For example, 50 percent of ELI alumni said that their expectations were exceeded, and the other 50 percent said it met their expectations. As for the action projects, fully 98 percent said that the projects provided a meaningful opportunity to apply models and insights to a real ARAMARK issue; 99 percent felt that they gained personal benefit from participating in the project; and 98 percent said they gained insights that could be applied to their own current business environment. Lynn also attributes ELI as having played a critical role not just in the company's growth but in its transformation to a collaborative culture that values partnerships, teamwork, and innovation.

Grace Cocoa

A second comprehensive example of the use of work-based learning, the Leadership Forum of Grace Cocoa, has been reported by Leadership in International Management, Ltd. (LIM), which has adopted a form of work-based learning known as Action Reflection Learning (Flynn, 1997). Comparable to classic action learning, ARL emphasizes a reflective component that is initiated from responsible actions in real situations. It further stresses the value of learning from and sharing real-time experiences with others.

Grace Cocoa Associates, L.P., recently acquired by Archer Daniels Midland (ADM), processes more than 10 percent of the world's supply of cocoa beans. It is a truly global manufacturer, operating in five different continents in more than 16 locations. In 1990, however, it faced the need to increase collaboration by learning how to diffuse knowledge across its multiple companies, each operating within its own unique culture. Its solution was an action learning program called the Leadership Forum.

According to the program manager, Chris Dennis, 20 managers are selected for a series of four one-week meetings or forums over the course of six months. Each meeting is held in a different country where Grace has operations. In between the forums, the managers are assigned to an action learning group to work on a significant project that has been developed by a top executive who would otherwise have hired it out to a consultant. The Forum also insists that no manager work on a project in which he or she has had prior experience. The logic for this program feature is to expose managers to cross-functional work, giving them confidence that they will be able to operate in the future outside their area of expertise.

In one instance, an American manager of compensation and benefits was placed on a team charged with improving customer service. During the course of her project, she found herself engaging in such non-HR functions as buying cocoa beans and separating butter and powder. Another team focused on market diversification, concluding that Grace would have to move into a new South American market as well as intensify its efforts in the Asia-Pacific region (Flynn, 1997). This team also created a software program to guide market expansion efforts into new regions.

Although the action learning tenet of learning-to-learn is reinforced, the project teams also receive skill development training during their four meetings in such topics as consulting skills, managing conflict, dealing with resistance to change, conducting survey research, and augmenting communication skills. Each team is also assigned a learning coach, whose job it is to keep members as much focused on learning from the project experience as on solving the inherent problem. Using such action learning techniques as "stop-and-reflect," coaches slow team members down so they can examine the assumptions underlying their plans and actions.

The Grace Cocoa program also entails most of the other components associated with work-based learning. Participants maintain journals and share portions of their reflections with fellow team members. Teams make recommendations on their projects to top management, who decide whether or not to adopt them. Participants complete development plans, using such personal assessment devices as the Myers-Briggs personality profile, and receive multisource reviews on their strengths and weaknesses in management. There is also a substantive focus on leadership, but in the first program series, it was illustrated in a very dramatic manner. As they assembled for the initial week of instruction during the Forum, each participant received a leather-bound book entitled "Leadership." However, they were shocked to find that the book only contained blank pages. Dennis's explanation for this usage was that "truly successful leaders literally sit down and reflect on their experiences. They write them out, they think about them, they work on them and try to take it to a higher level" (Flynn, 1997).

When the effect of having multiple Leadership Forums are added together, it is no surprise that Dennis feels strongly that work-based learning has played a key role in changing the culture at Grace Cocoa. The company now functions as a global entity without operating divisions (Dennis, 1997).

Examples from University-Sponsored Programs

It may strike the reader as odd that universities, bastions of steeped conceptual knowledge, might have an interest in sponsoring work-based learning programs. However, this misconstrues the purpose of the university as that of teaching, not of learning. Where learning is thought to constitute praxis as much as the development of theory, work-based learning can become a legitimate domain of higher education.

Certainly professional schools have been long committed to field experiences. Using such terms as internship, externship, residency, practicum, co-op, and the like, there is a recognition that students need practical experience before becoming independent professional practitioners. Such components, nevertheless, without a conscious public reflective experience, do not constitute work-based learning in the way characterized in this book.

Some university programs have become committed to work-based learning methods, especially applied to the domain of management. I have reported on Penn State's ELI with ARAMARK. Here are a few additional examples.

Ballarat University

Ballarat University College, Australia, has a Master of Business Management program, which besides its provision of conventional managerial skills and competencies makes extensive use of work-related assignments and action learning projects (Ballarat University, 1994). Forty percent of the curriculum is action learning- and project-based and, in turn, 40 percent of this component derives from a final presentation to a client who also plays a significant role in evaluating the end product. The other major component of the action learning experience is the thesis, in which students are required to reflect on their learning as well as report the results of their project intervention.

Boise State University

The College of Business and Economics in its part-time MBA program offers a series of courses called "issues in." As business issues change—a decline in sales, a change in tax laws—the curriculum adjusts accordingly. Since the school is the only public university for three hundred miles in any direction, it believes it needs to make its educational provision responsive and real-time for its corporate customers such as Micron, Boise Cascade, and Hewlett Packard (*Newsline*, 1996).

Boston College

Boston College's Carroll Graduate School of Management provides a 12-credit graduate certificate program called "Leadership for Change." The program focuses on leadership and change through social reflectiveness at four levels of experience: individual, group, organization, and society. A one-year program, it features six modules of coursework combined with a six-month action project in the participant's own organization. Learning teams of six to seven participants meet throughout the entire experience.

Carnegie Mellon University

Carnegie's Bosch Institute delivers custom programs for its client companies focusing on their specific environment and problems. Its programs emphasize teamwork and learning by doing and are designed to be fully integrated with the companies' overall management development strategy (Brickers, 1997).

Columbia University

The Graduate School of Business at Columbia tailors its offerings by addressing students' work-based problems. Not only is this approach used in its Global Leadership Program but in its open enrollment executive education courses. According to the director of executive education, Kathleen McGahran, participants come to their classes with a one-page description of an issue or a problem that they are currently facing. These problems are addressed as part of the class discussion. Participants develop specific plans for change to address their workplace issue. McGahran further notes that at the end of the course students might also have one-on-one sessions with the professors about their company's problems (Wines, 1996).

Copenhagen Business School

The Human Resource Management (HRM) Master Program has a number of work-based learning features. One unique approach links first-year students organized into learning groups with an HRM mentor in a private or public organization. Throughout the term, the group has frequent meetings with the mentor to test course concepts against the reality of the organization. In addition, specific current issues of interest to the mentor are passed on to the students, who are then asked to analyze and suggest solutions to the problems of the mentor.

Durham University

The Durham (U.K.) University Business School has been offering a Graduate Associates Programme (GAP) since 1988 and awards the associates who complete the program with a Diploma in Enterprise Management. Working in small and medium-sized enterprises, associates complete company-specific projects, which are focused on developing a new process or product or on developing and strengthening the overall management structure of the company. Learning support groups are assembled to provide the associates with peer support. In addition to working at company sites, the graduate also takes part in a 40-day training program, spread out over the entire academic year (Ahmed et al., 1995).

FENIX

FENIX is a graduate-level research program offering both doctorate and master's degrees through three academic partners (Chalmers University of Technology of Göteborg, Institute for Management of Innovation and Technology at Göteborg, and the Stockholm School of Business and Economics) in association with several large Swedish corporations such as Astra Hässle, Ericsson, Telia, and Volvo. During the course of study, research projects are conducted in close cooperation with the sponsoring firms within the fields of leadership, strategy, and product and business development. The projects are designed to form a foundation for improvement and renewal processes within the partner companies.

Georgia State University

The Center for Executive Education strives to provide company- and industry-specific context to conceptual management issues. Courses use actual company data to present concepts in a hands-on manner. The intent is to make the subject matter immediately relevant to the job at hand. Faculty have even made sales calls and deliveries for one major client to develop a firsthand understanding of the company's culture (Brickers, 1997).

Helsinki University of Technology

A program called ExIma, developed through the Department of Industrial Management, sponsors both masters and doctoral degrees. Both degree programs require a thesis, which focuses on real and important issues pertinent to the candidate's company. Each candidate also works with a personal tutor who guides the research work of the candidate, is committed to the problem, and works a couple of days a month in the student's company.

International Institute for Management Development (IMD)

IMD, located in Lausanne, Switzerland, tailors programs for more than 100 international firms registered in its partnership scheme. With commitment at the senior level, partners are involved at every stage of the program, and programs are designed to meet their clients' specific objectives. Action learning is the preferred delivery mode because it transcends the boundaries between formal development and on-the-job learning (Lorange, 1994; Brickers, 1997).

International Masters Program in Practicing Management (IMPM)

The IMPM is offered by five universities (Lancaster, McGill, Indian Institute of Management, Hitotsubashi, and INSEAD), each of which sponsors a two-week program module. Each module is organized around a mindset: the reflective in England, the analytic in Canada, the wordly in India, the collaborative in Japan, and the catalytic in France. The focus of the program is on the development of managers in their own contexts—their jobs and organizations. As the program is spread over a year and a half, assignments between the modules are designed to deepen and continue the learning process. For example, before each module, participants prepare a brief statement of the issues they see in their job and in their companies related to the particular mindset. This enables the faculty to tailor the module to their concerns. Participants work on a "venture" throughout the program, which is an activity designed to bring about some substantial change in their organization. Participants are also supported by tutorial group meetings, which are held both during and in between each module.

Lancaster University

The Management Development Division sponsors two types of part-time or post-experience MBA programs. Single-company programs are tailored to corporate clients, with much of the instruction taking place on-site. The Consortial MBA attracts managers from a number of companies in a common geographic region. While instruction in the consortial programs takes place at the university, like the single-company program, action learning projects are solicited and managed as in-company projects designed to have strategic impact within the client's workplace. Participants also take part in six-person learning teams that help members appraise their own learning. Tutors from the university facilitate the learning teams and also supervise the preparation of a dissertation based on the participant's project.

Leeds Metropolitan University

Leeds offers both a diploma and a master's degree as part of its management development program known as the Company Associate Partnership Scheme (CAPS). CAPS associates are assigned to work full-time on a strategic project in a small or medium-sized business. Projects are chosen by the company on the basis that they could not be completed by existing personnel. Although there is no formal commitment to employ associates at the end of their scheme, it is expected that many will be offered permanent positions. Each associate is also assigned a mentor who spends a half-day each week working with the associate on technical, academic, and professional development matters (Ahmed et al., 1995).

Nene College of Higher Education

Nene–University College Northampton (U.K.) houses the SOLAR Centre (The Centre for Social & Organizational Learning and Re-animation), which in turn offers both MPhil and Ph.D. degrees. SOLAR's postgraduate program aims to provide a stimulating research and development opportunity for managers, professionals, consultants, and practitioners who are actively engaged in processes of learning and change within organizations and communities. The primary emphasis is on public and voluntary service organizations. Participants undertake projects that have personal and professional meaning to them as well as have impact within their fields of action. They also join supervisory/support teams, which are cross-disciplinary and internationally diverse but made up of members who are committed to generating new understandings of quality and practice in participatory action research.

University of Chicago

The Office of Corporate Education specializes in the design and delivery of customized offerings that attempt to address the client's specific needs. As participants acquire tools for analyzing business problems, faculty make sure that they also acquire an understanding of how to apply them within their work setting (Brickers, 1997).

University of Michigan

The University of Michigan, whose MBA program is recognized for the innovation of placing MBA students in corporations for an entire quarter, also sponsors a Global Citizenship Program (Hill, 1997). A values-driven program, Global Citizenship is designed to provoke critical thinking on the troubling social and environmental issues that surround the world. Starting with an orientation program based on action learning principles and then subsequently throughout the academic year, students work in the community on a variety of projects, ranging from developing business and marketing plans for community agencies to mentoring students within the local high school system (Mercer, 1996).

University of North Carolina at Chapel Hill

The Center for Custom Programs at the Kenan-Flagler Business School customizes its offerings to the extent of establishing strategic alliances with its clients. In this process, students from client organizations develop action learning plans that assist them in leveraging learning to business problems back in the world of work.

University of Salford

The Revans Centre for Action Learning & Research at Salford, U.K., offers a Ph.D. Programme, a Master of Science Degree, and a post-graduate diploma in action learning and research. All programs are firmly based on action learning principles. In particular, students form immediately into sets of five to six people with varied backgrounds and diverse interests, but each having a strong commitment both to their own research and to that of their fellow researchers. In working to fulfill their degree requirements, participants engage in short-term action projects, often within their current job role.

University of Texas at Dallas

The School of Management Executive Programs sponsors a program in organization development and change management designed for corporate change agents, consulting professionals, and interested managers. The program ensures translation of classroom lessons immediately into the workplace through company projects. A capstone four-month project is featured in which participants conduct an organizational assessment, design an organization development and change program, and develop an implementation and assessment plan.

Virginia Commonwealth University

The Adult Education and Human Resource Development Program frames learning in the context of one's life and personal learning style, not as a generic "one size fits all" methodology. Students keep learning journals and also submit reflective essays at the end of each course. The program of study is flexible, with an individualized portfolio assessment making up one-third of the students' comprehensive examination and a report of an intensive 15-week action learning project making up the remaining two-thirds (Dilworth, 1996).

Washington University

The John M. Olin School is known for leading its corporate partners through in-depth, thorough problem definition, needs assessment, and objective setting before embarking on program development. In this way, the programs combine leading-edge theory with real-world practicality, offering the client a chance to work on proprietary issues. Team projects are developed by both faculty and senior managers and officers in order to incorporate real problems and issues faced by the company (Brickers, 1997).

Global Programs

Although most experiments in work-based learning have taken place in the West, it is an approach that has applications for the developing world as well. Nevertheless, work-based learning needs to be adapted to observe the customs and predispositions toward learning in the new cultures in which it might be introduced.

Experiments in the Developing World

In developing countries, public enterprises are typically the engines of development, so it is not surprising that most work-based learning experiments concentrate on developing managerial and business practices in the public sector and among NGOs (nongovernmental organizations). The Centre for Socio-Eco-Nomic Development in Geneva, Switzerland, has developed management capability programs for many developing nations—most recently Slovenia and China. Most of the programs, in the words of their directorate, are based upon action research and action learning principles. Working with their clients' host training institutions, projects are completed and trainees, most of whom are responsible government officials, end up making recommendations that have wide policy implications. Some examples of work-based learning projects in China are:

- improving the competence of Chinese county magistrates in decision making, coordination, and organization;
- establishing an intrinsic motivational mechanism within Chinese state enterprises;
- determining how to manage the training of Chinese civil servants;
- conducting a needs analysis for Chinese training institutions;
- surveying the teaching capabilities of junior teaching staff among China's economic cadre training institutions.

Another successful program in the developing world using work-based learning, has been the PIP (Planning for Improved Performance) program originally started in Egypt by the International Labour Office in Geneva. Wallace (1985) reports that it has been used in hundreds of public enterprises in more than 20 countries and seems to be remarkably successful in establishing a forum where the rules of the game can be clarified between enterprise managers and government/political officials. In one developing country, PIP held action planning workshops for six public enterprises, involving government officials at the beginning and at the conclusion of a five-day exercise. During the workshop, teams met to plan substantive managerial (as opposed to policy) actions they would like to undertake in their public administrations. The teams also took turns presenting their plans to each other.

The plans included revising staff recruitment procedures in a Public Service Commission; ironing out delays in procuring and stocking spare parts; facilitating procedures for constructing and commissioning new facilities; and developing incentives and disciplinary discretion in training and career advancement policies. When the government officials came back to the session, they were presented with some specific proposals that the managers wished to execute in exchange for increased autonomy. In fact, the proposals resulted in some modification of government policies. Management morale and commitment improved. Furthermore, some government officials were replaced by professionals more familiar with management problems. Wallace disclosed that a year later evaluations showed that several enterprises were making good progress in reducing costs and improving productivity and service.

Although there are opportunities for wide application of work-based learning principles in developing countries, Merrick Jones (1990), former adviser to the Sri Lanka Institute of Development Administration, advises educational policymakers wishing to undertake experiments in work-based learning to proceed cautiously. In order that we be careful about possible implicit ethnocentrism, I would add that many of Jones's cautions could be inserted in organizational subcultures within the developed world. The principal concern is that in many cultures throughout the world, learners are viewed as (and may even view themselves as) passive and dependent, whereas teachers are active and authoritative. In such environments, learners have difficulty with pedagogical approaches such as work-based learning that ask them to take responsibility for their own learning. In a similar vein, teachers find it difficult to let go of their control of the learning process for fear that it would undermine their authority. Indeed, in some cultures there is wide deference to those with presumed expert authority. Moreover, there is also tremendous respect, as is the case in Sri Lanka, for book knowledge over knowledge emanating from work itself.

Mike Marquardt (1998) has offered some very specific cautions in using work-based learning in the non-Western world. Nevertheless, he doesn't advise barring ongoing experimentation with some of this book's principles and practices, but rather that they be introduced while keeping in mind some of our inherent Western-based assumptions. Let's consider three specific instances:

1. *Learning teams.* In constituting learning teams, we tend to mix people of differing ages, genders, and roles. The inherent philosophy of such teams recognizes such Western values as egalitarianism and informality, and such practices as offering different perspectives and promoting give-and-take among members. In many other cultures, however, mixing people of differing status groups may disturb their sense of hierarchy, their respect of differences, and the role of power and authority in the workplace. Further, formality among the differing statuses in groups may be the expected communication mode.

2. *Projects.* As we have seen, action projects tend to focus on real organizational problems within real time frames. The project team is advised to assume authority to act within its sphere of responsibility. Yet in some non-Western cultures, having a group take on a managerial task might reflect poorly on the manager, who might lose face if having to admit an inability to handle the problem oneself. In addition, the sharing of personal difficulties might be seen as culturally crass. Having someone outside one's immediate environment work on an internal problem might also be seen as problematic.

3. *Public reflection.* Public reflection, by promoting a thinking about one's thinking, calls for public examination of the most fundamental assumptions and premises behind our practices. Co-participants in work-based learning are viewed as learning resources who can help us bring things into perspective and draw out our questioning insight. In some cultures, however, a manager's authority, professional competence, and information are seen as personal possessions. He or she may be reluctant to share information. Moreover, questioning one another, especially pointing out a weakness to those of superior status, would be seen as insulting. One also does not wish to be seen asking a foolish question. There is also value, among some Asian countries for example, to hiding one's feelings and thoughts and to not prying into the feelings and thoughts of others.

Nevertheless, transformation in these cultures toward more reflective practices is possible, especially as these practices are contextually adapted. A good example is the work of Arphorn Chuaprapaisilp (1989), who combined action research with the Buddhist teaching known as Satipatthana to transform nursing education at the Department of Medical Nursing, Prince of Songkla University, in Thailand. Chuaprapaisilp reported that there are few work-based learning components in clinical teaching in Thailand, that content learning and academic excellence are stressed. Chuaprapaisilp's intervention entailed moving the traditional approach to learning—based on observing, remembering, and copying—to a critical approach represented by reflection on experience. According to the new approach, known as the Critical Experiential Learning Model, teachers initially created a democratic learning atmosphere wherein they clarified together with their students the objectives, structures, processes, roles, and assumptions in the conduct of the students' subsequent clinical work. The model included a process of gaining emancipation through experience such that teachers and students together challenged existing structures, identified contradictions, established clear communication, and engaged in the reflective process of Satipatthana, or "mindfulness." Satipatthana promotes contemplation of the body, feelings, mental states, and mental events. In Buddhist terminology, Chuaprapaisilp points out that productive Contemplation, supported by Virtue, will ultimately lead to Wisdom. The Critical Experiential Learning Model, according to Chuaprapaisilp, not only demonstrated that participants in this Eastern culture were able to improve their learning practices but that such practices could enhance the quality of nursing care.

The Centre for Socio-Eco-Nomic Development, cited earlier, has also been successful importing work-based learning principles to the non-Western world. Their project in China entailed developing a core group of organizational trainers and consultants who could improve the effectiveness of management training among China's economic and administrative cadres. The project challenged a number of Chinese cultural assumptions in such domains as the role of adult learning, the use of the workplace as a training site, the instruction style of the trainer/instructor, evaluation of training designs, the institutionalization of self-renewal processes in training organizations, and the integration of theory and practice. The principals, Lichia Yiu and Raymond Saner (1998), reported that the project was largely successful but only after modifying the program based on some adaptations to the Chinese culture:

1. The native instructional team performed more effectively after receiving personal tutoring in work-based learning.
2. Considerable attention needed to be devoted to identify individuals with a sufficient psychological consciousness and interpersonal skills to deal with the social processes inherent in learning teams.
3. Senior supervisors supported projects after experiencing a training program of their own and after having more personal contact with the trainers.

In contrast to the view that work-based learning is potentially inaccessible to the developing world, a branch of action learning, sometimes referred to as the "Southern School," suggests that any deficiency of learner proactivity in the Third World is as much due to oppression as to adherence to cultural values. Freire (1970), for example, believed that learning starts when people can begin to construct their own reality as opposed to receiving the wisdom of the dominant culture; therefore, learning is very much tied to the process of empowerment. Fals-Borda and Rahman (1991) delve into the relationship between knowledge and power, arguing that control over the production of knowledge can further isolate disenfranchised groups from those in intellectual power who maintain a monopoly over the supply of knowledge, just as the wealthy maintain a monopoly over material resources. In this case, work-based learning also has a political dimension such that collaboration is sought between those from privileged groups who have academic or conceptual knowledge and those among the economically disadvantaged who have experiential knowledge.

Multinational Sensitivity
Work-based learning is ideally designed to help firms develop their cross-cultural sensitivity, a competency that has become critical in our age of the global marketplace. Many of our national corporations are looking to establish a global identity and strategy for their businesses. Accordingly, they are interested in expanding their domestic markets, especially as local demand becomes satiated. Not only are they seeking new markets for their products and services, but they are also intent on acquiring new resources, be it physical or labor. However, global expansion requires much more than "showing up." Managers need to develop a sensitivity in working across boundaries. They need to know how to develop trusting relationships with managers from host countries. This includes more than learning how to speak their language. It also requires addressing those subtle cultural differences that exist below the surface.

 One of GE's action learning projects was to come up with ways to increase the company's share of the lighting market in Western Europe. There were questions about whether the market was ready for a new player or whether GE could actually change the market. To get a handle on these questions, the team went into the field and began to interview customers, suppliers, and other stakeholders. Their interviews touched on a wide range of issues from consumer preferences, tax laws, currency fluctuations, and legislation to the nuances of language. Reporting on this and other global projects,

Dotlich and Noel (1998) suggested that the experience taught program participants that globalization was:

> not a matter of *where* the company did business but *how*. . . . Being a global company . . . is a mindset rather than a location. . . . [The program helped] future leaders come to terms with the subtleties and ambiguities that come with a global marketplace.

Nancy Adler (1991) believes that a great deal of cross-cultural miscommunication derives from misperception, especially caused by stereotypes, subconscious cultural blinders, lack of self-awareness, and projected similarity. Without direct exposure to the other culture, one tends to use one's own meaning to make sense out of the other person's reality. Adler tells the story of a Japanese businessman who wants to tell his Western client that he is uninterested in a particular sale. To be polite, the businessman says, "That will be very difficult." The client interprets this statement to mean that there are still unresolved problems but that they can be overcome. He responds by asking how his company can help solve the problem. The Japanese businessman, meanwhile, is mystified since he believes he has sent the message that the sale is off.

Americans are often surprised to discover that they are often seen by foreigners as hurried, overly explicit, quite hard-working, law-abiding, and often too inquisitive. They may come across as businesslike and inauthentic. Miscommunication caused by such impressions needs to be addressed or it may have unintentional consequences that could affect relationships and, ultimately, business performance.

One benefit of work-based learning is that it requires direct exposure on the part of participants to other cultures when projects take place in other parts of the world. Further, global teams can be used to constitute these projects. Such teams can give participants a broad understanding of the company's international business, can open up informal networks of communication throughout the organization, and provide a unique opportunity for employee development. Using social learning theory (introduced in Chapter 4), Black and Mendenhall (1990) argue that cultural sensitivity is best learned from experience because individuals use the consequences of their experiences to shape current and future behavior. Having exposure to projects in other cultures gives work-based learning participants a chance to make sense of their interactions, teaching them, for example, what is appropriate and inappropriate in these settings or which behaviors to execute or suppress. The resulting cross-cultural experience is not simulated as in a classroom exercise but is real, emanating from the rough-and-tumble of actual practice in the field. Participants gain experience in a number of ways, be it from on-site interviews to inquire about the viability of a project prospectus or from having to sell the findings from a project to a local management.

W. H. Brady Co. uses global long-range planning teams to address key strategic issues. Teams meet for approximately six months, and although participants are taken out of their normal work environment for brief periods, they continue to perform their regular job responsibilities. One team looked at the impact of the Internet on sales channels in 10 years. This global team assembled participants from R&D, MIS, marketing, sales, and new products, and also drafted a computer expert and some experts outside the company. Northern Telecom Ltd. used global executive teams in the early 1990s to initiate its globalization efforts and to change mindsets. Teams met for nine-month periods and about five teams were active at any given time. One of the teams included two sales people from the United States, a country manager from France, an R&D professional from Canada, a manufacturing manager from England, and a senior HR professional from Canada. The team's charge was to determine the best strategy for externalizing product development. Consequently, members traveled to Europe, the Far East, and North America to benchmark best practices and put their recommendations together (Axel, 1996).

The experience of working with a global, cross-cultural team can present participants with critical lessons in intercultural competence. According to Beamer (1992), intercultural competence entails the ability to analyze communication behavior within a new culture, resulting in an ability to respond to messages *as if from within* that culture. Working in learning teams, Smith and Berg (1997) found that there are three processes that can lead early on to growing intercultural competence. First, the team members need to learn how to learn together. As members think of situations in which they had the opportunity to learn something of value but did not, they gradually learn to be more patient with each other when group crises occur. For example, they begin to recognize that some environments are not hospitable to productive group life.

Second, members need to explore their interdependence, which can be accomplished by exploring each other's unique cultural contributions. As they reflect upon the sociopolitical issues within their respective cultures, for example, they may begin to recognize their connectedness. Finally, they also need to learn to work through their differences as they consider cultural norms that are sacred to each respective culture. In this way, they can deal with the inevitable polarities embedded within the group environment, such as confrontation versus conciliation, or individuality versus collectivity. In the former case, some members may strive to accommodate differences whereas others may believe that it is preferable to confront conflicts or irritations directly. In the latter instance, some members may be culturally disposed to preserve the centrality of the individual whereas others may expect individuals to subordinate themselves to the well-being of the group.

Consider the challenge general manager Michael Burchett faced when opening the Four Seasons Resort in Bali, Indonesia. Blunt senior managers like himself from Australia and from other Western societies had to learn how to manage—but more important, empower—indirect, subtle, and exceptionally polite Indonesians. According to Burchett, expatriate senior managers perceived the local managers as not being sufficiently direct with their staff—that is, as not managing (Solomon, 1997). Meanwhile, the managers were frustrated with senior management because they felt they weren't letting them manage in their own way. The expatriates countered that they had to help them learn to "manage" by instructing them in detail. This in turn led the managers to believe that they were being talked down to.

The reflective elements of work-based learning can help senior managers like Burchett and his staff overcome these cultural barriers by exposing them to their implicit cultural biases and assumptions. In the safety of the learning team, for example, they can explore with their peers from different cultures how their social constructions of reality differ based upon their cultural upbringing and predispositions. Be it in one's own culture or in a global environment, work-based learning can serve as a first step in helping our managers learn to anticipate and work through the complex human conditions faced in our twenty-first century organizations.

References

Ackoff, R. L. (1981). *Creating the Corporate Future*. New York: Wiley.

Ackoff, R. L. (1994). *The Democratic Corporation*. New York: Oxford University Press.

Adams, J. D. (1993). The hurrier I go the behinder I get. *Vision/Action*, 12 (1): 7–11.

Adler, N. J. (1991). *International Dimensions of Organizational Behavior*. Boston: PWS-KENT.

Alder, H. (1992). The bottom line. *Training Tomorrow*, November, 33–34.

Ahmed, S., Campell, R., Greenwood, D., Milner, C., Webb, I., and Whitehouse, N. (1995). The company associate partnership scheme. *Education + Training*, 36 (7): 1–27.

Albanese, R. (1989). Competence-based management education. *Journal of Management Development*, 8 (2): 66–76.

Allen, T. D., Poteet, M. L., and Burroughs, S. M. (1997). The mentor's perspective: A qualitative inquiry and future research agenda. *Journal of Vocational Behavior*, 51 (1): 70–89.

Anderson, J. R. (1983). *The Architecture of Cognition*. Cambridge, MA: Harvard University Press.

Antonacopoulou, E. P. (1995). Mathophobia and philomathia: A new perspective and its implications for management education. Paper presented at the 1995 Annual Meeting of the Academy of Management, Vancouver, Canada, August 7.

Antonioni, D. (1996). Designing an effective 360-degree appraisal feedback process. *Organizational Dynamics*, 25 (2): 24–38.

Argyris, C. (1982). *Reasoning, Learning and Action*. San Francisco: Jossey-Bass.

Argyris, C. (1983). Action science and intervention. *The Journal of Applied Behavioral Science*, 19 (2): 115–140.

Argyris, C., and Kaplan, R. S. (1994). Implementing new knowledge: The case of activity-based costing. *Accounting Horizons*, 8 (3): 83–105.

Argyris, C., Putnam, R., and Smith, D. M. (1985). *Action Science: Concepts, Methods, and Skills for Research and Intervention.* San Francisco: Jossey-Bass.

Argyris, C., and Schön, D. A. (1974). *Theory in Practice: Increasing Professional Effectiveness.* San Francisco: Jossey-Bass.

Argyris, C., and Schön, D. A. (1978). *Organizational Learning. A Theory of Action Perspective.* Reading, MA: Addison-Wesley.

Arkin, A. (1996). Lessons from life. *People Management*, 2 (2): 41.

Aryee, S., Chay, Y. W., and Chew, J. (1996). The motivation to mentor among managerial employees. *Group and Organization Management*, 21: 261–277.

Axel, H. (1996). Company experiences with global teams. The Conference Board's *HR Executive Review*, 4 (2): 1–18.

Axelrod, D. (1992). Getting everyone involved: How one organization involved its employees, supervisors, and managers in redesigning the organization. *Journal of Applied Behavioral Science*, 28: 499–509.

Badaracco, J. L. (1991). *The Knowledge Link: How Firms Compete through Strategic Alliances.* Boston: Harvard Business School Press.

Baird, L., Henderson, J., and Watts, S. (1997). Learning from action: An analysis of the Center for Army Lessons Learned (CALL). *Human Resource Management*, 36 (4): 385–395.

Baldwin, T. T., Danielson, C., and Wiggenhorn, W. (1997). The evolution of learning strategies in organizations: From employee development to business redefinition. *Academy of Management Executive*, 9 (4): 59–72.

Ballarat University (1994). *Master of Business (Management),* Programme Brochure, Prospective Student Services, Ballarat University College, Victoria 3353.

Bandura, A. (1977). *Social Learning Theory.* Englewood Cliffs, NJ: Prentice-Hall.

Bandura, A. (1986). *Social Foundations of Thought and Action.* Englewood Cliffs, NJ: Prentice-Hall.

Bateson, G. (1972). *Steps to an Ecology of Mind*. London: Paladin.

Bateson, G. (1979). *Mind and Nature: A Necessary Unit*. New York: Bantam.

Bazerman, M. (1990). *Judgment in Managerial Decision Making*. 2d ed. New York: Wiley.

Beamer, L. (1992). Learning intercultural communication competence. *Journal of Business Communication*, 29 (3): 285–303.

Beaty, L., Bourner, T., and Frost, P. (1993). Action learning: Reflection on becoming a set member. *Management Education and Development*, 24: 350–367.

Bell, C. R. (1996). *Managers as Mentors*. San Francisco: Berrett-Koehler.

Bell, D. (1974). *The Coming of Post-Industrial Society*. London: Heinemann.

Bell, S. (1998). Self–reflection and vulnerability in action research: Bringing forth new worlds in our learning. *Systemic Practice and Action Research*, 11 (2): 179–191.

Bereiter, C., and Scardamalia, M. (1993). *Surpassing Ourselves*. Chicago: Open Court.

Berger, P., and Luckmann, T. (1967). *The Social Construction of Reality*. Garden City, NY: Anchor Books.

Bernstein, R. J. (1976). *The Restructuring of Social and Political Theory*. Philadelphia: University of Pennsylvania Press.

Berryman, S. E. (1992). Apprenticeship as a paradigm for learning. In J. E. Rosenbaum et al. (eds.) *Youth Apprenticeship in America: Guidelines for Building an Effective System*, 25–40. Washington, DC: William T. Grant Foundation Commission on Youth and America's Future.

Black, J. S., and Mendenhall, M. (1990). Cross-cultural training effectiveness: A review and a theoretical framework for future research. *Academy of Management Review*, 15 (1): 113–136.

Blackler, F. (1993). Knowledge and the theory of organizations: Organizations as activity systems and the reframing of management. *Journal of Management Studies*, 30: 863–884.

Block, P. (1993). *Stewardship*. San Francisco: Berrett-Koehler.

Bohm, D. (1985). *Unfolding Meaning*. Loveland, CO: Foundation House.

Bolman, L. G., and Deal, T. E. (1997). *Reframing Organizations: Artistry, Choice, and Leadership.* 2d ed. San Francisco: Jossey-Bass.

Boody, R., East, K., Fitzgerald, L. M., Heston, M. L., and Iverson, A. M. (1998). Talking teaching and learning: Using practical argument to make reflective thinking audible. *Action in Teacher Education*, 19 (4): 88–101.

Botham, D. (1997). Action learning and the programme at the Revans Centre. Unpublished manuscript. University of Salford, United Kingdom.

Boud, D., Keogh, R., and Walker, D., eds. (1985). *Reflection: Turning Experiences into Learning.* New York: Nichols.

Boudreau, J. W., and Ramstad, P. M. (1997). Measuirng intellectual capital: Learning from financial history. *Human Resource Management*, 36 (3): 343–356.

Boyatzis, R. (1982). *The Competent Manager: A Model for Effective Performance.* New York: Wiley.

Boyce, M. E. (1996). Teaching critically as an act of praxis and resistance. *Electronic Journal of Radical Organizational Theory*, 2 (2): 2–9.

Boyett, J. H., and Conn, H. P. (1988). Developing white-collar performance measures. *National Productivity Review*, 7: 209–218.

Brancato, C. K. (1995). *New Corporate Performance Measures.* New York: The Conference Board, Report No. 1118-95-RR.

Branch, J., and Smith, B. (1992). Project-based management development: The Volvo story. *Journal of European Industrial Training*, 16 (1): 3–9.

Brenneman, W.B., Keys, J. B., and Fulmer, R. M. (1998). Learning across a living company: The Shell Companies' experiences. *Organizational Dynamics*, 27 (2): 61–69.

Brickers International Directory (1997). *University-Based Executive Development Programs.* 28th ed. Princeton, NJ: Peterson's.

Briggs, R. O., Ramesh, V., Romano, N. C., Jr., and Latimer, J. (1994–1995). The exemplar project: Using group support systems to improve the learning environment. *Journal of Educational Technology Systems*, 23 (3): 277–291.

Bright, B. (1996). Reflecting on "reflective practice." *Studies in the Education of Adults*, 28 (2): 162–184.

Brinkerhoff, R.O., and Gill, S. J. (1994). *The Learning Alliance: Systems Thinking in Human Resource Development.* San Francisco: Jossey-Bass.

Brookfield, S. (1992). Uncovering assumptions: The key to reflective practice. *Adult Learning*, 3 (4): 13–18.

Brookfield, S. (1993). Self-directed learning, political clarity, and the critical practice of adult education. *Adult Education Quarterly*, 43: 227–242.

Brown, J. S., and Duguid, P. (1991). Organizational learning and communities of practice: Towards a unified view of working, learning and organization. *Organizational Science*, 2 (1): 40–57.

Brown, J. S., and Duguid, P. (1996). Universities in the digital age. *Change,* 28 (4): 11–19.

Brown, J. S., and Gray, E. S. (1995). The people are the company. *Fast Company*, Premier Issue: 78–82.

Broughton, J. (1977). Beyond formal operations: Theoretical thought in adolescence. *Teachers College Record*, 79 (1): 87–97.

Bunker, B. B., and Alban, B. T. (1997). *Large Group Interventions.* San Francisco: Jossey-Bass.

Bunning, C. (1992). Turning experience into learning. *Journal of European Industrial Training*, 16 (6): 7–12.

Burgoyne, J., and Stuart, R. (1977). Implicit learning theories as determinants of the effect of management development programmes. *Personnel Review*, 6 (2): 5–14.

Burgoyne, J., & Hodgson, V. E. (1983). Natural learning and managerial action: A phenomenological study in the field setting. *Journal of Management Studies*, 20: 387–399.

Burnside, R. M., and Guthrie, V. A. (1992). *Training for Action: A New Approach to Executive Development.* Greensboro, NC: Center for Creative Leadership.

Burrell, G. (1994). Modernism, postmodernism and organizational analysis 4: The contribution of Jürgen Habermas. *Organization Studies*, 15 (1): 1–19.

Caie, B. (1987). Learning in style—Reflections on an action learning MBA programme. *Journal of Management Development*, 6 (2): 19–29.

Carew, D., Parisi-Carew, E., and Blanchard, K. (1990). *Group Development and Situational Leadership II*. Escondido, CA: Blanchard Training and Development.

Carr, W., and Kemmis, S. (1986). Becoming critical: Education, knowledge, and action research. Geelong, Victoria, Australia: Deakin University Press, 1986.

Cell, E. (1984). *Learning to Learn from Experience*. Albany: State University of New York.

Checkland, P. B. (1985). Achieving "desirable and feasible" change: An application of soft systems methodology. *Journal of the Operational Research Society*, 36 (9): 821–831.

Chidambaram, L. (1996). Relational development in computer-supported groups. *MIS Quarterly*, 20 (2): 143–163.

Chief Executive. (1995). The learning organization: *CE* roundtable. 101 (March): 57–64.

Choo, C. W. (1998). *The Knowing Organization*. New York: Oxford University Press.

Chuaprapaisilp, A. (1989). Improving learning from experience through the conduct of pre- and post-clinical conferences: Action research in nursing education in Thailand. Unpublished Ph.D. thesis. The University of New South Wales, Australia.

Collins, A., Brown, J. S., and Newman, S. E. (1989). Cognitive apprenticeship: Teaching the crafts of reading, writing, and mathematics. In L. B. Resnick (ed.) *Knowing, Learning, and Instruction: Essays in Honor of Robert Glaser*, 453–492. Hillsdale, NJ: L. Erlbaum.

Constable, J., and McCormick. R. (1987). *The Making of British Managers*. London: BIM/CBI.

Cooper, R., and Burrell, G. (1988). Modernism, postmodernism, and organizational analysis: An introduction. *Organization Studies*, 9: 91–112.

Coutu, D. L. (1998). Trust in virtual teams. *Harvard Business Review*, 76 (3): 20–21.

Cunningham, I. (1990). Beyond modernity—Is postmodernism relevant to management development? *Management Education and Development*, 21: 207–218.

Daft, R. L., and Weick, K. E. (1984). Toward a model of organizations as interpretation systems. *Academy of Management Review*, 9: 284–295.

Dalton, M. A. (1998). Using 360-degree feedback successfully. *Leadership in Action*, 18 (1): 2–11.

Davenport, T. H., De Long, D. W., and Beers, M. C. (1998). Successful knowledge management projects. *Sloan Management Review*, 39 (2): 43–57.

De Bono, E. (1986). *Six Thinking Hats: An Essential Approach to Business Management from the Creator of Lateral Thinking*. Boston: Little, Brown.

De Bono, E. (1994). *De Bono's Thinking Course*. New York: Facts on File.

de Geus, A. (1997). The living company. *Harvard Business Review*, 75 (2): 51–59.

Dennis, C. (1997). Action Reflection Learning at Grace Cocoa. Paper presented at the Action Learning for Executive Development Conference, International Quality and Productivity Center, Chicago, July 21–22.

Deshler, D. (1985). Metaphors and values in higher education. *Academe*, 71 (6): 22–29.

Dewey, J. (1916). *Democracy and Education*. Toronto: Macmillan.

Dewey, J. (1933). *How We Think*. Chicago: Regnery.

DiBella, A. J., Nevis, E. C., and Gould, J. M. (1996). Understanding organizational learning capability. *Journal of Management Studies*, 33: 361–379.

Dilworth, R. L. (1996). Action learning: Bridging academic and workplace domains. *Employee Counseling Today*, 8 (6): 48–56.

Dilworth, R. L. (1998). Personal learning goals. Personal correspondence, July 11.

Dixon, N. M. (1990). Action learning, action science and learning new skills. *Industrial and Commercial Training*, 2 (4): 10–16.

Dixon, N. M. (1995). A practical model for organizational learning. *Issues and Observations*, 15 (2): 1–4.

Dixon, N. M. (1997). The hallways of learning. *Organizational Dynamics*, 25 (4): 23–34.

Dixon, N. M. (1998). The responsibilities of members in an organization that is learning. *The Learning Organization*, 5 (4): 161–167.

Donaghue, C. (1992). Towards a model of set adviser effectiveness. *Journal of European Industrial Training*, 16 (1): 20–26.

Dotlich, D. L., and Noel, J. L. (1998). *Action Learning: How the World's Top Companies Are Re-Creating Their Leaders and Themselves*. San Francisco: Jossey-Bass.

Dovey, K. (1997). The learning organization and the organization of learning. *Management Learning*, 28: 331–349.

Drath, W. H., and Palus, C. J. (1994). *Making Common Sense*. Greensboro, NC: Center for Creative Leadership.

Dreyfus, K. L., and Dreyfus, S. E. (1986). *Mind over Machine*. New York: Free Press.

Driscoll, M. C. (1995). Never stop learning. *CFO—The Magazine for Senior Financial Executives*, 11 (2): 50–56.

Eby, L. T., and Dobbins, G. H. (1997). Collectivist orientation in teams: An individual and group-level analysis. *Journal of Organizational Behavior*, 18: 275–295.

Eden, C. (1988). Cognitive mapping: A review. *European Journal of Operational Research*, 36 (1): 1–13.

Eden, C. (1989). Using cognitive mapping for Strategic Options Development and Analysis (SODA). In J. Rosenhead (ed.) *Rational Analysis for a Problematic World*, 21–42. Chichester, UK: John Wiley.

Emery, F. (1995). Participative design: Effective, fexible and successful, now! *Journal for Quality and Participation*, 18 (1): 6–9.

Emery, M., and Purser, R. E. (1996). *The Search Conference: Theory and Practice*. San Francisco: Jossey-Bass.

Enderby, J. E., and Phelan, D. R. (1994). Action learning groups as the foundation for cultural change. *The Quality Magazine*, 3 (1): 42–49.

Fals-Borda, O., and Rahman, M. A. (1991). *Action and Knowledge: Breaking the Monopoly with Participatory Action Research*. New York: The Apex Press.

Ferry, N. M., and Ross-Gordon, J. M. (1998). An inquiry into Schön's epistemology of practice: Exploring links between experience and reflective practice. *Adult Education Quarterly*, 48 (2): 98–112.

Fisk, A. D., and Gallini, J. K. (1989). Training consistent components of tasks: Developing an instructional system based on automatic/controlled processing principles. *Human Factors*, 31: 453–463.

Flood, A. L. (1993). The business of business is learning. Address to the Canadian Payments Association, Vancouver, Canada, April 26.

Flynn, G. (1997). Competing with grace. *Workforce*, 72 (6): 52–56.

Frank, H. (1996). Will the future of management development involve action learning? *Education + Training*, 33 (8): 4–9.

Frank, H. (1998a). Action learning at work: The learning experiences of British managers in Yorkshire. Unpublished manuscript.

Frank, H. (1998b). Another review of the Revans Centre seminar. *Link-Up with Action Learning*, 1 (4): 21–22.

Freire, P. (1970). *Pedagogy of the Oppressed*. New York: Seabury Press.

Fulmer, R. M. (1997). The evolving paradigm of leadership development. *Organizational Dynamics*, 25 (4): 59–72.

Fulmer, R. M., and Vicere, A. A. (1995). *Executive Education and Leadership Development: The State of the Practice*. University Park, PA: The Pennsylvania State University.

Fulmer, R. M., and Vicere, A. A. (1996). Executive development: An analysis of competitive forces. *Planning Review*, 24 (1): 31–36.

Fulwiler, T., ed. (1987). *The Journal Book*. Portsmouth, NH: Boynton/Cook.

Galagan, P. A. (1993). The search for the poetry of work. *Training & Development Journal*, 47 (10): 33–37.

Garratt, B. (1991). The power of action learning. In M. Pedler (ed.) *Action Learning in Practice*, 2d ed., 45–61. Aldershot, UK: Gower.

Gerber, R. (1998). How do workers learn in their work? *The Learning Organization*, 5 (4): 168–175.

Gherardi, S., Nicolini, D., and Odella, F. (1998). Toward a social understanding of how people learn in organizations. *Management Learning*, 29 (3): 273–297.

Giddens, A. (1991). *Modernity and Self-Identity: Self and Society in the Late Modern Age*. Cambridge, UK: Polity Press.

Giroux, H. A. (1981). *Ideology, Culture and the Process of Schooling*. London: Falmer Press.

Goleman, D. (1996). *Emotional Intelligence*: *Why It Can Matter More Than IQ*. New York: Bantam Books.

Gordon, E. F. (1997). Work-based learning in America: Solutions for a new century. *Corporate University Review*, 5 (6): 36–38.

Gordon, R. A., and Howell, J. E. (1959). *Higher Education in Business*. New York: Columbia University Press.

Gore, L., Toledano, K., and Wills, G. (1995). Leading courageous managers on. *Journal of Management Development*, 14 (9): 54–56.

Gouldner, A. W. (1970). *The Coming Crisis of Western Sociology*. London: Heinemann.

Graham, W., Osgood, D., and Karren, J. (1998). A real-life community of practice. *Training & Development*, 52 (5): 34–38.

Grant, R. M. (1996). Prospering in dynamically-competititve environments: Organizational capabilty as knowledge integration. *Organization Science*, 7: 375–387.

Greco, J. (1997a). Corporate home schooling. *Journal of Business Strategy*, 18 (3): 48–52.

Greco, J. (1997b). Long-distance learning. *Journal of Business Strategy*, 18 (3): 53–54.

Green, R. E. A., and Shanks, D. R. (1993). On the existence of independent explicit and implicit learning systems: An examination of some evidence. *Memory and Cognition*, 21: 304–317.

Griffith, W. (forthcoming). The reflective team as an alternative case teaching model: A narrative, conversational approach. *Management Learning*.

Habermas, J. (1971). *Knowledge and Human Interests*. Boston: Beacon Press.

Habermas, J. (1984). *The Theory of Communicative Action. Vol. 1: Reason and the Rationalization of Society*. (Trans. T. McCarthy.) Boston: Beacon Press.

Hall, E. T. (1977). *Beyond Culture*. New York: Doubleday.

Halper, M. (1997). Everyone in the knowledge pool. *Computerworld Global Innovators*, December 8.

Hamilton, M. A., and Hamilton, S. F. (1997). When is work a learning experience. *Phi Delta Kappan*, 78 (9): 682–689.

Hammer, M., and Stanton, S. A. (1997). The power of reflection. *Fortune*, 136 (10): 291–296.

Handy, C., et al. (1988). *The Making of Managers*. London: Pitman.

Hanfling, O. (1981). *Logical Positivism*. New York: Columbia University Press.

Hayes, J., and Allinson, C. W. (1998). Cognitive style and the theory and practice of individual and collective learning in organizations. *Human Relations*, 51 (7): 847–871.

Hayes, N. A., and Broadbent, D. E. (1988). Two modes of learning for interactive tasks. *Cognition*, 28: 249–276.

Heifetz, R. A. (1994). *Leadership Without Easy Answers*. Cambridge, MA: The Belknap Press.

Heifetz, R. A., and Laurie, D. L. (1997) The work of leadership. *Harvard Business Review*, 75 (1): 124–134.

Henderson, L., and Casey-Higgins, G. (1997). Xerox uses online learning to push change and deliver needed business skills. *Corporate University Xchange*, (March/April): 4–5.

Hendry, C. (1996). Understanding and creating whole organizational change through learning theory. *Human Relations*, 49 (5): 621–641.

Heron, J. (1989). *Six Category Intervention Analysis*. 3rd ed., Human Potential Research Group, University of Surrey, Guildford, United Kingdom.

Hersey, P., and Blanchard, K. H. (1988). *Management of Organizational Behavior*. 5th ed. Englewood Cliffs, NJ: Prentice-Hall.

Hesselbein, F., Goldsmith, M., and Beckhard, R., eds. (1996). *The Leader of the Future*. San Fransciso: Jossey-Bass.

Hibbard, J. (1997). Knowing what we know. *Informationweek*, 653 (October 20): 46–64.

Hill, A. (1997). Business schools show they can learn to adapt. *Puget Sound Business Journal*, 17 (45): 11.

Hofman, M. (1997). Facilitating multi-disciplinary teams through cognitive mapping. Unpublished thesis. Nijenrode University, Breukelen, The Netherlands.

Hollenbach, D. (1998). Is tolerance enough? The Catholic university and the common good. *Conversations*, 13 (Spring): 5–15.

Hollenbeck, K. M. (1997). School-to-work: Promise and effectiveness. *Upjohn Institute Employment Research*, 4 (2): 5–6.

Holman, D., Pavlica, K., and Thorpe, R. (1997). Rethinking Kolb's theory of experiential learning in management education. *Management Learning*, 28 (2): 135–148.

Honey, P. (1994). Establishing a learning regime. *Organisations and People*, 1 (1): 6–9.

Honey, P., and Mumford, A. (1992). *Manual of Learning Styles*. 3rd ed. Maidenhead, UK: P. Honey.

Höpfl, H., and Linstead, S. (1997). Learning to feel and feeling to learn: Emotion and learning in organizations. *Management Learning*, 28 (1): 5–12.

Hoshmand, L. T., and Polkinghorne, D. E. (1992). Redefining the science-practice relationship and professional training. *American Psychologist*, 47 (1): 55–66.

Houlder, V. (1997). Group therapy for business leaders. *The Financial Times,* March 20, p. 26.

Howard, J. H., and Ballas, M. (1980). Syntactic and semantic factors in the classification of nonspeech transient patterns. *Perception and Psychophysics*, 29: 431–439.

Huff, A. S. (1990). *Mapping Strategic Thought*. Chichester, UK: John Wiley.

Hutcheson, P. G. (1996). Ten tips for coaches. *Training and Development*, 50 (3): 15–16.

Humphries, S. (1998). Assessing to learn—learning to assess. The Society for Organizational Learning, Cambridge, MA. http://www.sol-ne.org/pra/pro/assessment/progrep98.html.

IFAL (1996). What is Action Learning? International Federation of Action Learning, Lancaster, UK. http://www.metalearning.com/ifal-usa/ifal-usa_frm.htm,

Inman, P. L., and Vernon, S. (1997). Assessing workplace learning: New trends and possibilities. *New Directions for Adult and Continuing Education*, 75 (Fall): 75–85.

Jackall, R. (1983). Moral mazes: Bureaucracy and managerial work. *Harvard Business Review*, 61 (5): 118–130.

Jacobs, R. (1989). Getting the measure of management competence. *Personnel Management*, 21 (6): 32–37.

Janis, I. L. (1971). Groupthink. *Psychology Today*, 5 (6): 43–46, 74–76.

Janov, J. (1995). Creating meaning: The heart of learning communities. *Training & Development*, 49 (5): 53–59.

Jensen, M. C. (1997). Non-rational behavior, agency costs, and organizations. Paper presented at the Boston-Cambridge Seminar on Economics of Organizations. Harvard Business School, May 9.

Johnson, C. (1997). *The Essential Principles of Action Learning.* In electronic conference, New Approaches to Management Education and Development (NAMED), MCB University Press, UK. http://www.mcb.co.uk/services/conferen/sept97/named/paper1-4.htm.

Jones, A., and Hendry, C. (1994). The learning organization: Adult learning and organizational transformation. *British Journal of Management*, 5 (2): 153–162.

Jones, M. L. (1990). Action learning as a new idea. *Journal of Management Development*, 9 (5): 29–34.

Jordan, B. (1987). Modes of teaching and learning: Questions raised by the training of traditional birth attendants. Report No. IRL87-0004. Palo Alto, CA: Institute for Research on Learning.

Joyce, B., and Showers, B. (1988). *Student Achievement Through Staff Development*. London: Longman.

Judge, W. Q., and Cowell, J. (1997). The brave new world of executive coaching. *Business Horizons*, 4 (4): 71–77.

Kanter, R. (1989). The new managerial work. *Harvard Business Review*, 67 (6): 85–92.

Katzenbach, J. R., & Smith, D. K. (1993). *The Wisdom of Teams*. Boston: Harvard Business School Press.

Kaydos, W. (1991). *Measuring, Managing, and Maximizing Performance*. Portland, OR: Productivity Press.

Kaye, B., and Jacobson, B. (1995). Mentoring: A group guide. *Training & Development*, 49 (4): 22–27.

Keen, E. A. (1975). *A Primer in Phenomenological Psychology*. Lanham, MD: University Press of America.

Kegan, R. (1982). *The Evolving Self*. Cambridge, MA: Harvard University Press.

Kelly, A. (1993). Measuring payback from human resource development. *Industrial & Commercial Training*, 25 (7): 3–6.

Kelly, G. A. (1955). *The Psychology of Personal Constructs*. New York: Norton.

Ketelhorn, W. (1996). Mastering management: Toolboxes are out, thinking is in. *Financial Times*, March 22.

King, P. M., and Kitchener, K. S. (1994). *Developing Reflective Judgment*. San Francisco: Jossey-Bass.

Kirkpatrick, D. L. (1975). *Evaluating Training Programs*. Alexandria, VA: American Society for Training and Development.

Kleiner, A., and Roth, G. (1997). How to make experience your company's best teacher. *Harvard Business Review*, 75 (5): 172–177.

Knowles, M. S. (1975). *Self-Directed Learning: A Guide for Learners and Teachers*. New York: Association Press.

Kolb, D. A. (1984). *Experiential Learning as the Source of Learning and Development*. Englewood Cliffs, NJ: Prentice-Hall.

Kolb, D. A., Osland, J. S., and Rubin, I. M. (1995). *Organizational Behavior: An Experiential Approach*. Englewood Cliffs, NJ: Prentice-Hall.

Kolb, D. A., and Plovnick, M. S. (1977). The experiential learning theory of career development. In J. Van Maanen (ed.) *Organizational Careers: Some New Perspectives*, 65–87. London: Wiley.

Korey, G., and Bogorya, Y. (1985). The managerial action learning concept—theory and application. *Management Decision*, 23 (2): 3–11.

Kram, K. E. (1985). *Mentoring at Work: Developmental Relationships in Organizational Life*. Glenview, IL: Scott Foresman.

Krim, R. (1988). Managing to learn: Action inquiry in city hall. In P. Reason (ed.) *Human Inquiry in Action: Developments in New Paradigm Research*, 144–162. London: Sage.

Labich, K. (1996). Elite teams get the job done. *Fortune*, 133 (3): 90–99.

Lakoff, G., and Johnson, M. (1980). *Metaphors We Live By*. Chicago: University of Chicago Press.

Lancaster, H. (1996). You might need a guide to lead you around career pitfalls. *Wall Street Journal*, July 30.

Langer, E. (1997). *The Power of Mindful Learning*. Reading, MA: Addison-Wesley.

Lauriala, A. (1998). Reformative in-service education for teachers (Rinset) as a collaborative action and learning enterprise: Experiences from a Finnish context. *Teaching and Teacher Education*, 14 (1): 53–66.

Lave, J. (1988). *Cognition in Practice: Mind, Mathematics, and Culture in Everyday Life*. New York: Cambridge University Press.

Lave, J. (1993). The practice of learning, in S. Chaiklin and J. Lave (eds.) *Understanding Practice: Perspectives on Activity and Context*. Cambridge, UK: Cambridge University Press.

Lawler, E. E., III, Nadler, D. A., and Cammann, C. (1980). *Organizational Assessment*. New York: Wiley.

Lawton, S., and Ernesti, D. (1998). Are staffers headed in the right direction? *Nursing Management*, 29 (7): 28–30.

Lee, A. S. (1991). Integrating positivist and interpretive approaches to organizational behavior. *Organization Science*, 2: 342–365.

Leibowitz, Z. B., Schultz, C., Lea, D. H., and Forrer, S. E. (1994). Shape up and ship out. *Training & Development*, 48 (8): 39–42.

Lessem, R. (1991). A biography of action learning. In M. Pedler (ed.) *Action Learning in Practice*, 2d ed., 17–30. Aldershot, UK: Gower.

Lewicki, P. (1986). *Nonconcious Social Information Processing*. New York: Academic Press.

Lewicki, P., Hill, T., and Czyzewska, M. (1992). Nonconscious acquisition of information. *American Psychologist*, 47: 796–801.

Lewin, K. (1951). *Field Theory in Social Science*. (ed., D. Cartwright.) New York: Harper and Row.

Lewis, A., and Marsh, W. (1987). Action learning: The development of field managers in the Prudential Assurance Company. *Journal of Management Development*, 6 (2): 45–56.

LIM, Leadership in International Management Ltd. (1997). Developing Global Business Leaders Through Action Reflection Learning™. Pennington, New Jersey.

Linn, S, and Snyder, W. M. (1997). Deploying and Building Knowledge at the Front Line. Working paper. Cambridge, MA.

Long, D. G. (1990). *Learner Managed Learning*. New York: St. Martin's Press.

Lorange, P. (1994). Back to school: Executive education. *Executive Education*, 92 (March): 36–39.

Luft, J. (1969). *Of Human Interaction*. Palo Alto, CA: National Press Books.

Lukinsky, J. (1990). Reflective withdrawal through journal writing. In J. Mezirow et al. (eds.) *Fostering Critical Reflection in Adulthood*, 213–234. San Francisco: Jossey-Bass, 1990.

McCrudden, C. (1998). One year in action learning. *Link-Up with Action Learning* (A Publication of the Revans Centre for Action Learning and Research), 1 (3): 13–15.

McDermott, L. (1996). Wanted: Chief executive coach. *Training & Development,* 50 (5): 67–70.

McDougall, M., and Beattie, R. S. (1997). Peer mentoring at work. *Management Learning*, 28: 423–437.

McGill, I., and Beaty, L. (1992). *Action Learning—A Practitoner's Guide*. London: Kogan Page.

McKernan, J. (1991). Some developments in the methodology of action research: Studied enactments. In C. J. Colins and P. J. Chippendale (eds.) *Proceedings of the First World Congress on Action Research and Process Management. Volume 1: Theory and Praxis Frameworks*, 43–56. Brisbane: Acorn Publications.

McMaster, M. D. (1996). *The Intelligence Advantage: Organizing for Complexity*. Boston: Butterworth-Heinemann.

Maclagan, P. (1995). Ethical thinking in organizations. *Management Learning*, 26 (2): 159–177.

Marquardt, M. J. (1998). Using action learning with multicultural groups. *Performance Improvement Quarterly*, 11 (1): 113–128.

Marsick, V. J. (1988). Learning in the workplace: The case for reflectivity and critical reflectivity. *Adult Education Quarterly*, 38 (4): 187–198.

Meehan, M., and Jarvis, J. (1996). A refreshing angle on staff education: Action learning at Britvic Soft Drinks. *People Management*, 2 (14): 38.

Meisel, S. I., and Fearon, D. S. (1996). Leading learning. In S. A. Cavaleri and D. S. Fearon (eds.) *Managing in Organizations that Learn*, 180–209. Cambridge, MA: Blackwell.

Mennecke, B. E., Hoffer, J. A., and Wynne, B. E. (1992). The implications of group development and history for group support system theory and practice. *Small Group Research*, 23 (4): 524–572.

Mercer, G. (1996). The global citizenship MBA orientation program: Action learning at the University of Michigan Business School. *Journal of Business Ethics*, 15 (1): 111–120.

Mercer, J. R. (1990). Action learning: A student's perspective. *Industrial and Commercial Training*, 22 (2): 3–8.

Meyer, A. D. (1982). Adapting to environmental jolts. *Administrative Science Quarterly*, 27 (4): 515–537.

Mezirow, J. (1981). A critical theory of adult learning and education. *Adult Education*, 32 (1): 3–24.

Mezirow, J. (1991). *Transformative Dimensions of Adult Learning*. San Francisco: Jossey-Bass.

Mezirow, J., et al., (eds.) (1990). *Fostering Critical Reflection in Adulthood*. San Francisco: Jossey-Bass.

Morgan, G., and Ramirez, R. (1984). Action learning: A holographic metaphor for guiding social change. *Human Relations*, 37 (1): 1–28.

Mott, V. W. (1996). Knowledge comes from practice: Reflective theory building in practice. *New Directions for Adult and Continuing Education*, 72 (Winter): 57–63.

Mumford, A. (1996). Effective learners in action learning sets. *Employee Counseling Today*, 8 (6): 5–12.

Nelson, R. R., and Winter, S. G. (1982). *An Evolutionary Theory of Economic Change*. Cambridge, MA: Belknap Press.

Newsline (1996). Part-time MBA programs echo changes in full-time counterparts. *AACSB Newsline*, 27 (1): 1–4.

Newton, R., and Wilkinson, M. J. (1995). When the talking is over: Using action learning. *Health Manpower Management*, 21 (1): 34–39.

Noel, J. L., and Charan, R. (1992). GE brings global thinking to light. *Training & Development*, 46 (7): 29–33.

Noel, J. L., and Charan, R. (1988). Leadership development at GE's Crotonville. *Human Resource Management*, 27 (4): 433–447.

Nonaka, I. (1991). The knowledge-creating company. *Harvard Business Review*, 69 (6): 96–104.

Nonaka, I. (1994). A dynamic theory of organizational knowledge creation. *Organization Science*, 5 (1): 14–37.

Nonaka, I., and Takeuchi, H. (1995). *The Knowledge-Creating Company*. New York: Oxford University Press.

Nowack, K. M. (1993). 360-degree feedback: The whole story. *Training & Development*, 47 (1): 69–72.

O'Dell, C., and Grayson, C. J. (1998). If only we knew what we know: Identification and transfer of internal best practices. *California Management Review*, 40 (3): 154–174.

Ohmae, K. (1982). *The Mind of the Strategist*. New York: McGraw-Hill.

Olian, J. D., Durham, C.C., Kristof, A. L., Brown, K.G., Pierce, R. M., and Kunder, L. (1998). Designing management training and development for competitive advantage: Lessons from the best. *Human Resource Planning*, 21 (1): 20–31.

Orr, J. E. (1990). Sharing knowledge, celebrating identity: Community memory in a service culture. In D. S. Middleton and D. Edwards (eds.) *Collective Remembering*, 169–189. Newbury Park, CA: Sage.

Owen, H. (1993). *Open Space Technology*. Potomac, MD: Abbott Publishing.

Paul, R. W. (1992). *Critical Thinking*. Santa Rosa, CA: Foundation for Critical Thinking.

Pearce, D. (1991). Getting started: An action manual. In M. Pedler (ed.) *Action Learning in Practice*, 2d ed., 349–366. Aldershot, UK: Gower.

Pedler, M., ed. (1991). *Action Learning in Practice*. 2d ed. Aldershot, UK: Gower.

Pedler, M., Burgoyne, J., and Boydell, T. (1978). *A Manager's Guide to Self Development*. Maidenhead, UK: McGraw-Hill.

Peters, H. (1996). Peer coaching for executives. *Training & Development*, 50 (3): 39–41.

Peters, J., and Smith, P. (1997). Action Learning and the Leadership Development Challenge. In *Electronic Conference, New Approaches to Management Education and Development (NAMED)*, MCB University Press, United Kingdom.

Pierson, F. C. (1959). *The Education of American Businessmen*. New York: McGraw-Hill.

Pitcher, P. (1997). *The Drama of Leadership*. New York: Wiley.

Pleasants, N. (1996). Nothing is concealed: De-centring tacit knowledge and rules from social theory. *Journal for the Theory of Social Behaviour*, 26 (3): 233–255.

Polanyi, M. (1966). *The Tacit Dimension*. Garden City, NY: Doubleday.

Popper, K. (1959). *The Logic of Scientific Discovery*. New York: Basic Books.

Powers, E. A. (1983). The AMA management competency programs: A development process. *Exchange: The Organization Behavior Teaching Journal*, 8 (2): 16–20.

Progoff, I. (1975). *At a Journal Workshop*. New York: Dialogue House Library.

Putnam, R. (forthcoming). Transforming practical discourse: An action science view. *Management Learning*.

Quinn, J. B., Anderson, P. and Finkelstein, S. (1996). Managing professional intellect: Making the most of the best. *Harvard Business Review*, 74 (2): 71–80.

Quinn, R. E., and Spreitzer, G. M. (1997). The road to empowerment: Seven questions every leader should consider. *Organizatoinal Dynamics*, 26 (2): 37–49.

Raab, N. (1997). Becoming an expert in not knowing. *Management Learning*, 28 (2): 161–175.

Rackham, N., and Morgan, T. (1977). *Behaviour Analysis in Training*. London: McGraw-Hill.

Raelin, J. A. (1990). Let's not teach management as if it were a profession. *Business Horizons*, 33 (2): 23–28.

Raelin, J. A. (1991). *The Clash of Cultures: Managers Managing Professionals*. Boston: Harvard Business School Press.

Raelin, J. A. (1993a). The Persean ethic: Consistency of belief and action in managerial practice. *Human Relations*, 46 (5): 575–621.

Raelin, J. A. (1993b). Theory and practice: Their roles, relationship, and limitations in advanced management education. *Business Horizons*, 36 (3): 85–89.

Raelin, J. A. (1997a). Individual and situational predictors of successful outcomes from action learning. *Journal of Management Education*, 21 (3): 368–394.

Raelin, J. A. (1997b). A model of work-based learning. *Organization Science*, 8 (6): 563–578.

Raelin, J. A. (1994). Whither management education: Professional education, action learning, and beyond. *Management Learning*, 25 (2): 301–317.

Raelin, J. A., and Cooledge, S. (1995). From generic to organic competencies. *Human Resource Planning*, 18 (3): 24–33.

Raelin, J. A., and Lebien, M. (1993). Learn by doing. *HRMagazine*, 38 (2): 61–70.

Ranier, T. (1978). *The New Diary*. Los Angeles: Jeremy P. Tarcher.

Reason, P. (1994). *Participation in Human Inquiry*. London: Sage Publications.

Reason, P., and Rowan, J., eds. (1981). *Human Inquiry: A Sourcebook of New Paradigm Research*. Chichester, UK: Wiley.

Reber, A. S. (1976). Implicit learning of synthetic languages: The role of instructional set. *Journal of Experimental Psychology: Human Learning and Memory*, 2: 88–94.

Reber, A. S. (1989). Implicit learning and tacit knowledge. *Journal of Experimental Psychology: General*, 3: 219–235.

Redding, J. C., and R. F. Catalanello (1994). *Strategic Readiness*. San Francisco: Jossey-Bass.

Reed, R. (1997). Action learning at Knight-Ridder. Paper presented at the Action Learning for Executive Development Conference, International Quality and Productivity Center, Chicago, July 21–22.

Reilly, R. F. (1982). Teaching relevant management skills in MBA programs. *Journal of Business Education*, 57 (4): 139–142.

Reingold, J., and Bongiorno, L. (1997). Where the best B-school is no B-school. *Business Week*, October 20, pp. 68–69.

Revans, R. W. (1982). *The Origin and Growth of Action Learning*. Brickley, UK: Chartwell-Bratt.

Rifkin, G. (1996). Leadership: Can it be learned? *Forbes ASAP*, April 8, pp. 100–112.

Rigano, D., and Edwards, J. (1998). Incorporating reflection into work practice. *Management Learning*, 29 (4): 431–446.

Rimanóczy, I. (1998). What does it mean to be a learning coach? Leadership in International Management Ltd., http://www.limltd.com/frame.htm.

Robertson, S. (1995). Meier: Education, communicaton seen as key. *American Metal Market*, September 27, p. 7.

Rogoff, B. (1990). *Apprenticeship in Thinking*. New York: Oxford University Press.

Rose, J. (1998). How a virtual company creates cohesiveness and commitment. *At Work*, 7 (4): 16–17.

Rosenau, P. M. (1992). *Postmodernism and the Social Sciences*. Princeton: Princeton University Press.

Russell, J. E. A., and Adams, D. M. (1997). The changing nature of mentoring in organizations: An introduction to the special issue on mentoring in organizations. *Journal of Vocational Behavior*, 51 (1): 1–14.

Ryder, J. M., and Redding, R. E. (1993). Integrating cognitive task analysis into instructional systems development. *Educational Technology Research and Development*, 41 (2): 75–96.

Ryle, G. (1945). Knowing how and knowing that. *Aristotelian Society Proceedings*, 46: 1–16.

Salaman, G., and Butler, J. (1990). Why managers won't learn. *Management Education and Development*, 21: 183–191.

Schaffer, R. H. (1998). Outside experts, internal learning opportunities. *Leverage* (Pegasus Communications), 21 (November): 1–4.

Schein, E. (1967). *Process Consultation, Volume I*. Reading, MA: Addison-Wesley.

Schön, D. (1983). *The Reflective Practitioner: How Professionals Think in Action*. New York: Basic Books.

Schön, D. (1988). *Educating the Reflective Practitioner*. San Francisco: Jossey-Bass.

Schroder, H. M. (1989). *Managerial Competencies: The Key to Excellence*. Dubuque, IA: Kendall/Hunt.

Scott, C. D., and Jaffe, D. T. (1989). *Managing Organizational Change*. Los Altos, CA: Crisp Publications.

Scribner, S. (1986). Thinking in action: Some characteristics of practical thought. In R. Sternberg, and R. K. Wagner, (eds.) *Practical Intelligence: Nature and Origins of Competence in the*

Everyday World, 13–30. Cambridge, UK: Cambridge University Press.

Senge, P.N. (1994). *The Fifth Discipline: The Art and Practice of the Learning Organization*. New York: Currency/Doubleday.

Sherman, S. (1995). How's tomorrow's best leaders are learning their stuff. *Fortune*, 132 (11): 90–102.

Shor, I. (1992). *Empowering Education: Critical Teaching for Social Change*. Chicago: The University of Chicago Press.

Smith, K., & Berg, D. (1997). Cross-cultural groups at work. *European Management Journal*, 15 (1): 8–15.

Smith, P. (1988). Second thoughts on action learning. *Journal of European Industrial Training*, 12 (6): 28–31.

Smith, P. A. C. (1997). Performance learning. *Management Decision*, 35 (10): 721–730.

Solomon, C. M. (1997). When training doesn't translate. *Workforce*, 76 (3): 40–44.

Stack, J., and Burlingham, B. (1994). *The Great Game of Business*. New York: Doubleday.

Stamps, D. (1997). Communities of practice: Learning is social. Training is irrelevant? *Training*, 34 (2): 34–42.

Sternberg, R., and Wagner, R. K., eds. *Practical Intelligence: Nature and Origins of Competence in the Everyday World*. Cambridge: Cambridge University Press.

Stewart, T. A. (1996). The invisible key to success. *Fortune*, 134 (3): pp. 173–176.

Stuller, J. (1993). Practical matters: Executive training programs. *Across the Board*, 30 (1): 36–40.

Sutton, D. (1989). Further thoughts on action learning. *Journal of European Industrial Training*, 13 (3): 32–35.

Sveiby, K. E. (1997). *The New Organizational Wealth*. San Francisco: Berrett-Koehler.

Tannenbaum, S., and Yukl, G. (1992). Training and development in work organizations. *Annual Review of Psychology*, 43: 399–441.

Taylor, E. W. (1997). Building upon the theoretical debate: A critical review of the empirical studies of Mezirow's transformative learning theory. *Adult Education Quarterly*, 48 (1): 34–59.

Thorpe, R. (1988). An MSc by action learning: A management development initiative by higher degree. *Management Education and Development*, 19 (1): 68–78.

Tobin, D. R. (1998). *The Knowledge-Enabled Organization*. New York: AMACOM.

Torbert, W. R. (1983). Initiating collaborative inquiry. In G. Morgan, (ed.) *Beyond Method: Strategies for Social Research*, 272–291. Newbury Park, CA: Sage Publications.

Torbert, W. R. (1987). *Managing the Corporate Dream: Restructuring for Long-Term Success*. Homewood IL: Dow Jones–Irwin.

Toulmin, S. (1990). *Cosmopolis: The Hidden Agenda of Modernity*. New York: Free Press.

Townsend, A. M., DeMarie, S. M., and Hendrickson, A. R. (1998). Virtual teams: Technology and the workplace of the future. *Academy of Management Executive*, 12 (3): 17–29.

Trochim, W. M. K. (1989). Concept mapping: Soft science or hard art? *Evaluation and Program Planning*, 12 (1): 87–110.

Tucker, V. M., and Taylor, M. W. (1997). Action project: Common pitfalls and ways around them. ISOE Working Paper, WP-97/001. The Pennsylvania State University, University Park, PA.

Tuckman, B. W. (1965). Developmental sequences in small groups. *Psychological Bulletin*, 63: 384–399.

Twain, M. (1948). *The Adventures of Huckleberry Finn*. New York: Grosset & Dunlap.

Twigg, C. A. (1994). The need for a national learning infrastructure. *Educom Review*, 29, nos. 4, 5, 6.

Tyre, M. J., and von Hippel, E. (1997). The situated nature of adaptive learning in organizations. *Organization Science*, 8 (1): 71–81.

Urban, T. F., Ferris, G. R., Crowe, D. F., and Miller, R. L. (1985). Management training: Justify costs or say goodbye. *Training and Development Journal*, 39 (3): 68–71.

U.S. Department of Labor (1994). *Road to High-Performance Workplaces: A Guide to Better Jobs and Better Business Results*. Washington, DC: U. S. Department of Labor.

Vaill, P. B. (1997). *Learning as a Way of Being*. San Francisco: Jossey-Bass.

Van Horn, C. E. (1995). *Enhancing the Connection Between Higher Education and the Workplace: A Survey of Employers*. Denver: State Higher Education Executive Officers and the Education Commission of the States.

Varney, G. H. (1998). Guidelines for Entry Level Competencies to the Field. *Academy of Management ODC Newsletter*, Winter: 9–11.

Vazquez, S. (1977). *The Philosophy of Praxis*. New York: Humanities Press.

Ventetuolo, J. (1998). Opening space for your organization. *Leverage* (Pegasus Communications), 10 (May): 1–3.

Vicere, A. A., Taylor, M. W., and Freeman, V. T. (1994). Executive development in major corporations: A ten-year study. *Journal of Management Development,* 13 (1): 4–22.

Viljoen, J., Holt, D., and Petzall, S. (1990). The MBA experience: Participants' entry level conceptions of management. *Management Education and Development*, 21 (1): 1–12.

Vince, R., and Martin, L. (1993). Inside action learning: An exploration of the psychology and politics of the action learning model. *Management Education and Development*, 24: 205–215.

Vygotsky, L. (1988). *Thought and Language* (Trans. A. Koulzin). Cambridge, MA: MIT Press.

Waldroop, J., and Butler, T. (1996). The executive as coach. *Harvard Business Review*, 74 (6): 111–117.

Wallace, J. B. (1985). Fostering management growth in developing countries. *Training and Development Journal*, 39 (1): 67–73.

Warkentin, M. E., Sayeed, L., and Hightower, R. (1997). Virtual teams versus face-to-face teams: An exporatory study of a web-based conference system. *Decision Sciences*, 28 (4): 975–996.

Watkins, K. E., and Shindell, T. J. (1994). Learning and transforming through action science. *New Directions for Adult and Continuing Education*, 63 (Fall): 43–55.

Weaver, R. G., and Farrell, J. D. (1997). *Managers As Facilitators*. San Francisco: Berrett-Koehler.

Weick, K. E. (1979). *The Social Psychology of Organizing*. 2d ed. New York: Random House.

Weil, S. Romm, N., and Flood, R. (1997). *Critical reflexivity: Multi-dimensional conversations*. Northampton; UK: The SOLAR Centre, Nene–University College Northampton.

Weinstein, K. (1995). *Action Learning: A Journey in Discovery and Development*. London: Harper/Collins.

Weisbord, M. R., and Janoff, S. (1995). *Future Search*. San Francisco: Berrett-Koehler.

Wenger, E. (1998). *Communities of Practice: Learning, Meaning, and Identity*. Cambridge, UK: Cambridge University Press.

Wertsch, J. (1985). *Vygotsky and the Social Formation of Mind*. Cambridge, MA: Harvard University Press.

Wholey, J. S. (1991). Using evaluation to improve program performance. *The Bureaucrat*, 20 (2): 55–59.

Wilmott, H. (1993). Breaking the paradigm mentality. *Organization Studies*, 14: 681–719.

Wilmott, H. (1994). Managing education: Provocations to a debate. *Management Learning*, 25 (1): 105–136.

Wines, L. (1996). Class of '96: Pragmatic courses for trying times. *Journal of Business Strategy*, 17 (2): 26–36.

Wintermantel, R. E., and Mattimore, K. L. (1997). In the changing world of human resources: Matching measures to mission. *Human Resource Management*, 36 (3): 337–342.

Wishart, N. A., Elam, J. J., and Robey, D. (1996). Redrawing the portrait of a learning organization: Inside Knight-Ridder, Inc. *Academy of Management Executive*, 10 (1): 7–20.

Witherspoon, R., and White, R. P. (1996). Executive coaching: What's in it for you? *Training & Development*, 50 (3): 14–15.

Wolff, J. (1975). Hermeneutics and the critique of ideology. *The Sociological Review*, 23: 811–828.

Woodruffe, C. (1991). Competent by any other name. *Personnel Management*, 23 (9): 30–33.

Wright, R. W. (1994). The effects of tacitness and tangibility on the diffusion of knowledge-based resources. *Proceedings of the 1994 Academy of Management Annual Meeting,* Dallas.

Wyatt, S. (1997). John Dewey meets the bottom line. *OD Practitioner*, 29 (4): 5–12.

Yiu, L., and Saner, R. (1998). Use of action learning as a vehicle for capacity building in China. *Performance Improvement Quarterly*, 11 (1): 129–148.

Young, D. P., and Dixon, N. M. (1996). *Helping Leaders Take Effective Action*. Greensboro, NC: Center for Creative Leadership.

Name Index

Subject Index